'When someone we love dies, we lose not or an organising principle of our assumptive w that moment, we had taken for granted. Grie dead; it is about discovering a new narrative, a new source of meaning to our lives. Jane Moss here shows us a way of helping bereaved people to do just that. She gives us a choice of techniques and suggestions, exercises and insights, that are well supported by research and which we can adapt to the particular needs of individuals at this turning point in their lives.'

*— Colin Murray Parkes, OBE, MD, FRCPsych, psychiatrist,*
*author and Life President of Cruse Bereavement Care, UK*

'Here is a wealth of ideas and inspiration for those of us aspiring to work creatively with bereaved people using the written word. I found my creative juices begin to flow as I read the ideas for the exercises and how to use them. These will be of enormous benefit for those wanting to start working in this way and will provide added incentive and encouragement for those who already use creative tools. I could use the ideas not only with the bereaved person but also with volunteer supporters in their supervision. The example of the fictional Greenbank writing group will be of special interest to those who want to offer support groups for bereaved people and there is much practical help offered for setting up such a group. I am sure this will prove to be a truly useful volume to have for reference and advice for those of us working in the field of bereavement support and counselling.'

*— Dodie Graves, counsellor, bereavement service co-ordinator*
*and author of* Talking with Bereaved People *and* Setting
Up and Facilitating Bereavement Support Groups

'Moss helps mourners reach deeply into the wordless silence at the heart of grief, and render what they discover in language that is resonant with meaning and emotion. From acrostics to villanelles, and from the opening group warm up to the final wind down, she scaffolds a structure for *Writing in Bereavement* that fosters continuity and connection in life narratives rewritten by the experience of loss. Whether you work with bereavement support groups or in the intimate crucible of grief therapy, you will find in this book an indispensable muse to your clinical creativity.'

— *Robert A. Neimeyer, PhD, editor of* Techniques of Grief Therapy: Creative Practices for Counselling the Bereaved

'Bereavement can be a dark and lonely place. This book shows how writing in groups can help bereaved people to find companionship and to begin to map out their own paths through this alien landscape. The book is thoroughly researched and offers a clear and systematic toolkit for professionals. On top of this, it is an engaging read that should leave readers feeling inspired to try this approach within their own work.'

— *Anne Cullen, Manager of Psychosocial and Spiritual Care, Princess Alice Hospice, Esher, UK*

# WRITING in BEREAVEMENT

## Writing for Therapy or Personal Development Series

*Edited by Gillie Bolton*

Writing for Therapy or Personal Development, a foundation library to a rapidly developing field, covers the theory and practice of key areas. Clearly exemplified, engaging and accessible, the series is appropriate for therapeutic, healthcare, or creative writing practitioners and facilitators, and for individual writers or courses.

# WRITING in BEREAVEMENT

## A Creative Handbook

Jane Moss

Jessica Kingsley *Publishers*
London and Philadelphia

The poem on p.147 from Robert Seatter, 2006 is reprinted with permission from Seren Books.
The quote on p.165 from Eva Wiseman, 2010 is reprinted with permission from the Observer Magazine.
'The Magic Box' poem on pp.171–172 from Kit Wright, 2009 is reprinted with permission from Kit Wright.
Permission for poems, writing, comments and case studies was kindly granted by the writing group members in this book.

First published in 2012
by Jessica Kingsley Publishers
116 Pentonville Road
London N1 9JB, UK
and
400 Market Street, Suite 400
Philadelphia, PA 19106, USA

*www.jkp.com*

**Library of Congress Cataloging in Publication Data**
Moss, Jane.
  Writing in bereavement : a creative handbook / Jane Moss.
    p. cm. -- (Writing for therapy or personal development)
  Includes bibliographical references and index.
  ISBN 978-1-84905-212-2 (alk. paper)
  1. Graphotherapy. 2. Creative writing--Therapeutic use. I. Title.
  RC489.W75M67 2012
  616.89'165--dc23
                                    2012006343

**British Library Cataloguing in Publication Data**
A CIP catalogue record for this book is available from the British Library

ISBN 978 1 84905 212 2
eISBN 978 0 85700 450 5

Printed and bound in Great Britain

# Contents

# *Acknowledgements*

—◆•◆•◆—

Many people have contributed to the ideas and practical work reflected in this handbook. The exercises and techniques set out in its pages have arisen from writing groups including those run in partnership with the Macmillan Bereavement Service at Meadow House Hospice in the London Borough of Ealing and the Bereavement Service at Princess Alice Hospice in Esher, Surrey. Members of the Avenue Club writers group in Kew Gardens, Surrey, have also contributed. I am grateful for permission to quote from examples of writing by members of these groups and others; we have enjoyed many poignant and insightful moments together, as well as plenty of humour, comfort and joy as people share their stories, poems and memories.

In some cases (with permission), I have included people's comments on their writing and on the effects of writing, rather than quoting directly from the writing itself. Sometimes these references are paraphrased or presented as composites, where a single illustration would be too revealing of personal circumstances, or in cases where there is a common response expressed by many.

I am always struck by participants' willingness to share their writing with each other and for publication, some of it referring to difficult and sad experiences. In a bereavement writing group the ground rules always include a commitment to confidentiality but, as many have said to me, 'if it helps other people in my situation I'm happy for it to be included.' Perhaps the idea that others may read their words and benefit from their experience carries its own therapeutic worth.

The counsellors with whom I have collaborated, Anne Rivers, Alison Glynne-Jones (both at Princess Alice Hospice) and Marianne Kolbuszevski (at Meadow House Hospice), and my colleagues from

Cruse Bereavement Care, have been generous with their time and advice. I hope this book does justice to their support and wisdom.

I would like to thank Emily McClave and Lisa Clark, my editors at Jessica Kingsley Publishers. Gillie Bolton has kept a wise and watchful eye over the handbook's development, to its considerable benefit, and has been encouraging from the start; also Professor Robyn Bolam and Peter Dewar, both formerly at St Mary's University College, Strawberry Hill, for firing my initial interest in this topic.

Beverly Frydman, a *Journal to the Self* (Adams 1990) practitioner and bereavement counsellor, has provided endless inspiration. My friend and writing colleague Jess Kidd's gentle cajoling has been essential to the writing process.

Finally, thank you to my family and friends, especially in this instance Nicholas Barker, Sheila McGill, Helen Ross McGill, Rosemary Seagrief, Robert Seatter and Ruth Tompsett.

# *Preface*

I have always been a person who writes. I write when I am happy, I write when I am sad. I write when I am troubled, I write when I am carefree. At times of uncertainty I reach for the pen, laptop or mobile phone notebook. If I need to reflect or have a conversation with myself, the page is my listening friend.

It seems I am not alone. The urge to put pen to paper, or fingers to keyboard after a significant loss is common and strong. Every day in the media, in weekend supplements and magazines from tabloid to highbrow we find people writing about bereavement as a traumatic life change. Check the best seller lists; you will see novels, autobiographies and poetry in which the author expresses his or her experience of grief. The famous and the obscure, celebrities and those who describe themselves as ordinary or normal (as opposed to public figures or professional writers), turn to the written page after a loss.

In recent years, the literary end of the spectrum has given us *The Year of Magical Thinking* (Didion 2005), the American writer Joan Didion's poignantly forthright account of her husband's sudden death and her experience of the early stages of shocked grief. In *Blue Nights* (Didion 2011), she relates the subsequent death of her daughter; a heartrending sequel.

Christopher Reid's *A Scattering* (Reid 2009), offers a poetic memoire of loss in a structured meditation on the process of grieving for his wife. Penelope's Shuttle's collection of poems *Redgrove's Wife* (Shuttle 2006), is a tour de force of reflection and re-adjustment. Her poems are a striking example of what the American psychologist and grief theorist Robert Neimeyer has termed 'meaning reconstruction' (Neimeyer 2007); the process, in other words, of reflecting on one's altered identity in the wake of bereavement and moving into a new sense of self.

The urge to continue a conversation with the one who has died is movingly captured by Natascha McElhone whose account of her husband's unexpected death weaves memoire with unsent letters to him in *After You* (McElhone 2010). Ted Hughes's *Birthday Letters* (Hughes 1998) is a one-sided conversation in poetic letters that record the process of adjustment over decades following the suicide of his wife, the American poet Sylvia Plath. In *Diary of a Grief* (Woods 1998), Peter Woods (a pseudonym) keeps a searingly honest diary of the three years following his wife's death.

A poem can work as a howl of grief; look at Thomas Hardy's 'The Voice', which was written as part of a series known collectively as *Poems of 1912–1913* (Hardy 1994 [1914]), following the death of his wife, Emma. Emma died without her husband realising the seriousness of her illness and her death shocked him to the core. The opening line 'Oh woman much missed, how you call to me, call to me' (Hardy 1994, p.315), reads as a wail of despair and yearning.

Shakespeare puts it best, of course:

> *Give sorrow words: the grief that does not speak*
> *Whispers the o'er-fraught heart, and bids it break.*
>
> (*Macbeth*, IV. iii. 209–210)

I offer these examples from what some might call 'proper' writers not to imply that everyone should aim to write like them (if only...), but to suggest that everyone, from the habitual or professional writer to the novice keeper of a journal or diary, may feel the urge to write in times of trauma and loss. Grief is a great leveller. Nothing in life is as certain as death and taxes, to paraphrase Defoe (or was it Franklin? The sources disagree so I shall leave them to fight it out together), and because we are human our impulses are the same. In grief, as in love, we act out of the ordinary.

In bereavement support we listen as people talk about their grief. For some the words run like rivers. People talk to fill the silence at home and to make sense of what weighs heavy in heart and head. Talking is, for many, the most needed and effective therapy. Some, however, struggle to give sorrow words. When talking is not possible, or is not enough, the page offers a place of safety in which we can listen to ourselves and start to make sense of sad and difficult experience. As time goes on, the activity of writing can be the bridge to a new way of life in which creativity helps fill the space left by the one who has died.

Some of the leading practitioners in the field of writing for health and well-being have referred to ways of coping with loss on the page. Gillie Bolton writes authoritatively and persuasively about the value of writing for medical staff and those in caring professions who deal almost daily with others' bereavements (Bolton 2008). Dodie Graves's work on how to talk to the bereaved is grounded in compassion and common sense (Graves 2009).

Kathleen Adams's *Journal to the Self* (Adams 1990) is an inspiring well from which to draw up ideas for journal writing. Kate Thompson's *Therapeutic Journal Writing* (Thompson 2011) considers some of the specific applications for journaling in grief. Diana Hedges (2005) makes a compelling case for the power of poetry as a means of expression in the context of loss. I draw on these and others like them on a daily basis.

## Why this handbook?

The idea for this handbook came from two spurs. The first was my sense that there is a gap in the literature about the value of writing in mental health, palliative care and other health and social contexts, when it comes to the specific context of bereavement. Many of those who offer support to the bereaved, including counsellors, therapists, volunteers, pastors and health workers, suggest writing as an intervention when it seems helpful to the person struggling to pinpoint or verbally express an issue in their grieving. The unsent letter is widely used and journaling is acknowledged as being of value to people as they move through their grief. Yet I often hear people speculate about other creative techniques that could be offered, and about where to find guidance and ideas that are appropriate to bereavement. Training and workshops I have facilitated in trialling some of the material for this book have drawn enthusiastic participants. Feedback always seems to ask for 'more please'. This handbook is my attempt to offer practical guidance and inspiration to meet this apparent need.

The second more personal spur came from my own experience. My interest in the value of writing in bereavement was first awakened through creative research at St Mary's University College in 2008. I accompanied this by training as a bereavement support volunteer with Cruse Bereavement Care and running a writing group with the

Bereavement Counselling team at Princess Alice Hospice. Through these activities I began to understand the respective roles of counsellor and bereavement support, and the role of the writer. Cruse stresses the distinction between the role of volunteers in bereavement support and that of fully trained and professional counsellors. I would never call myself a counsellor nor, I think, a therapist. I am writer who works in bereavement support.

Cruse provides its volunteers with practical tools to listen, talk to and support people, wherever they might be on their journey through the experience of significant loss and the profound life changes that entails. With Cruse's training and further practical experience with bereavement writing groups, and others, I have been able to bring my ideas together.

Inevitably, I bring my own experience of loss to bear on this work. During the Cruse ABC course, a worksheet invited us to circle the types of loss we had experienced in our lives to date. The sheet contained examples of significant losses: everything from the death of a grandparent, parent, sibling, friend, spouse, partner, child or pet, to less obvious bereavements such as being made redundant or losing one's home or business. The exercise invited us to reflect on the nature of loss and the way certain losses can seem like bereavement or can bring back earlier unresolved experiences of grief.

In a trainee group of diverse ages it surprised me to find, when we shared our worksheets, that I had circled the highest number. I had not thought of myself as someone who had experienced a great deal of loss, but this simple exercise made me reflect on the different ways we define bereavement, and the personal path we take through it as we adapt to each loss.

I have been fortunate, perhaps, in finding a natural way to process loss through my innate tendency to put pen to paper. To someone like me metaphor and imagery come naturally. This is not the case for everyone, but my own experience of writing makes me a natural champion for the role pen and page can play in assisting people through the profound changes that bereavement brings.

In setting these ideas down in handbook form and offering them to others engaged in supporting people in bereavement I am conscious, too, that this practice is constantly developing. For me, the learning will never cease. I hope that others will feel inspired to develop their own approaches based on the groundwork presented here.

# Who is this handbook for?

You do not need to be a writer, or even be of a particularly literary mindset, to make use of the advice in these pages. Everybody with some degree of literacy has the ability to express themselves on the page.

My hope is that the handbook will be of use to a diverse range of practitioners in bereavement support, whether counsellors or volunteers, representatives of faith communities, mental health workers, nurses, GPs, social workers, life coaches, funeral directors, and others who come into contact with bereaved people.

If you are reading this book, you are probably from one of two principal readerships. Even if you are not, please keep reading; there is plenty for a mixed range of skills and background here; bereavement support is a broad church.

Those two readerships are:

1. Those regularly engaged in bereavement support, whether as professional counsellors, in their capacity in the healing professions, as volunteers or others providing support in the community.

2. Writers working in health and social care, including palliative care, hospices, partnerships with counselling services, and the criminal justice system. Writers in adult or community education, or those who work with reminiscence and family history may also find themselves dealing with people's expressions of loss.

Perhaps you are a counsellor or volunteer who already uses writing to enable people – individually or in a group – to express the feelings that dominate following a loss. Whether you are new to the idea of writing in bereavement, or already familiar with some of its benefits, I hope you will find inspiration here and be encouraged to incorporate writing into your practice.

If you are skilled in enabling people to talk, and to listen to them as they do, I suggest that creative and expressive writing can provide further tools to enable people to communicate thoughts and feelings. The ideas in this handbook are offered for you to adapt to your own work and clients' circumstances.

I hope that writers working in community settings will pick up this book too. Some will be qualified in psychotherapy and other relevant disciplines; others may be writers skilled in residency work and group facilitation. The theme of loss will often arise in the writing classroom or group, whether focused on bereavement or not. Among the networks and communities of writers working in health and social care the call often goes out for 'anyone who has experience of writing with bereaved people? I need ideas!' As these requests acknowledge, particular skills and sensitivity are needed when working with bereaved people.

A residency in, for instance, palliative care can lead to a request to facilitate writing among bereaved families and friends following a death. Writers working in prisons may find that bereavement is a significant theme for prisoners for whom incarceration can trigger the loss of family ties and contact with children. The inability to attend the funerals of family members and friends while in prison is one sad example of disenfranchised grief.

It is an inexact science. No one can predict how a group of differently bereaved people, or an individual, will respond to a writing prompt. Still, with awareness of the ways in which people might be thinking or feeling at any given stage after their bereavement, and guidance on how to facilitate and contain the writing in structured exercises and with carefully chosen themes or prompts, the results can be astounding. I have lost count of the number of people, writing from a stuck point in their grieving, who have looked up from the page and said, 'I never thought I would write about that.'

I have worked principally with adults aged from their 20s to 80s; people with a diverse range of life experience, social background and education. The handbook is consequently written with adults in mind. Bereavement in children deserves a handbook to itself, although those who provide bereavement support for children, or work with them in the context of family support, may find inspiration here.

I would not necessarily recommend this book to individual bereaved people. It is written for practitioners rather than a readership interested in self-help. My aim is to enable counselling professionals, trained volunteers and writers with appropriate skills, to plan, deliver and evaluate writing activities with their clients and writing groups.

In attempting to identify the potential users of this handbook, I am immediately aware that nothing in life is ever as straightforward as these categories suggest. Some counsellors are also writers and use the written word and other creative techniques as part of their toolkit. Many use journaling for self-care and as a means of reflection and development. Some writers are trained in counselling and other therapeutic skills.

Nothing is ever black and white. Rather than seeing separate roles for bereavement counselling and writing, I prefer to think of the place where they meet as a place of depth, insight and colour. It is anything but a grey area.

## What this handbook contains

You will find a mixture of theory and practice in these pages. In the Introduction you will meet the Greenbank group, a fictional writing group. This entirely made up group of people serves as a way of illustrating how writing exercises may be applied in a given situation and with people showing different styles and at different stages of grieving. I hope this imaginary scenario will encourage you to consider how you might use writing with such a selection of bereaved people. The Introduction also introduces the idea of a toolkit of writing techniques which are referred to throughout the handbook and described in full in Chapter 13; a kind of user's guide to the principal tools.

In Chapter 1, I provide an overview of current grief theories and present ideas on how writing may assist with the work of grieving. Chapter 2 offers ways to enable people to start writing. In Chapter 3 you will find guidance on journal writing. In Chapter 4, I offer some literary forms and techniques, not because I expect people to turn into poets or experts in metaphor and simile overnight (although some take to these like a duck to water), but because accessible forms such as the acrostic, alpha poem and haiku offer valuable containment; little vessels in which to hold thoughts and describe a mountain of emotion in relative safety. Consider the use of form in poetry and prose to contain writing about difficult thoughts and feelings. Chapter 5 offers themes and structured exercises for writing in bereavement. Chapter 6 considers ways of writing about a life, drawing on material from family history and the life story of the deceased as well as the life story of the bereaved. Chapter 7 considers ways to reflect upon change and readjustment following a death. Chapter 8 surveys some of the ways in which writing can contribute to memorialisation, from park benches to website. The fast-evolving phenomena of online memorials and the use of social networking sites come with its own warning about instant obsolescence. I have drawn together some examples of organisations and charities in the field of bereavement support whose websites include written memorials, forums and blogs. The way new technologies are being adopted by the bereaved to create online shrines and other forms of remembrance (the bereavement blog and the continued conversation with the deceased through social networking sites, for instance), is gathering popularity across the generations and is worth considering as writing activity.

Chapter 9 suggests ways to bring a group to an appropriate end, while Chapter 10 offers ways to evaluate and seek feedback on the experience of writing for your participants; an important part of developing your own approach and understanding the value of writing in bereavement support. Chapter 11 provides an example of a facilitator's reflexive journal (my own), kept during a series of writing sessions with a closed group. Chapter 12 provides a nuts and bolts approach to setting up and running a bereavement writing group, with practical guidance on everything from recruiting group members, to the time of day, layout of the room, roles of the facilitators and ethical considerations. Chapters 13 and 14 respectively offer helpful terms and a series of sample writing sessions for you to adapt for your own use, with an indication of timings, support materials and how to introduce and close a session. I always like to have a plan. Even if I depart from it, it serves as a rudder to steer a group through an hour or so together. The sense that someone has a plan and is in charge is reassuring to a group of bereaved people who are likely to be feeling shaky, to say the least.

At the end of the handbook you will find sources of further reading including anthologies and published texts to provide inspiration for your own writing groups.

Finally a postscript; my reflections on the value of this work and the need for more research to understand its effectiveness in bereavement support. I hope that others with the resources and expertise will take up the challenge of testing these and other methods of creative intervention in a systematic way. I have learned as I have gone along, supported by collaborators and participants in the counselling teams and writing groups I work with; yet I know that I would have benefited considerably from someone whispering, 'Try this... it'll work' in my ear when I set out on this path.

I hope this book can do that for you.

# Introduction

Before setting forth on the practical advice that is at the heart of this handbook, I want to offer some writing tools and introduce you to a fictional group of people who between them exhibit the models and stages of grief work you will commonly encounter in a bereavement writing group. I have called this collection of people the Greenbank group. They are entirely made up; any resemblance to actual people living or dead is coincidental. I have, of course, drawn on my experiences and understanding of grief theory, but imagination has been my biggest influence in creating these characters.

## The Greenbank group

Imagine a typical setting for a writing group: the Greenbank Hospice in a large converted Victorian building in an outer suburb of a large town. The hospice's catchment area includes post-war former local authority housing and, on its outer edges, semi-rural greenbelt. The hospice is a charity. Patients are referred to it by their GPs and from NHS hospitals. Its services include end of life care, home support and a day hospice. Its bereavement service provides support to family and friends.

The group is new. It will be meeting weekly on Thursday evenings over ten weeks from September to December, in a conservatory that looks out on the garden at the back of the building. To reach it, participants walk along a corridor from which the ward rooms can be glimpsed. There is a small kitchen close by and an office with a photocopier.

The members of the Greenbank group are:

## Cynthia

Cynthia's mother died six months ago following a short illness. Cynthia is an only child. She cared for her mother whilst also working full-time as an office manager. Since her bereavement, Cynthia's employer has allowed her to return to work part-time. She has rented out her own flat and has moved into her mother's house (which she herself grew up), in the hope that this will make it easier for her to sort out the estate. She now has a longer commute to work and the move to her mother's house has taken her some distance away from her friends. Her mother never threw anything away and the amount of clutter in the house is overwhelming.

## Alan

Alan's wife Ali died a year ago, three months after their marriage, of a bacterial illness she contracted on their honeymoon. They had been together for six years and had two children, now aged two and four. Alan, who is 35, has taken time off work to be a full-time parent. He has some support from his sister who lives nearby. He attends two other groups run by the hospice's counselling service; a monthly drop-in group for around 20 people and a weekly men's group attended by five others, which Michael runs. Alan has difficulty sleeping but finds that if he is busy enough in the day he can tire himself out.

## Bobbie

Bobbie is 72. She is widowed with two adult daughters. Six months ago her 22-year-old grandson Angus died while on active service in Afghanistan. She heard about the attack on his platoon on the radio, but did not learn of his death until three days later when her youngest daughter called to tell her. Bobbie feels angry with her eldest daughter, Angus's mother, for not telling her in person, and angry with the army for mishandling (as she experienced it) the communication of Angus's death to his close family.

## Anna

Anna is in her mid-60s. Pat, her partner of 30 years, died of breast cancer shortly after retiring. Anna blames herself for not having insisted they go together for mammograms. She has no history of illness in her own family and assumed that nothing like that would ever happen to her or to someone she knew. Pat's family arranged the funeral without consulting Anna. Anna's mother died when she was ten. She has never known the cause of death and feels angry with her father for not telling her (he too, has since died). Anna has been seeing Michael for bereavement counselling off and on for more than two years but feels stuck.

## Ros

Ros's 26-year-old husband Dan died of a blood clot following a game of rugby, six months ago. She had recently given birth to their first child, a girl. She is supported at home by her mother, who has moved in with her, and she has a close circle of friends, most of whom are young married women. She still sends text messages to Dan's mobile phone (often at night when she cannot sleep), and posts messages on his Facebook wall.

## Marielle

Marielle is 68 and was born in Portugal. She has lived in the UK for ten years, having retired here with her husband to be near his family. Marielle's husband died suddenly nearly a year ago, on New Year's Day. Marielle has a distant relationship with her late husband's relatives and his children from his first two marriages. She has no children of her own.

## Riaz

Riaz's twin brother took his own life three years ago, when he was 42. Riaz supports their parents financially as well as running the family business which he and his brother used to manage together. Since his brother's suicide he has put in long hours keeping the business afloat. He has high blood pressure and has recently been diagnosed with type 2 diabetes. His wife has (as he sees it) pestered him to seek help. He has been referred to Michael's team by his GP and has had some sessions with Michael as his counsellor, but is finding it hard to talk openly about his feelings.

The facilitators are Fiona and Michael:

## *Michael*

Michael is 38 and has worked at the Greenbank Hospice for four years. He is a qualified counsellor, registered and accredited by the BACP. He manages a team of volunteers who provide bereavement support at the hospice and in the community. He lives with Tim, his civil partner. Between them they care for Tim's elderly mother who has dementia.

## *Fiona*

Fiona is a published writer of short stories. She has previously collaborated with an art therapist and a specialist in oral reminiscence, working with patients and their families to produce a book of life stories as part of the Hospice's end of life care. The idea of providing a writing group for bereaved families and friends arose from that project, for which funds were raised from the Hospice's trustees and network of supporters. Fiona is 41 and married, without children. Her best friend committed suicide when she was 18.

This is the cast of characters. You will spot the grief models among them; for example, Bobbie's anger and (possibly) disenfranchised grief, Anna's guilt and unresolved grieving for her mother, Riaz's complex and stuck grief following bereavement suicide, Alan's tendency to frantic activity while on the verge of exhaustion, Cynthia's sense of being overwhelmed, Marielle's isolation, and Ros's bereft need to communicate with her husband. The facilitators' personal circumstances, too, hint at some of the ways in which they may need to exercise self-care or maintain boundaries between themselves and the group as the writing work gets underway.

Having introduced them, I invite you to hold these imaginary people in your mind as you work through or dip into the handbook. At the end of each chapter you will find a box headed 'Greenbank group' in which I summarise key points and questions to consider. I shall offer scenarios and examples at intervals to illustrate the ways in which a chapter's guidance might be applied to the group; the issues that might arise, some of the dos and don'ts, and the outcomes (or even surprises) that might occur. My aim is to bring the theory and practice alive and to offer insight through a group experience which, although imagined, is rooted in real experience.

I immediately ask myself how writing might help the Greenbank group's members.

# The writing toolkit

Throughout this book I refer to expressive writing and creative writing. Bereavement support providers may be familiar with some of the techniques of expressive writing (the unsent letter is one example), but may be less sure of what is meant by creative writing. For writers reading this book it may be the other way round, although those accustomed to working in health and social care settings will almost certainly be fluent practitioners of both.

In attempting to define the different types of writing, I have selected forms, genres and techniques which I find to be of value in the context of bereavement. Whether you are familiar with these terms or not, it is worth considering what is meant by expressive and creative writing (there is a more detailed listing of these in Chapter 14).

## Expressive writing

Expressive writing does what it says on the tin in the sense that it provides a means for the writer to express what is on their mind and the emotions they are experiencing.

Some of the best known and most robustly evaluated examples of expressive writing can be found in the work of the American psychologist James Pennebaker. His clinical trials, carried out in the 1990s, offer evidence of tangible health benefits including the lowering of blood pressure and reduced susceptibility to illness such as the common cold (Pennebaker 1990, pp.145–146).

In his written exercises Pennebaker was not asking people to use creative imagination or to work with metaphor, fiction or literary form. He simply asked people to describe how they were feeling or what they were thinking about and to reflect on aspects of their mood or situation. The prompts offered by Pennebaker (2004) invite people to express what is going on in their lives in quite literal terms:

> Day 1: Writing Instructions... for today's work, your goal is
> to write about your deepest thoughts and feelings about the
> trauma or emotional upheaval that has been influencing your
> life the most. (Pennebaker 2004, p.26)

For the bereaved, this approach may be too blunt and directive. It is like being instructed to write directly about one's grief. My observation is that few people wish to stare their grief in the face on the page; they live with it all the time and know it well. This is not to say that people will avoid writing about their loss, but the choice of whether or not to do so is a personal one.

For some, writing in a journal provides the ultimate place of safety and privacy in which to express sometimes dark thoughts. Expressive writing is the backbone of journal writing in bereavement, as Chapter 3 will consider in detail. When someone who is bereaved attends a writing group with others, their conscious need may be to explore other aspects of life and experience, including the imagination, memories, hopes and dreams for the future (if the writer is ready for that). More oblique and flexible forms of stimuli, including themes and creative techniques for writing, can offer gentler ways into difficult subject matter. When someone starts to write, they often do not know where the pen will lead them.

## Techniques for expressive writing in bereavement

This handbook makes use of certain tools and techniques, among them dialogue (Adams 1990, pp.102–122), which enables the writer to have a conversation on the page; diaries which in bereavement can provide routine and structure as well as a means to track the passage of time through grief; entrance meditations (Adams 1990, p.100) to help clear the mind before writing; guided writing in which the facilitator uses images and prompts to stimulate writing and enable subject matter to emerge gently; journal writing which can contain thoughts and feelings daily or when the mood strikes; lists, an accessible and familiar way to get pens flowing; postcards which can contain a short message to the self or someone else (texts, tweets and emails can perform the same function); sprint writing (Thompson in Bolton *et al.* 2004, p.76) in timed bursts of a minute or two; the time line which enables the writer to see the shape of a story or the events of a life; and the unsent letter, a way to say what needs to be said to those who cannot be spoken to directly.

These expressive techniques offer choices to enable the writer to address difficult thoughts and feelings on the page, whether by addressing their grief directly, or writing about other experiences, people and memories. Over time, people will find the techniques that suit them best.

## Techniques for creative writing in bereavement

If expressive writing is too challenging for those whose emotions are raw in grief, creative writing techniques can offer a gentler way to explore thoughts, emotions and memories.

Techniques such as metaphor enable the writer to describe a difficult thought or feeling or a mood in terms of something else. Somebody who is stumped for words to describe an emotion may be able to describe their mood as a kind of weather, or water or a colour. In bereavement, even happy memories can be too painful to recall. I have heard many people, in the early stages of grief, say that they cannot bear to remember happy times. The memories remain painful for a long time. Creativity provides an alternative, whether through the ability to imagine alternative ways of being, or to take people outside their current pain into a different real or imagined story.

The listing provided among the useful terms in Chapter 13 includes acrostics and alpha poems (Butler in Bolton, Field and Thompson 2006, pp.46–50), both useful forms of containment; free writing (Hilsdon in Bolton *et al.* 2004, pp.212–220), in which the writer simply starts to write with no particular aim in mind; life writing which embraces memoire, biography, autobiography and family history (something to which bereaved people often feel drawn as a way of processing their loss); metaphor in which something is described as something else (e.g. weather used to describe a mood), simile in which a comparison is made to something else; nano fiction or flash fiction in which a story is told in very few words; and poetry, which can take a range of forms and styles.

The writers' toolbox is endlessly flexible. Once someone hits on the right technique, the pen will fly across the page, or the fingers over the keyboard.

## The value of containment

Bereavement can feel like chaos, but certain forms bring a kind of order to the expression of chaotic and painful thoughts and feelings. One of the best examples of containment is the haiku. These minimalist and calming little poems are from a classical Japanese tradition dating back to the 17th century. Typically, they describe an event in nature in 17 syllables arranged in lines of five, seven and five. They do not rhyme. In Japanese, where the arrangement and juxtaposition of syllables can alter the sound and meaning of the words, they can be fiendishly hard to accomplish. English is a more pliable language and haiku are an ideal way to enable those who protest that they could never write a poem, to do just that.

Short forms, whether in poetry or fiction, provide manageable space in which to imply and express more expansive subject matter. The American writer Ernest Hemingway famously won a bet with his friend the playwright Eugene O'Neill, that he could write a novel in six words. Hemingway won his bet with this:

> For sale: baby shoes, never worn.
>
> (Hemingway in Ferleischer and Smith 2008).

It is hard to imagine a more moving or succinct expression of loss, whether fictional or real.

## Managing risks

Some reading this handbook will be concerned about when and how to use certain forms of writing, and whether to steer away from or fly close to certain themes and topics. Contra-indications are not always easy to identify in bereavement work; what one grief-stricken person finds distressing may leave another unmoved. One thing is certain however, in a bereavement writing group people will cry. People will also laugh and smile, however, as they share writing and talk together. Genuine laughter (rather than the sort that arises from social awkwardness or nervousness) can be a surprisingly common feature of group work amongst bereaved people. Bonnano's study of laughter in bereavement looked at 'the possible role in the recovery process played by positive emotional experiences, such as laughter,' and concluded that 'genuine laughter seems to help' (Bonnano 1999). Laughter is catching: 'it tends to induce positive emotions in other people through contagion' (ibid, pp.19–22). Those skilled in bereavement support will be used to the sometimes rapid movement from distress to calm via humour and back again.

As a facilitator, you will draw on your own expertise and understanding of the individuals in the room with you. In many respects, this is your best guide. If you have doubts about the suitability of a theme or technique for someone in, for instance, a blocked state of grief, or perhaps at too early a stage in their bereavement, listen to your doubts before deciding how to proceed.

Bear in mind that not everyone responds well to the invitation to write. This can be for any number of reasons. Perhaps it is too early in their grief for the activity to be of benefit. Someone for whom memories are too painful in the early stages of bereavement may struggle to put pen to paper when every prompt and theme seems to lead them down the path of painful associations. This can be hard for the facilitators to judge. An apparently harmless exercise around writing about flowers, for instance, might trigger distress in someone who has spent the weekend trying to get to grips with the overgrown garden, or may bring back memories of wreaths or a bridal bouquet. Someone who struggles to string a sentence together in the disorganised stage of grief may find the page is no better. Difficult thoughts and feelings can be stirred; sleep may be disrupted.

Such experiences are likely to be in the minority, but no one should be expected to write if it does not suit them. It is worth offering a reminder at the start of each session that the choice of what to write about is the writer's alone; also that each participant is responsible for their own feelings and responses. If someone does not wish to write about a given subject, they must feel able to allow a prompt to take them in another direction.

If you have doubts, always be prepared to enable the one who is struggling to opt out. Some people wait for permission; some feel they must continue at all odds. After all, a writing session can offer somewhere to go, which may be more attractive that the silence or chaos of home. Be guided by your observations of the participants in a group, by your understanding of the individuals in front of you and the feedback their behaviour suggests. The best advice I can offer is to trust them and trust yourself. It is worth persevering.

Whatever your perspective in picking up this handbook, I hope you will greet it in a spirit of adventure. The tools described here are offered to those who are prepared to try something new, to experiment with creative writing techniques, genres and forms, to enrich their own practice and enable others to make progress in their grief.

# CHAPTER 1

# An Overview of Writing in Bereavement

Let me tell you a story. This is an anecdote of the sort often shared among writers who run workshops in care and therapeutic settings. I offer it because it illustrates how a guided writing exercise can enable a bereaved person to access and express thoughts and feelings which may surprise them and enable a shift to take place in their grief process.

In the summer of 2009 I facilitated a writing group with the Bereavement Counselling Service at Princess Alice Hospice (Moss 2010, p.24). I worked with Anne Rivers, the (then) Counselling Co-ordinator, and a group of five women who ranged in age from their early 30s to late 60s. Before coming to our group they had not met before, but had in common the experience of having had someone close to them die within the last two years; some at the hospice, others at home with hospice support or elsewhere. The women had subsequently sought either counselling or other kinds of support through the hospice's counselling team. Some were receiving one to one counselling; others attended support groups in which they could meet and talk with others. The writing group had been set up to offer a supportive group with a creative focus. It met fortnightly on a weekday evening.

One evening one of the younger members of the group arrived late and flustered. She had had a bad day at work and was stressed. She had struggled through traffic to get to us and as she entered the hospice she spilled her bottle of water all over herself. By the time she had dried herself, the session had started (we had waited for her and had asked if it would be alright to begin without her). As she sat down she appeared a little tearful, but soon settled as the group got underway.

Our theme that evening was journeys. I guided the group through a structured exercise in which they wrote about a journey to their dream destination; perhaps somewhere they had visited in the past, or somewhere they had always wanted to visit. The exercise (which is provided in full in Chapter 5, p.111), began with five minutes of free writing. Each participant wrote a description of their destination using sensory detail: the scents, tastes, sounds, textures and sights of the place they were imagining. Then I gave them the good news that their tickets had arrived and they were about to set off.

First, they had to pack. They could take up to five items with them. I encouraged them to be imaginative in their choice: anything from sunglasses to their pet Labrador or a best friend; a positive outlook or a happy mood might be included in the packing. Once they had assembled their imaginary luggage in the form of a short list I told them that, because the baggage allowance had been reduced, they must choose just one item (there was laughter as they heard this). Once they had chosen what to take, I invited them to write an invitation.

In the second part of the exercise I asked the group to sit with eyes closed, picturing themselves arriving at their destination. I again invited them to experience the senses of scent, taste, touch, sight and sound; to savour the feeling of their feet on the ground, to sniff the air, taste the food and enjoy the look and feel of the place they were picturing for themselves. I invited them to open their eyes and write freely about the sensation of arriving, what it would mean to them and how they might feel having made the journey.

Finally, I asked them to write a postcard to whatever it was they had decided to leave behind. The exercise took 50 minutes, with further time for reading out, sharing and reflection on the writing that the group had produced. This was accomplished comfortably within a session lasting an hour and a half with some time at the start for welcomes and warm up, and time to wind down at the end.

This exercise can produce moving insights among bereaved people who are reshaping their lives following the death of someone close. This occasion was no exception. An hour after her late arrival, the young woman read out her account of a journey she had planned to take with her late husband; a trip of a lifetime which would have taken them to the Space Centre at NASA. She wrote about it as something that could happen in her future; a different future to the one she had imagined with her husband, but her future, nonetheless. She described what she would take with her – a camcorder to record the experience – and she imagined how she might feel having made that journey, whether on her own or with the support of family and friends.

As we listened, we recognised something in the writing which none of us had expected. Seeing her words on the page and hearing herself read them out to us, the young woman put it best herself when she said, 'I didn't expect to find myself writing about hope this evening, but that is what I feel.'

Writing can surprise us with its ability to uncover deep and unexpected feelings and realisations. The skill of the facilitator rests in how these moments of unexpected catharsis are contained and managed within the group or with individuals.

If you do search online for terms such as 'poems about loss' or 'bereavement writing', streams of titles appear. Websites and blogs are devoted to online memorials, whether offered as a service by charities or set up by families and individuals. One of the first in the UK, www. muchloved.com, is proving to be enduring. Facebook© – also achieving longevity among social networking sites – has developed an unexpected role as a space in which people write their messages about and to the departed (the young media entrepreneurs who conceived Facebook probably did not think of that one in their early planning meetings).

The journey exercise described above demonstrates, for me, that while emotions such as sadness and anger are bound to be expressed in bereavement writing, so too are hopefulness and the ability to look to the future. Good humour, kindness, positive memories and the ability to experience gentle enjoyment of small pleasures, both past and present, can also arise, often to the surprise and unexpected pleasure of the writer. Writing in a group enables people to explore and contain their experience within a place of safety. In this sense, bereavement writing groups have much in common with the writing that takes place in other areas of palliative care and counselling. By sharing their writing and comparing responses to writing exercises with others, participants can feel less isolated. In bereavement this has special value in terms of the sense of release people can feel and the pleasure of creativity. Two examples occur to me to illustrate this: a participant in a Princess Alice Hospice group in 2010 described the benefit of writing for her as, 'feeling I can lay my thoughts to rest.' For Teresa, in the same group, it felt 'so good to create something new.'

## The experience of bereavement

When we are bereaved we go inside ourselves. We go to a place which no one but the grieving can imagine; a place without present, past or future, in which the possibility of feeling different or better seems remote. Grief pitches us into unknown territory where nothing is as it was. No wonder some feel unnerved.

The experience of loss through the death of someone close to us is, sadly, inevitable. We all experience it; no one can avoid it. Those who go through it several times, and at different times of life, through the death of parents, partners, children, friends and even pets, come to understand that it takes many forms. Any loss, whether expected or sudden, can leave the griever bereft and distraught. The experience is both intensely personal and universal.

The shock of a sudden death is different from the sense of release and completion that can be experienced with the peaceful death of an elderly person; yet even those deaths that are expected and prepared for can weigh heavy in their finality for those who are left. The loss of a young person or a child through ill health or accident, or an untimely death at any age through suicide, murder or violence, leaves complex grieving to be done. If the relationship with the person who has died was fraught, the process of grieving for them can be especially difficult, regardless of the manner of the death. Anger, guilt and feelings of profound devastation may linger for years; an emotional roadblock impeding progress into future life.

Everyone's experience is unique to them, yet in the aftermath of a death, all bereavements have features in common. These can include the need to understand and accept the loss, to adapt to it in continuing daily life, and to move on into a different future in which the person who has died is remembered but is no longer physically present. There is a deep need to be understood, to be listened to and supported while the work of grief is carried out. Grief is a lonely place, no matter how many well-meaning and supportive people surround the bereaved person.

The process (if it can be called that) of grieving takes time. If you are skilled in bereavement theory you will understand that there are no hard and fast rules to determine how long it should take to feel better or how to go about grieving. For some it is a linear process, for some a process of one step forward, two steps back. Some get stuck and find it hard if not impossible to make a new life without the person who has died. Adjustment may not be easy and many seek help through counselling in the months and years – sometimes many years – after a death. The feeling of 'I ought to be over it by now' can be strong. Unfortunately, some find themselves feeling judged by others who imply that they should be 'over it'. Who can ever know how it feels until they are in that place themselves? Grief, like love, is not a tap to be turned on and off.

## Models of grief work

Those engaged in bereavement support are familiar with the theories of grief work. I recommend that others, such as writers entering this field, familiarise themselves with the most widely accepted models.

Here are some I have found helpful in approaching writing in bereavement (in no particular order).

### Kübler-Ross

Elizabeth Kübler-Ross was the first to identify five stages (Kübler-Ross 2009 [1970]):

1. shock and denial

2. anger

3. bargaining

4. depression and

5. acceptance.

In this model, the focus is on the one who is preparing to die. It is helpful in understanding the thoughts and feelings of the one who is faced with terminal illness, and can also be applied to the responses of those who are bereaved.

## Bowlby

John Bowlby describes four stages (Bowlby 1998):

1. numbing

2. yearning and searching

3. disorganisation and despair and

4. reorganisation.

Bowlby's model focuses on the early stages of numb shock or disbelief (the 'I just can't believe he's gone' feeling), the sense of longing which Thomas Hardy's poem 'The Voice' (Hardy 1994 [1914]), captures so heartrendingly, and the chaotic sense of life turned upside down before a semblance of order is restored. Bowlby's work on attachment is also important to an understanding of grief work.

## Murray Parkes

Colin Murray Parkes describes the stages of shock, separation and pain, despair, acceptance, resolution and reorganisation (Murray Parkes 1987). As Parkes observes, acceptance can be experienced intellectually before it is fully experienced emotionally. The bereaved person may swing back and forth between acceptance and feeling as bereft as ever (see Stroebe and Schut, below). 'I'm having good days and bad days' sums this up in terms with which we can all identify.

## Worden

J. William Worden defines 'four tasks of mourning' (Worden 2004):

1. to accept the reality of the loss

2. to work through the pain of grief

3. to adjust to an environment in which the deceased is missing

4. to emotionally relocate the deceased and move on with life.

You may find, as I do, that some of these models resonate with you personally. When I read Worden's theory I have a palpable sense of recognition. Having said that, the idea of a process in which the bereaved person moves in a straight line from one stage or task to the next (rather like ticking off the items on a list) does not fit everyone's experience. We humans are not built to be linear in our emotional responses.

## Stroebe and Schut

This leads us to Stroebe and Schut's Dual Process model (Stroebe and Schut 1999). Now widely accepted in bereavement support, this describes the bereaved person oscillating between a focus on grief and loss, and trying to restore themselves by reaching out into the world and seeking meaning and enjoyment in new activities.

## Tonkin

Then there is Tonkin's model (Tonkin 1996, p.10), which describes the process of accommodating a loss and building a new life around it. This acknowledges that the significance of the life being mourned does not necessarily diminish in its importance over time. Instead, the one who has died still occupies their place in the bereaved person's life, while the rest of life grows around it. Those who struggle with the idea that they are expected to move on from their loss can find this model helpful. It releases them from the pressure of 'getting over it' and allows them to acknowledge the continuing importance of their relation to the deceased, while being able to build new relationships and enjoy new experiences around and alongside their memory.

I am an enthusiast for Worden, the Dual Process and Tonkin's models and I have found it useful to reflect on my own experience of loss in relation to these theories. I recommend you do the same and give thought to the ways in which writing might enable someone at any given stage or task to express themselves or derive benefit from writing creatively. One size does not necessarily fit all when you are facilitating writing among a group of bereaved people with different experiences of loss and at differing stages in their grief work.

Thinking about your clients, consider these questions:

- What sort of writing activity in the early numb or shocked stage of grief might be either difficult or fruitful?

- What themes or topics might work well for someone who has reached a stage of acceptance, but is still oscillating between adjustment and pain?

- If someone's dominant emotion is anger, what does that suggest about their grief work, and how might writing help them to express it and find a balance for some of their worst thoughts and feelings?

In the early stages of grief, some people will reach for the diary or journal to get themselves through the dark days; others will write letters to the deceased, seeking a way to carry on or conclude the conversation that has been interrupted by death. Others may reach for these at later stages or find consolation in writing stories about the life of the one who has died, or in writing a family history based on photograph albums or family anecdotes. Delia, a Princess Alice Hospice group member reflected that after her mother's death she was 'unable to talk about things. Everything was just too raw. It was easiest for me to work through things in writing.' As time passed, Delia found writing about her current experiences and happier memories to be a kind of balm, following this difficult and sad period. Her journal 'helped me to look more positively at life. It made me focus on all my daily achievements and it even inspired me to achieve more, so that I had more to write about each evening (consequently the busier you are, the less time you have to focus on the sadness).'

The techniques for writing are variable and adaptable. As you find your way with a group or an individual, be mindful of the theories around grief work alongside the tools for self-expression which writing offers. Finding the mix is a skill but you will most likely find that the more you work with people and encourage them to experiment with writing, the more fruitful it will be.

Bear in mind that you are working with people whose lives are undergoing a seismic shift. For most, nothing will ever be the same again, or at least it may feel that way. This may include their very own sense of self; for instance the wife who now finds herself described as a widow, or the bereaved father who is no longer a parent in the physical day-to-day sense of bringing up a child. People's expectations of the future will have been altered. The parent whose only adult son dies will not become a grandparent. The husband who took early retirement to enjoy time with his wife finds himself alone after her death following a short illness. Neimeyer describes this readjustment like 'a novel that loses a central character in the middle chapters, the life story disrupted by loss must be reorganised, rewritten, to find a new strand of continuity that bridges the past with the present in an intelligible fashion' (Neimeyer 2007, p.263).

# Men and women: What's the difference?

Another ingredient to bear in mind is awareness of the gender difference in the ways women and men grieve and the different emotional, cognitive and practical responses they may exhibit. Walter observes, 'Women tend to prefer social support and emotionally oriented styles of coping, while men prefer to be active and to solve problems' (Walter 1996). Similarly, Doka and Martin pinpoint the difference in grieving styles between men and woman in terms of instrumental and intuitive grieving (Doka and Martin 2010). An instrumental griever will immerse themselves in practicalities (think of Alan, the suddenly single parent in our fictional Greenbank group, signing up for every activity he can, to keep busy). Intuitive grieving, on the other hand, is exemplified by the grandmother who weeps with her grandchildren over the death of their mother (her daughter). In the Greenbank group, Ros perhaps exemplifies this intuitive grieving with her tendency to send text messages to her late husband's phone and talk to her close circle of female friends.

These may seem like gender stereotypes, but reality bears them out. The bereaved person who establishes a memorial fund, or runs a marathon to raise money for charity, is immersing themselves in an activity which, consciously or not, they hope will help to counter their loss. Others may embark on legal action or a campaign. As Doka and Martin observe, instrumental grievers '...focus on the problems caused by the loss, actively trying to find appropriate solutions or engaging in activity related to the loss' (Doka and Martin 2010, p.9).

Cognitive grieving describes a reaction in which someone is preoccupied with the loss, going over it again and again in their minds. Cognitive grief can find relief in the written word; 'getting it out of my head is such a relief', as some put it.

In a mixed gender group, men may be in the minority, yet they are just as likely (from my observation) to be as keen as women to write about memories, thoughts and feelings, to write poetry and express themselves through the written word. Dave, the lone man in an otherwise all women bereavement writing group at Meadow House, commented, 'I felt a certain amount of apprehension and nervousness, and being the only male presence in the group didn't help my initial uncertainties. However, the fact that we all shared the same feelings of grief and loss, and that common bond, soon lessened any doubts I may have had.' Dave felt that attendance at the writing group had enabled him to 'talk about subjects

I may have avoided in the past... [I] am more inclined to reveal what I'm really thinking and feeling, especially with close family members.'

## The core skills

Rather than attempt to analyse specific models of grief in terms of writing as an intervention, I suggest that the core counselling skills used in bereavement support provide the best clues in terms of when and how writing can help with grieving.

Those trained in bereavement support will possess the core skills of:

- listening – the ability to listen actively and attentively

- exploring – the ability to explore and understand what is being expressed or experienced

- clarifying – the ability to challenge and reflect on what is being expressed, especially those thoughts and feelings which may seem complex or contradictory, both to the speaker or writer and to the listener.

Threaded through these essential skills is the concept of 'unconditional positive regard' (Rogers 1967). This is the listener's ability to listen, be present, show empathy and remain congruent (in other words, to show sincere rapport with someone), with whatever is being expressed, no matter how painful, distressing or perhaps at odds with the listener's own experience and values.

The fear of being misunderstood or not heard in a supportive non-judging way is a barrier to many people when considering how to talk about their bereavement. The risk of talking to friends and family about the most desperate and sad aspects of bereavement and being met with a baffled or embarrassed response, can feel too great.

When people seek support in bereavement they tend to do it for three reasons. Drawing on the models described above, I would pinpoint these reasons as:

1. To be listened to. This can be at any stage of the grief process.

2. To make sense of what has happened. This is likely to take place further into the process, for example during the period of yearning and searching for meaning, or as someone begins to feel able to adjust to and accept the loss.

3. As part of reorganisation and making a new life. This includes the process of revising the bereaved person's narrative about their life, although this work is likely to occur under reason 2 as well.

In each of these, writing can aid self-expression and can offer a complement to, or a replacement for, talking. It can do this both as a means of expression on the page – literally talking and listening to oneself – and also as a creative activity; something to try for oneself and share with others as steps are taken to reorganise life and move into the future without the person who has died. Many people cite this sense of wanting to try something new, as a means of getting out of a stuck place in their grief and enabling, even kick-starting, their efforts to move on.

After the initial shock of the loss, after the phone calls, funerals and flowers, the visits from family and friends, the real work of grieving begins. It is then, in the small hours and quiet afternoons, when the phone doesn't ring and the old routines are redundant, or as a complement to the talking therapy found in the counselling room or on the phone, that the pen and paper of a journal, or a letter to the person who is no longer present in body, can offer comfort and a way to accept and adapt to the profound change that loss brings. Bolton says, memorably:

> Writing is different from talking… It can allow an exploration of cognitive and spiritual areas otherwise not accessible, and expression of elements otherwise inexpressible. (Bolton *et al.* 2004, p.1)

In feedback following a writing session, I have often heard people comment that the page has felt like an unfailingly sympathetic friend who listens to them, no matter how dark or sad the words. Often, people will liken the page to a private place in which they can say anything at any time, without fear of censorship or rebuke. Jean, an enthusiast for journal writing, put it well when she said 'my journal will never judge me.' For someone like Jean, dealing with difficult feelings lingering from the loss of a parent for whom she was principal carer and companion, the page offers freedom and a shelter in which to hold a conversation with oneself and others; to rant, rage, express anger, guilt, regret and whatever other raw and painful emotions need to be expressed. Yet it is also the vessel for reflections of love, longing, kindness, gratitude, hopefulness and comfort. The page will not argue or challenge; it will hear the writer out as they express some of the most painful feelings that human beings can experience.

What is written can be as private or as shared at the writer wishes. It can be available at any time of day or night for as long or as brief a burst of writing as feels necessary. It can be kept and read back, or it can be torn up, burned or thrown away. The writer is in control. This flexibility is one of writing's great strengths. In terms of offering unconditional positive regard, the written word has few equals.

People who seek bereavement support sometimes ask 'am I going mad?' In the great majority of cases, the answer, of course, is 'no', but in the worst moments of despair and exhaustion grief can certainly feel like illness, both physical and emotional. Murray Parkes has questioned whether bereavement is an illness and whether it should be treated as such. He concluded that grief, although not an illness in itself, can give rise to symptoms of illness, and can affect both physical and mental health; 'On the whole, grief resembles a physical illness more closely than any other type of illness' (Murray Parkes 1987, p.25). Worden likens mourning to the process of recovery from injury or trauma and notes that there can be an increase in 'symptoms such as headaches, trembling, dizziness, heart palpitations and various gastrointestinal symptoms' (Worden 2004, p.2) after a loss.

Bereaved people may feel sad, tired, joyless and burdened by their loss; they may be stuck in the present, unable to remember the past with happiness or look forward to the future. In the early days they may feel numb; as time passes they may feel anger, exhaustion and distress. They may exhibit symptoms of physical ill health, but they are not ill *per se*, nor are they necessarily without hope. As one participant said to me, 'I've had enough of the sadness. I want to look forward now and write about happy things.'

Death may still be taboo in our society and people will cross the road to avoid talking to someone recently bereaved, but the bereaved are among the most willing to look it in the face and be honest about its effect on the living. This honesty gives the rest of us our cue in listening, talking and writing with them.

## Writing expressively, writing creatively

The question of when writing may be of value to someone working through grief has no straightforward answer. It seems fair to say (from observation and feedback), that different forms and techniques of writing can come into play at different stages, for different people. Then again, it may be the case that people respond differently to the same techniques, either because of their natural tastes and tendencies or because the right technique at the right time will provide a valuable trigger for them. I have seen this happen often in writing groups and with individuals. Someone will look as if a light bulb has gone on inside them and they will start to write at speed, filling the page as if they can hardly get the words out fast enough. Others may sit unmoved and eventually make a few cautious marks on the paper (those marks can, in themselves, be significant, however). I am reminded of one example; a quiet member of a bereavement writing group, who would sometimes pause for a long time before writing. She rarely spoke in the group but when she did there was always insight and precision in her contributions. Asked to compare herself with an animal, she wrote that she felt 'like a lost cat that can't find its home.'

Some will cite the desire to 'do something creative' among their reasons for taking pen to page in bereavement. Others will mention 'needing to express myself, somehow.' Teresa, a participant at Princess Alice Hospice, expressed frustration at only being able to write in blunt, staccato words. Writing close observations of nature enabled her to move on a little from her blocked state.

In a typical group, few will be experienced as writers beyond memories of school or college essays, letter writing or keeping a diary or journal. The difference between writing as a creative activity and writing as a means of self-expression is a distinction that few will make consciously. It is worth, however, considering the distinction from the facilitator's point of view.

Expressive writing can enable a bereaved person to vent their feelings of anger and distress on the page. By finding words, metaphors and images to express the pain of loss, and seeing them written down, it may become possible to understand those feelings and begin accepting the reality of the loss. For the individual, writing in a journal can be especially effective.

As the bereaved person adjusts to their loss, personal writing of a more creative kind can provide comfort. Many people turn to art, music, poetry or works of fiction in times of illness, stress and sadness (Walter forthcoming 2012). The consumption of art, music and literature provides comfort, solace and distraction. Having said that, many will also comment that they are unable to concentrate on reading anything as lengthy as a novel after a loss. The inability to watch the news ('too sad') or listen to music ('too emotional') is also common. Short stories, magazine articles, websites and poems can offer more digestible reading material for those who find themselves unable to focus for more than a few sentences or pages at a time. This is a normal response in the earlier stages of grief and can last for some considerable time, in tandem with feelings of numbness, exhaustion and disorientation.

For a bereaved person, the act of exploring or rediscovering their creativity can signal an important stage in adjusting to loss. When the product of the creative process, whether a poem, short story or a piece of well-crafted dialogue, enables the writer to communicate something of importance to them, the value of the creative act is two-fold.

Writing can be a private activity or a shared one. Someone who needs to have their experience acknowledged and heard following a death can find a useful personal space on the page in which to record their feelings and thoughts about the loss. Someone from a large family, who finds it harder to talk about the loss of a parent than their siblings, or where one person's experience of the bereavement is dominant, can find writing a helpful way to record their own loss and its meaning for them. Whether or not they choose to share it with others is up to them. The act of writing it down and being heard on the page by themselves, can offer a way of rehearsing what they wish to say to the wider family, as well as being comforting and a release in itself.

---

## Greenbank group

Bearing in mind the different models and stages of grief represented by members of the group, the facilitators, Fiona and Michael, will think about the ways in which writing may benefit them as a group activity, or as individuals.

- The group contains instrumental, intuitive and cognitive grievers. This may make a difference to the ways in which the participants use writing. For instance, Alan who is talkative and tends to throw himself into lots of activity may take a while to focus on writing.

- Cynthia might find that writing creatively can help her to relax, while some of the expressive techniques such as lists might help her organise her time and feel more in control of the gargantuan task she faces in sorting through her mother's cluttered home.

- Bobbie, who is angry with some members of her family and with the army, might find ways to express her anger and understand its roots. This may help her feel less guilty that she was not able to support her daughter when she first received news of Angus's death.

- Riaz, who is dealing with difficult and complex grief arising from suicide, and whose background and circumstances suggest he must keep up a brave face might find it hard to disclose feelings in the group at first, but poetry and journal writing may help him find a form of expression and share his writing in the supportive group atmosphere away from the pressures of family and business responsibility.

CHAPTER 2

# Starting to Write

A mixed group of people meeting for the first time will exhibit all the signs of trepidation mingled with cautious excitement and more. The facilitator's role is to act partly as host, partly as director, but above all to be welcoming, to put people at ease and ensure that the writing gets off to a positive start. It will have taken some people a lot of effort and courage to attend. In bereavement, it will represent not just the start of new social or learning experiences, but a real step into the unknown; tangible proof that their lives have changed. If they had not been bereaved, they probably would not be doing this.

In the first meeting you will begin to find out how individuals behave and how the group will work together. In this chapter I offer ways for you to break the ice and ease everyone into writing.

## Welcome and introductions

When everyone is seated and settled, it is natural to begin with a welcome. If you are working in partnership (a team of writer and bereavement support practitioner for example), this is best coming from the host who should also provide house-keeping information such as the location of fire exits and directions to the cloakroom.

As facilitator you can then begin by saying something about your skills whether as a writer, or as a bereavement support practitioner with an interest in and skills for writing. Mention your interest in writing as an aid in bereavement and any track record you have of work in this context. This will reassure the group that they are in safe hands.

Bereaved people are particularly sensitive to the feeling that other people may be upset or feel they have to tread on eggshells around them. By letting them know that you have relevant training and skills, you put them at ease.

Introductions over, it is time to invite the group to introduce themselves. Depending on numbers, you can invite them to work in pairs, or speak directly to the whole group. Working in pairs at the outset helps encourage the nervous or shy; either way, this first exercise in group work ensures that everyone contributes and is heard.

## Name games and icebreakers

Here are some suggestions to get the ball rolling:

1. Invite the group to write their name on the first page of their notebook, adding an adjective beginning with the same letter as their name. This makes use of alliteration (a string of words beginning with the same letter), and keeps the introductions brief but focused. At this early stage, some may feel uneasy if they hear others going into detail. They may not yet wish to disclose personal information to strangers. I often provide my own example to get the ball rolling, even though J is not the easiest of letters to work with.

---

### Greenbank group

Some of the group introduce themselves with their alliterations:

*All over the place Alan.*

*Miserable Marielle.*

*Sad Cynthia (who is allowed to cheat with the 's' sound).*

---

2. Invite participants to write their name and describe something about it; perhaps its meaning, or who gave it to them, or what they like (or not) about it. This will encourage a flow of information about family, married or maiden

names (for women), nicknames, and anecdotes about their parents' choices. Some may disclose information about adoption or other aspects of their upbringing.

3. Invite participants to write their name and say what has brought them here; again, using alliteration and zeugma (where two contrasting nouns agree with the same verb). Again, I would offer my own example to help get the ball rolling:

*I'm Jane and I've come here in hope and a Honda.*

---

## Greenbank group

Bobbie and Riaz come up with these examples:

*Bobbie on a bus and with a broken heart.*
*Riaz in a rush and a red Renault.*

---

These can produce the groups' first laughter, as well as sympathy and the beginnings of group bonding as people start tentatively to reveal information about themselves and their reasons for attending.

People's answers to the question 'what has brought you here?' can be revealing of mood, purpose and expectation. Someone who says they have come because someone else said they might enjoy it may mean that they have been told to come, rather than choosing it for themselves. Be alert for clues that they might not (yet) be convinced that a writing group is right for them (I can envisage Riaz in the Greenbank group saying that his wife has been nagging him to come to something like this. He probably feels it is taking him away from valuable time at the office).

4. Invite participants to write about their route to get here and anything unusual they noticed or encountered on the way. This can produce short written sketches (timed by the facilitator as a sprint write) that get people writing quickly and freely, and start to stimulate their powers of observation.

## Greenbank group

Someone like Bobbie, whose grandson died on active service, might mention seeing a newspaper headline about the latest army losses while on the bus and flinching at the sight.

Alan might mention that his normal route would take him past the school where his wife Ali used to work. His journey took longer than necessary because he had to go a longer way round to avoid it.

 5. In a more direct approach, invite people to share their names and write for three minutes (a sprint write) about their reasons for attending the group. This may produce a variety of reasons for attending a writing session, and many similarities.

## Greenbank group

Members of the group write about their reasons for attending:

> Ros: 'I write to my husband everyday on his Facebook wall and I send him text messages. It comforts me. I'd like to do other sorts of writing; maybe write about him for our daughter to read when she's old enough.'

> Cynthia: 'I feel blank. I want to feel like myself again but the words won't come at the moment.'

> Bobbie: 'I feel so angry I can't sleep. I want to get it all out of my system and on to the page.'

> Alan: 'I need to get out of the house. It's chaos with the kids.'

Fiona notices that Alan does not mention the desire to write specifically. He may be attending the group because of his desire to stay busy and engage with lots of different activities.

Common reasons that emerge from this exercise include:

- the desire to meet others who share a similar experience
- the urge to attempt something new and creative after a period of desolation

- in order to return to or recover a version of themselves from before their bereavement

- because someone has told them they should, or that they might enjoy it

- to get out of the house

- to learn different ways to express themselves.

You may hear others being articulated. Not all of them will focus on writing as an activity, so it is important that the facilitator stresses this and enables everyone to pick up the pen from the earliest stages.

## The principle of sharing

These introductory exercises enable the facilitator to establish the principle of sharing what has been written. This can induce nerves in the first meeting, yet those nerves may arise more from the thought that what they write will be scrutinised for spelling and grammar, than from anxiety around emotional disclosure. If sharing is encouraged from the very start, those fears can soon be allayed. The group will soon discover how much they have in common by reading their words and hearing others' words. Insights into everyday lives and what is important to them will start to be shared. It will soon be clear that everyone has stories to tell.

## Bonding the group

After the sharing that arises from the introductory writing exercises, you will have the beginnings of an established group and a way of working together. Empathy will emerge as people become interested in each other and start to discover things in common. Some may mention their bereavement, others may not, but the tone will have been set.

As a follow-up to sharing names, invite your participants to speak more generally about what they hope to do in the group, perhaps describing their interest in writing and whether they have written before. This can be done in pairs or, if there are enough people, in threes so that more of the group get to know each other. This is a further opportunity for them to mention some of their hopes and fears about joining the group, and their interests.

Typical expressions of anxiety will include:

- My spelling is terrible.

- My handwriting is illegible.

- I'm worried about having to read out what I've written.

- I'm embarrassed to cry or show emotion.

- My crying may make others feel uncomfortable or upset.

- I was never any good at school essays.

These are legitimate worries, but sharing anxieties round the table will enable people to relax.

You can broaden the discussion to include anything they enjoy reading, such as favourite authors, books or poems. Their suggestions will give you ideas for published texts to draw on and forms of writing to introduce in future sessions.

You may find at this stage that you have a room full of people who enjoy (or are terrified of) poetry. A comment such as, 'I'm not clever enough to write poetry' (which I have heard many times) tells me that this person may have had a bad experience at school, or may not have been introduced to accessible or contemporary forms of poetry. Perhaps it seems elitist to them. Some people's perception of poetry is so bound up in having been made to read 'difficult' work, or the expectation that a poem has to rhyme, that they cannot imagine being able to write recognisable poems for themselves.

A common interest in writing life histories or drawing on memories may emerge, or the desire to keep a journal (some may already keep diaries or journals). Such comments provide helpful pointers for planning future sessions, although do not discount the possibility of introducing people to other forms. As they become used to writing and more comfortable with experimentation they, and you, may be surprised by the results.

Another way to capture this information is through a short questionnaire. Here is one I have used to elicit information from new bereavement writing groups. I find this is a useful way to ensure that everyone contributes, even those who are reticent to speak up.

## QUESTIONNAIRE

Please help us plan our writing sessions over the next eight weeks by completing this short questionnaire.

Name: _____

1. What sort of writing are you interested in (do you like poems, stories, writing about your own life or others', or do you keep a diary or journal)?

   _____
   _____
   _____

2. What sort of writing have you done in the past, or do you do now?

   _____
   _____
   _____

3. What do you enjoy reading?

   _____
   _____
   _____

4. How do you hope writing might help you in your current situation? Please continue over the page if necessary.

   _____
   _____
   _____

Thank you.

*Note:* This questionnaire is available for download from the JKP website at www.jkp.com/catalogue/book/9781849052122/resources

If you can allow about ten minutes at the end of the first session for people to complete this, it can form part of the writing activity itself. Encourage your participants to complete the form within the session, rather than take it away with them for completion at home. This rarely works; people will forget, or will fail to bring it with them the following week.

---

## Greenbank group

Fiona gives the group a prompt: 'What can writing do for me now?'

Riaz writes: 'I talk to my brother in my head. I lie awake at night and I tell him how the business is doing. Sometimes I ask his advice. Sometimes I shout at him. My counsellor says it might help me to write some of this down because it stops me sleeping.'

Marielle writes: 'I had a wonderful life with my husband. We travelled the world together. I would like to be able to remember it all but at the moment it makes me too upset. Writing about it might be easier. I want to make a scrap book of our photographs and the mementoes from our travels. His grandchildren might be interested in it one day.'

Anna does not write, but says: 'I feel as if I want to apologise to Pat for letting her down. I'd like to write her a letter. It sounds ridiculous, but if I can write to her I might be able to get it off my chest. There are things I want to say to her family as well but I can't talk to them without getting upset and angry. They have been so cold and unkind to me since she died. Why? I'd like to rehearse to them what I'd like to say.'

From these, Michael notices that Riaz has taken on board his counsellor's suggestion that writing might help him with his complex grieving. When Riaz shares this with the group, Michael, Fiona and the others can affirm his idea of writing to his brother. Fiona may go on to suggest he writes a dialogue or an unsent letter. Marielle's wish to write about her husband's life and share it with his grandchildren suggests she wants to reach out to his family, who are not close to her at the moment. Her idea of producing a scrapbook is a tangible place for her to start and can be achieved creatively with stimulus from the group. Anna's desire to write to Pat would be a good exercise to follow up in her one to one bereavement support, although she might also wish to bring this to the group, where she would be listened to and affirmed. Dialogue may also help her to rehearse what she wants to say to Pat's family. Fiona may suggest journal writing techniques to help Anna explore her difficult thoughts and feelings about the family.

---

# Warming up

In the early sessions of group work, warm up exercises help put people at ease and settle down after the distractions of home or work. For those who are less confident about writing, these accessible exercises build confidence and reassure people that they have material to contribute and stories to tell. Think of these as limbering up or stretching before embarking on a swim or a run. Like exercise, writing is hard to do well from a standing start.

 ## SHOES, CLOTHES AND PERSONAL ITEMS

Invite the group to stand up or move their chairs so that everyone can see each other's shoes. Invite them to describe the shoes they are wearing and explain why they chose to wear them today.

This carries an element of surprise as well as offering the way into reflective writing and empathy. Once everyone has described their shoes you can draw out points of comparison; most people, for example, will have mentioned the desire for comfort and there is bound to be good humour in people's descriptions of their footwear.

When everyone has described their shoes, invite them to write from the prompt: 'How does it feel to stand in these shoes?' Some will take the question literally; others will seize the opportunity to write reflectively, using metaphor and imagery.

---

## Greenbank group

Alan writes: 'My shoes are old trainers. They should be comfortable but my feet are different sizes and the left one is too small. I don't want to be wearing these shoes but they're the only ones I can find to wear at the moment. I can't be bothered to get new ones. Ali was always the one who thought about things like that but since she died I haven't had time. I'm too busy looking after the children. It makes me realise how much she did for us all.'

As Alan reads this out to the group, others nod in sympathy. Anna says she can't be bothered to wear nice things anymore. Marielle says she always tries to look her best 'for my husband', even though he can no longer admire her. The group reflects together on the different responses. Some take little care of their appearance since their bereavement, others still try to look smart. Michael invites Alan to reflect on how he could make more time for himself, but Alan replies that he is better being busy. Riaz agrees with him: 'I have to keep going or the business and the family will suffer.' Hearing this, Alan acknowledges that perhaps he does need to slow down sometimes. He is comparing himself with Riaz, who is obviously stressed.

Listening to Alan's description of his shoes, Fiona wonders if he has unconsciously made a metaphor to describe his feelings about his current situation: 'I don't want to be wearing these shoes…'. She offers this to Alan but he does not immediately acknowledge it. Cynthia, hearing this, agrees and says she feels as if she is in a situation she has not chosen for herself, like wearing something constricting (her shoes are pinching her feet). Alan is quiet while she talks but others nod agreement. Michael makes a note to follow this up with Alan after the session.

---

A similar effect can be achieved with 'How does it feel to wear this coat?', or 'How does it feel to carry this bag?' Clothes and shoes can be the vehicle for exploration of mood and how the wearer is feeling in the present moment; a less abrupt way into the expression of feelings than 'How are you feeling?' or 'Tell us about yourself.'

Another approach is to invite people to say something about a favourite item they are wearing or which they always carry with them; for example a watch or ring, a photograph they keep in their wallet, or an item of personal significance which they always have with them. This can give rise to family stories and anecdotes, and to personal insight as they describe why the item carries the significance it does.

 ## THE FURNITURE GAME

This is a favourite creative writing exercise, often used to generate metaphor and imagery in poetry. Adapted from a word game (Sansom 2007, p.76), it invites people to describe themselves through metaphor; in other words, comparing themselves to something else. Try these prompts:

Describe yourself as:

- a piece of furniture
- an animal
- a flower
- a time of day
- a type of weather
- an item of clothing
- a song.

The insights that emerge can be startling and moving. Sarah, a young woman grieving for her mother, described herself as an old ladder:

> *I feel like an old ladder.*
> *It serves its purpose.*
> *It's strong, reliable and helps people to achieve their goal.*
> *Without it things would not get done – goals would not be achieved.*
> *The ladder has been frail for a little while now, but no one appears*
>     *concerned.*
> *As long as they can get their use out of it, then it is somebody else's*
>     *problem.*
> *It's a sturdy thing and that crack will hold for one more task – won't it?*
> *It needs to be tested. If it keeps working why add support? Why try to fix it?*
> *Let us see how much it can take.*
> *'One day it will break, but hopefully not on my watch', they will say.*
> *In any case, if it does, it can be temporarily fixed and bound together*
>     *ready to use – until the next time it fails.*

Sarah has taken her ladder metaphor and extended it into a reflective piece of writing about her sense of carrying the weight of many responsibilities which others around her assume can be borne. The ladder is frail but no one will take responsibility for looking after it; instead adding more burdens to it.

The furniture game uses a simple list approach; a form that enables even the most reticent to start writing. Here is another example, by someone whose husband had died. She chooses the metaphor of a lost cat to explore her mood:

> Today there seems to be so much negativity around; it's quite cold and now it has started to rain which seems to add to my lack of energy and motivation. I feel like a lost cat that doesn't really belong anywhere. I wander around from place to place and can't seem to organise myself. I know why but don't seem to have the ability (maybe that's not the right word) to resolve any of these tasks that need attending to.

The writer's disorientation and restlessness, is perhaps indicative of the yearning, searching stage of grief work (Bowlby 1998), and it finds an effective metaphor.

Variations on this technique can focus on specific feelings or emotions. For example:

'If you could describe your mood today as a soundtrack, what sort of music would it play?'

or

'What is your personal weather forecast today?'

This can be used to check in at the start of a writing session, and again at the end, to see whether people's general mood has shifted. Someone who arrives as a heavy storm cloud may leave as a light shower.

If you can encourage people to revisit their metaphors over a period of weeks, or to reflect on them in their own time, perhaps as part of journal writing, they may be able to see progress in their grieving or shifts in mood as their metaphors change.

---

## Greenbank group

Fiona invites the group to choose a style of music to describe themselves.
Riaz describes himself as a stuck record, endlessly replaying questions about his brother's suicide. Alan describes himself as a quickstep, always on the move, feet hardly touching the ground. Cynthia chooses a slow march for the time she is working through the clutter in her mother's house, and a gavotte for the hours she spends at work, trying to keep up.

---

 COLOUR

Colour is an effective way to express and understand the transitions that people may be making through their grief work. Try this:

- Think about the day you are having today.
- Choose a colour that represents it.
- Write about that colour and any associations it has for you.
- If the colour had a taste what would it be?
- If you could touch it how would it feel?
- If it had a scent what would it be?
- Is it hot or cold?

- How might it move?
- What might it sound like?

Ask the group to write freely about their colour, using lists and word associations until they are finished, for up to ten minutes, then invite them to compare notes.

In one example Liz, a woman with multiple sclerosis who had lost her husband almost a year ago, described the pain in her legs as 'red for pain, fire, strength and defiance.' A week later, after a visit to the specialist, Liz's vivid red pain had softened to 'a more pinkish glow' (see p.198).

Jan chose an orange rose to express her feelings about her daughter's forthcoming wedding:

> *It says that I am planning my older daughter's wedding in September (she is having cream coloured roses).*
>
> *But I am remembering my own wedding 37 years ago, when I had orange coloured roses.*
>
> *I am thinking of my mum and how she coped with the arrangements of my wedding, almost all on her own.*
>
> *How hard it must have been for her.*
>
> *Also my wedding day/anniversary is the same day as my grandmother's birthday – her mother.*
>
> *I am having to face my daughter's wedding without my mother there. I wonder how she felt without her mother there at my wedding?*

 **WHAT I KNOW**

This is another exercise used to generate poetry (Sansom 2007, p.77), which can be adapted to enable people to describe themselves without the pressure of being asked to disclose too much information before they feel ready or trusting of the group.

This may be introduced by inviting participants to name the various kinds of writing they do in their everyday lives. People typically offer the following as examples:

- letters
- notes
- emails
- texts

- postcards
- shopping lists
- daily 'to do' lists
- diary entry or journal.

Most people write lists of one kind or another, so this is a good form with which to demonstrate how easy it can be to start to write.

Offer the trigger 'what I know' or 'ten things I know' and invite the group to write for five minutes. If people look puzzled, offer 'I know my own name' as a starting point. Some will take the list idea literally and list 'things I know'. Others may interpret it in more subtle and personal ways.

When the lists are complete (let people know that it is alright to produce fewer or more than ten, although the challenge of reaching the number can induce momentum), invite people to read their lists back to themselves and choose one item to write about in more depth for a further five minutes. This will enable to them to explore anything that seems significant or has surprised them. When something that is written quickly surprises the writer, it often contains truth.

When you invite the writing to be shared, make it clear that they do not have to read their lists if they contain material they are not comfortable sharing with the rest of the group. Instead, invite them to comment or reflect on the exercise and any insights it has given them.

---

## Greenbank group

Cynthia writes her list of 'things I know':

I know I have to tackle Mother's wardrobe soon.

I know I have to organise someone to cut the hedge before winter.

I know I have to get up early to drive a long way to work in the morning.

I know I need to slow down and have a rest, but I can't.

I know I miss my own home.

I know I am drinking too much in the evenings.

Cynthia's list surprises her when she reads it back to herself. She chooses not to read it to the whole group, but comments that it has made her realise two very important things she needs to do. She needs to be easier on herself ('who says I have to sort out the wardrobe soon?'), and she needs to speak to her employer about taking more time off work so she can cope better. She does not mention her drinking, but thinks she may take this to her one to one bereavement support session next week.

---

These warm up exercises offer easy ways into writing, without the pressure of staring at a blank page. The activity of sitting together around a table and seeing how others begin to write, some swiftly and fluently, others a little more slowly and painstakingly, can provide reassurance that everyone is able to come up with something. The invitation to share may at first be accepted by just a few, but over time it would be unusual for everyone not to join in.

The effect of sharing writing creates the beginning of trust and a bond among the group. For people who feel isolated in their bereavement, this can be the start of feeling supported. The sharing of insights which spring off the page forms part of the benefits of writing in bereavement.

It is worth reflecting on this towards the end of the first session, thanking people for their contributions and acknowledging the group's achievement after just a short time together.

## Working with ground rules

The first session is the moment to invite the group to devise its ground rules (see Chapter 12, p.227). Rather than enforcing these at the start, I recommend introducing them at the start of the first session and leaving time towards the end to review them. This means that the group has had some experience of writing together before deciding how to fully express their rules. Confidentiality is likely to be raised and you should take the opportunity to reassure people that anything they disclose will remain confidential to the group. They must feel free to discuss their own writing with family or friends, or in one to one bereavement support, but should respect others' privacy and not talk about writing or information shared by others in the group.

# Review

Having completed the group's first session, the facilitator(s) should review how it has gone, while the experience is fresh in their minds.

Points to consider are:

- Did everyone attend who was expected to? If not, make contact with them and reiterate the invitation. They may feel they cannot come having missed the first session.

- Did the group gel? Was anyone dominant or quiet? How can you achieve balance in future sessions, so that everyone contributes and no one person is dominant?

- How was the timing? Do you need to adjust the number and duration of exercises?

- To what extent did people share information about their bereavement? Did anyone stand out as either over-sharing or not sharing? How can you handle this sensitively in future sessions?

- What sense do you have of where participants are in their progress through grief? Be alert to anyone who may be struggling with complex issues.

- Did everyone write? If someone seems reluctant to engage with the writing activity, preferring to talk, it will be necessary gently to remind them that this is a writing group. If they would rather join a group where the emphasis is on talking, perhaps that can be offered as an alternative.

- Does anyone have special requirements that were not apparent at the time of the invitation; for example is anyone hard of hearing or in need of large print materials?

- Has anything emerged that surprises you about this group or which is likely to present a challenge in future sessions?

- What interests do the group seem to have in common; for example, any interests they have expressed in types of writing or themes. How can these be worked into future sessions?

- Finally, did anything arise which you found personally upsetting or disturbing? In terms of your own self-care, be alert for subject matter that awakens difficult feelings or sadness for you.

If necessary, find someone to talk to about these feelings (ideally in supervision).

## Next steps

With the first session under your belt, and having gained insight into the group's interests and behaviours, you can start to plan further writing activities. A common concern among any writing group or individual, and indeed for most writers, is what to write *about*. Your group may have raised this in their introductions; some will be nervous about being made to write about sensitive subject matter (not necessarily just their bereavement). Whether and how they choose to write about their bereavement may be influenced by the nature of their loss and the stage they are at on their journey through grief.

With individuals, or in a group comprising people with a similar type of loss in common, the question of whether to write directly about the bereavement will be less of a challenge. In groups of a more mixed nature, you should give careful thought to the responses your exercises may elicit. You can never know for sure how someone will react to or interpret an exercise (therein lies the magic, but also the intrinsic risk). As a group settles and matures, new information may be disclosed that has not emerged in one to one support. It is important for people to feel that whatever they share of their writing will be heard and accepted by the group without judgement.

It is likely that participants will reflect through their writing the major and common themes of bereavement. Dodie Graves sets out a valuable commentary on themes that can provide a structure for working with bereaved people (Graves 2009). Although developed in the context of talking to bereaved people and supporting them through listening, I find Graves's ideas especially helpful in the context of writing.

Graves uses the metaphor of a journey to describe the client's experience of their grief. She sets out these three pointers (as she terms them), which are helpful in guiding the bereavement support provider in how to listen and talk:

1.  Reflect on what you would expect to see at the start of the journey of grief.

2.  What would you expect to hear from people as the experience of their loss becomes more of a reality to them?

3.  Consider what you would expect to hear from people as they are further along in their journey towards some measure of adjustment to their changed life circumstances.

(Graves 2009, p.147)

Graves talks about 'trying to plot this journey of grief' (ibid, p.147); an interesting allusion to the process of structuring a narrative in writing terms. Her approach suggests the following questions for facilitators of writing groups in bereavement to ask when presented with a group that is mixed in terms of individuals' stages on the journey she describes, or in terms of the different degrees of grief, whether difficult, complex or stuck:

1.  What might you expect people who are recently bereaved (up to six months) to express in their writing? (Be prepared to have those expectations challenged as well as met.)

2.  What might people who are experiencing complex or stuck grief express through their writing, or wish to explore?

3.  How might people with different experiences of grief find commonality through sharing their writing?

4.  What is your role as facilitator in enabling them to share their writing and reflect together on their experiences?

An understanding of the theories of grief is important to the approach you take as a facilitator of writing. Without repeating the theories summarised in Chapter 1, I want to pick out those I find useful for their relevance to the major themes which will almost certainly emerge through writing, and which can inform the way you plan and structure writing exercises.

Early stage: numbness, anger, disbelief.

Middle stage: pain, despair, yearning, guilt.

Later stage: acceptance, adaptation.

The Dual Process model (Stroebe and Schut 1999) embraces these stages and acknowledges that people move back and forth between them while attempting to reach out and create a new life following loss.

Tonkin's model acknowledges the continuing presence and significance of the loss to the bereaved person, while attempting to build a different existence after a death.

Threaded through these features of grief are:

- the need for comfort and solace

- the desire to look back through memory and reminiscence (while also acknowledging the pain and difficulty of doing this while grief is still raw)

- the feeling of isolation, the difficulty of anniversaries and, slowly, the awareness of the passage of time.

Each individual is likely to experience a mix of these emotions and needs. What follows is an attempt to map out some of the ways specific writing forms and techniques may be of value as people work through them. This is not to be prescriptive, but to suggest ways into writing around these themes and responses to grief. As you become familiar with the techniques and how they work in a live situation you will be able to devise and adapt your own.

**TABLE 2.1 WRITING AROUND THEMES AND RESPONSES TO GRIEF**

| Theme | Technique |
| --- | --- |
| Numbness | Diary, journal, lists |
| Anger | Metaphor, sprint writing, flow writing, dialogue, unsent letter |
| Disbelief | Diary, journal, dialogue |
| Pain | Diary, journal, haiku |
| Despair | Metaphor, journal, unsent letter |
| Yearning | Unsent letter |
| Guilt | Journal |
| Acceptance | Memoire, family history |
| Adaptation | Stories, poetry, memoire, journal |

You will find that people respond in different ways to the stimuli you provide. Be alert to the signals (enthusiasm, responsiveness, sometimes laughter, sometimes tears, and a feeling of energy in the room), and be guided by what your group tells you is working for them.

## Greenbank group

With the first session under their belts, Michael and Fiona will review how it went and how the group has bonded (or not). Their observations include that Anna seems anxious, Alan is talkative, Cynthia is distracted and Ros and Riaz are quiet. Fiona has noticed Ros using the keypad on her mobile phone; she assumed she was texting someone but realises she is using this instead of a notebook. Bobbie seems impatient and a little defensive. The group has started to bond; Alan and Riaz sit together and Michael notices Anna and Marielle talking to each other in the car park afterwards.

CHAPTER 3

# Keeping a Journal

A journal is the ultimate listening friend, available seven days a week, 24 hours a day. It can go with you or stay by the bed; be a few scribbled words or pages of outpourings. When there is no one else around to listen, the journal is a vessel for whatever needs to be expressed.

In this chapter I offer guidance for journal writing, something I introduce early in group work. Not everyone will choose to take it up, but for those who do the benefits can be remarkable. To illustrate its value in bereavement, I shall begin by telling Jean's story.

Jean attended a bereavement writing group at Princess Alice Hospice over eight sessions in the autumn and winter of 2010–2011. A year later, I met her again and she told me more about her bereavement. I had known little about her situation at the time of the writing group, other than that she had lost her mother four years earlier and had recently returned to the hospice for bereavement support. Our conversation revealed to us both the very powerful effect that writing had had on Jean's progress through her difficult grief; writing in the group, writing in her journal, and sharing her writing with her counsellor, Tania.

Jean was adamant about the difference writing has made to her and keen for her experiences to be shared with others. In her own words:

> I believe that I got an enormous amount from the creative writing and I will be forever grateful that I had the opportunity to do it. The writing…led to my starting my journal again and they both [the group and her journal] made a difference to the

sessions I had with Tania. She used to say that I talked from my head but wrote from my heart and by my reading my writing out to her, she could always see the things that I was struggling with. I know that I would have made progress with Tania anyway but I think the writing gave her a better insight into what I was trying to deal with… If my writing can help someone who is struggling with their loss to know that they aren't going mad and that what they're feeling is what they are feeling and that it is ok, then it has to be a good thing.

We arranged to meet one evening at the hospice. As I arrived I spotted Jean getting out of her car. I could see straight away that she was a different Jean to the one I had met almost a year ago. She looked less burdened. She looked well.

Jean had brought her journal with her and some of the writing she produced in our group sessions. She showed me the journal she had kept for about six weeks immediately following her mother's death and she read the opening passages to me. She told me about her close relationship with her mother as the youngest of eight siblings. She described how they had shared a house and that her mother had been involved in every part of Jean's life, whether in the background or as her best friend. Jean had looked after her mum during her illness and had been with her when she died.

Jean sought bereavement support in the first year after her loss. Her employer was sympathetic and suggested time off work when she was struggling to cope. Although Tania, her bereavement support volunteer, pointed out that grieving is 'not a race', Jean felt left behind by her older siblings whose lives seemed to return to normal quickly.

With support, she made some progress. For several years she felt she was getting on with her life. Then, in summer 2010 the washing machine broke down. It had been her mother's and they had bought it together. Somehow, its collapse signified a further loss for Jean and one which brought her grief back to the surface. Realising she had further deep grief work to do, she returned to the hospice's counselling service.

This coincided with the new writing group. In what Jean describes as a happy coincidence she began attending weekly bereavement support with Tania and fortnightly writing sessions with the group. I encouraged the group to write journals and offered techniques and prompts for people to try at home each week. I suggested that the group might like to reflect on their journal writing in one to one bereavement support (if they were having it). For Jean, this worked like a charm: 'The themes and writing we did in the group were uncanny. It came at just the right time for me.'

She came across the journal she had kept in the early weeks following her mum's death. This encouraged her to take up her journal again and she began bringing it to her meetings with Tania. Together, they were able to explore the thoughts and emotions that surfaced in the writing in a way which, in Jean's words, 'accelerated my progress.' In our meeting, Jean read the opening passages of the original journal to me:

### Monday 03/07/2006 8:10am

I have decided to keep a written record of my thoughts, feelings and day-to-day happenings to try and help me figure out what I am doing and whether I am healing as people want me to.

It has been 11 weeks since Mum passed. In some ways it seems forever since I have seen her but in others it feels like only yesterday when we were all at the hospital with her.

Life at the moment is confusing and at times frightening. Sometimes, even days, I can function reasonably well and I think I am coping with everything even if I can't remember what I've done or where I've been. Other times I feel so overwhelmed by everything and unable to make even the simplest of decisions.

Other people's views/thoughts also confuse me. I think I know where I am in my life, what I am doing and then someone will say something to help me and then I have what they say going round and round in my head. As I know I am away with the fairies sometimes, I worry that they are right and I should be 'just getting on with things.' This confusion continues until I speak with someone with a different opinion who will make a perfect argument for their views. The big debate at the moment is whether I should be back at work or not. Today my current thinking is that as I don't know, it is probably best that I am not (I think).

I worry that other people will think because I am off work, because I am seeing [Jean's bereavement support volunteer at the time], I am wallowing in it and that this means that I loved Mum more, which obviously is not the case at all. It is just that Mum and I were a team, a partnership. As well as being my Mum and being there to love me unconditionally, support me and encourage me, she was my best friend. We would discuss everything, we would do things together. Now there is just this big hole. No one to listen to my news, to share things with, to laugh with and to cry with; a gap bigger than she could ever have possibly known.

The sense of someone in the early, confused and disoriented state of grief is palpable in Jean's words; also the sense of loneliness and of struggling to cope with her sudden change in circumstances, not least of all the loss of her best friend and confidant.

In the writing group, I remembered Jean saying that she felt her journal 'would never judge me.' She repeated this as we reflected on her journal. She added that it had enabled her to work through thoughts and feelings that were troubling her and to rehearse things she might want to say to others.

Jean had found some of the prompts I offered as springboards into writing especially helpful. She showed me some examples, written during the winter when our writing group was in full swing:

### *29/10/2010*

I feel grateful for…

Having a loving and supportive family and some very special friends. [One of her sisters] has stepped in to support me in what I do and what I want to do. She has calmed me down when I have lost it (which was very often) in the early days without Mum. She has held me when I have been hysterical and has been hard when she needed to be. She has encouraged and accepted everything that I have wanted to do with regards to keeping Mum's memory alive; the endless walks, the memory box, the memorial tribute fund, etc. She has helped me and made suggestions. I am not where I would be without her and I'm not sure she knows how grateful I am to her.

[A friend's name] also deserves a mention in this despatch. She has cried with me, laughed with me and has welcomed me even further into her family life.

## 31/10/2010

What I really want to know...

Whether I did enough for Mum.

Whether I made the right decisions and if I didn't whether she understands that I did my best and whether she'll forgive me if I got it wrong.

Whether Mum knew I was there at the end.

Whether I stopped her saying anything that she wanted to at the end.

Whether my journal was right and that we did talk about the big things without talking about it.

Whether I'm going to be able to talk about Mum without constantly getting upset.

Whether I will ever be in a place where I can accept what everyone keeps telling me.

Whether I will ever be able to forgive myself.

As her response to 'what I really want to know...' shows, one of Jean's difficulties in her grief was a nagging feeling that, while her older siblings had visited their mother in her last weeks and days and had had a chance to say goodbye, she had not said those words to her mother herself. Writing about this in her journal, and prompted by a group exercise about opening a door (you can find the exercise in Chapter 5), she realised that because she and her mum were so close they had not needed to say goodbye in the same way. She worried, still, that she might have unwittingly denied her mother the chance to say other things she might have wished to. Realising there might be an unfinished conversation between them, she agreed when Tania suggested she write an unsent letter to her mother.

Since then, Jean told me, she had been working on her letter, although she had found it hard. She had decided, too, to write to her father, who died when she was 17. This, she thought, might be easier.

Talking to Tania, I learned that she too felt that writing had been effective in helping Jean move on in her grief work. She told me that when Jean shared her writing with her, it had assisted them both in identifying significant areas on which to focus in their work together. Tania echoed what Jean had told me; that when she wrote, Jean seemed to be 'speaking from her heart, whereas she talks with her head.' When Jean wrote, said Tania, she could 'hear her heart more clearly.' She said the breakthroughs and realisations that had emerged through Jean's writing were exciting to witness and a help to her in her task of bereavement support.

Jean read me the full version of the piece she had written in response to the door exercise. In it, she had pictured a door through which she was invited to enter. She wrote:

> It is extremely tall and it is in two parts. It is mahogany brown with detailed carvings that are smooth to the millions of touches and strokes it has endured over the years, the decades, the centuries. It has shiny brass furniture that shows no finger prints or smudges, no human touch. The door stands tall and proud, protecting, shielding, guarding the chosen few that have been allowed to enter through this imposing doorway.
>
> Entrance through this doorway is by invitation only; a strict code of admittance is adhered to. Many people want, need to go through this door but admittance is not usually allowed unless it is your time. I know that it is not my time to pass through the doorway but I have got this far without being stopped, without anyone telling me to go back. I take a look around me to make sure that no one is there to stop me and I gently put my hand out towards the door, expecting at any moment that either the door or I will disappear from this moment.
>
> My hand makes contact with the brass door handle and I push. I expect such big imposing doors to be heavy but the door moves easily inwards. The first thing I notice is the sweet light music that has drifted out of the door towards me. I then notice the sweet smell of stocks and notice that inside the door is a beautiful, amazing and well-tended garden. The colours of the hundreds of flowers all vie for my attention. I notice that despite the myriad of colours all blending together that it works, even though it really shouldn't. The grass is lush and vivid green, the sky a startling blue, the sun is shining. I can hear the faint trickle of water moving in the distance. I feel relaxed. I feel rested. I feel at peace.

Standing in the middle of the garden is Mum, looking healthy, able-bodied and just how she used to look when we were younger growing up. She's smiling and seems at one in her surroundings. She smiles and waves to me inviting me to move further through the doors and into the garden. I move through the doors cautiously, hesitantly, not wanting to spook her or frighten the garden into disappearing. I gently put one foot in front of the other and move closer and closer to Mum. She stands firm, her smile never wavers, the invitation to join her remains, her arms opening ready to welcome me to her.

As she read to me, Jean commented that this was the first time she had read the piece in full for herself since writing it. We recalled that she had wanted to share it with the rest of the group at the time, but had felt unable to continue beyond a certain point (we had also been short of time).

A week later Jean wrote to me that it had helped her to read her writing again. She said she had shared it with Tania as well and they had both seen different things in it compared to eight months ago, when it was first written. Jean reflected: 'I feel much more positive about it now.' She had shared her piece about the door with one of her sisters, who found it moving, and (I later learned) she went on to share it with one of her brothers who was moved by it and showed his emotion about the loss of their mother for the first time. Jean described the experience of re-reading it with these others as 'cathartic'.

As Jean's experience suggests, it is possible, even likely, that writing in a group will stimulate insights, self-revelation or catharsis for some. When this happens, it can signify a positive breakthrough. It may also bring to light difficult or complex feelings which require further exploration. Facilitators should be alert to this and ready to offer further support in one to one meetings, or suggest the client talks to their counsellor or seeks other appropriate support.

Why does the journal provide such safety and consolation? In her preface to *Therapeutic Journal Writing: An Introduction for Professionals*, Kate Thompson says this:

> ...journal writing is both a creative and a therapeutic act. Journal writing is broader than many people think... It encompasses many writing activities that may not have previously been considered to be journal writing; it is not necessarily a daily written record of activity. (Thompson 2011, p.15)

This touches on two important ideas for journal writing in the context of bereavement support.

1. Journal writing is a flexible vessel for containing a range of different writing techniques and styles. It offers freedom to express what needs to be expressed in whatever form feels appropriate.

2. It is different from keeping a daily diary. The individual is free to make of it what they will, without the need to complete a daily entry or stick to the regimen of dates. There are enough pressures in bereavement without feeling one has to keep up to date with a diary.

That said, for people used to the routine of keeping a diary, its pages can be a natural place to turn to in bereavement. In early bereavement, however, routines can feel impossible and oppressive. I have often heard people say 'I can't concentrate like that at the moment', or 'I can't bear to write about it; it makes it too real.' For some, the shock and numbness of early bereavement are simply not conducive to the discipline of diary writing.

Over time, however, the work of grief can start to find individual expression through resumption of a diary, or through keeping a journal of thoughts and feelings as they evolve. The journal offers space on the page for any kind of writing and the expression of those feelings or thoughts whose exploration feels necessary. Entries may be dated or not. Events may be described in detail, or the focus may be on emotions and thoughts. A journal can be anything the writer wants or needs it to be. I have seen a man's shoulders visibly relax on being reassured that he did not have to write in his journal every day.

The journal does, however, have one important characteristic in common with the diary: it can help capture the passage of time and with it the journal writer's progress in their grief work. Used over weeks and months and read back with hindsight, it is possible to see shifts in mood and perspective. The writer may be able to see that, although they are still grieving, their feelings are becoming less dark and intense as the months go by.

Kate Thompson and other practitioners of therapeutic journal writing in the UK are informed by the work of Kathleen Adams's *Journal to the Self* (Adams 1990), which sets out a structured framework for journal writing. This approach has much to offer in bereavement work.

One practitioner, Beverly Frydman, is taking an innovative approach that combines writing and yoga as a way to promote relaxation and stimulate insightful and expressive writing (Frydman 2010).

Julia Cameron has written extensively on the role journal writing can play in the daily creative lives of artists. Her ideas are relevant to others living less overtly 'creative' lives. *The Artist's Way* (Cameron 1995) and its sequel *Walking in this World* (Cameron 2002) offer models of creative journal writing including the concept of 'morning pages', in which the writer makes a three page journal entry each morning, offloading whatever is on their mind:

> There is no wrong way to do Morning Pages – they are not
> high art. They are about anything and everything that crosses
> your mind – and they are for your eyes only. (Cameron 1995)

Other writers working in health and social care and in writing for personal development cite the value of journal writing for both clients and practitioners. Reeves presents a framework for journal writing specific to bereavement (Reeves 2001). Bolton (1999) includes a valuable chapter on creative approaches to journaling. Bolton *et al.* (2004) offer guidance for therapeutic journaling and refer to the value of the reflexive journal in training for practitioners (ibid, pp.183–185). Etherington (2004) argues persuasively for the role of the journal at the heart of learning and development for students and practitioners. In bereavement support, the reflexive journal can be a valuable means of self-care.

# What is a journal?

Anyone new to journal writing should be encouraged to consider what they want their journal to be and what it will mean to them. The form a journal takes is a personal choice: a smart bound book or a decorative notebook kept in a private place, a password-protected computer file, or a loose collection of notes and scribbles in a box file. It might be accompanied by a special pen bought for the purpose. My own favourite pen was given to me by a fellow journal writer. It is small, Italian and purple. Its smooth ball point makes the act of writing a soothing experience.

Above all, the journal is a personal and private place for reflection on experiences, memories and people of significance.

## When and where to write?

The time and place for journal writing is a personal choice. Ideally it will be somewhere quiet, private and comfortable where the writer can enjoy repose before committing their thoughts and feelings to paper. In bereavement, where there is a strong possibility of emotion and tears, privacy is important.

A favourite cafe or park bench might work for some; for others it will be the seclusion of the bedroom or garden, or even the sanctuary of the car in the office car park during lunch break. Encourage clients and group members to find the conditions that suit them best. There is no right or wrong way to do this, only what works for them.

## Tools of journal writing

Between them, Adams (1990) and Thompson (2011) have devised some essential tools for journal writing, many of which lend themselves to writing in bereavement. I draw on these here as well as offering some I have devised. What follows is not comprehensive; I recommend you use these as sources of inspiration for your own work in bereavement support.

Thompson (2011) suggest several techniques for bereaved journal writers, among them:

1.  unsent letters

2.  captured moments

3.  writing from photographs

4.  dialogues.

I would also suggest:

1.  lists

2.  time perspectives

3.  expressions of gratitude.

As I explain these terms I shall offer some real and generic examples from actual participants in facilitated journal writing exercises. I shall also speculate on how members of the Greenbank group might respond.

## 1. The unsent letter

Practitioners in bereavement support and therapeutic or counselling settings will be familiar with the concept of the unsent letter.

The act of writing a letter to someone who cannot be spoken to, for whatever reason, can be a powerful way to say what needs to be said. Unsent letters can be one-offs or they can form a series. A bereaved parent might, for instance, write to a child who has died on the occasion of their birthday or the anniversary of their death for years. This might remain a ritual for the remainder of their lives. Letters to the miscarried, aborted, still-born, or those who die very young, can offer an outlet for the grieving parent as they express lost hopes and conduct the conversations they might otherwise have had with their growing child.

Like dialogue, the unsent letter offers a way for a conversation to be continued even though the person who has died does not respond. For some this can mean traditional letters, written in pen and ink or on the computer. For others it can mean emails and text messages.

---

### Greenbank group

Ros sends text messages to her late husband's mobile phone several times a day, just as she used to do when he was living. The only difference now, she feels, is that she does not receive a reply. It feels important to tell him things and let him know what she is doing. It helps her feel close to him still, although she acknowledges that she will eventually stop when she is ready.

---

An unsent letter can help people who are struggling with feelings of anger or guilt. The letter may be directed at the person who has died or to others; for example members of the family or friends by whom they feel let down or abandoned, or members of the medical profession or others in a professional capacity. Frustration with the slowness of probate, or annoyance with family members can be common themes. In one example, Delia wrote unsent letters to the hospital staff who she felt had let her mother and other patients down. She commented, 'These were hard to write. But the feelings of satisfaction and relief after writing them made it worthwhile.'

Unsent letters can help at various stages in the grief process. In the very early stages, in the first days and weeks involving the funeral and other rituals of leave taking, a letter to the departed can aid the farewell process. Some may start writing straight away, as a way of dealing with feelings of shock after a sudden loss. For others, a letter may help much later in the grief process (Jean's example above is one such), as a way of working through difficult or stuck feelings.

When considering when and how to suggest an unsent letter, listen for the client who says 'I wish I could have said...', or 'if he was here now I would tell him...'. If the feelings and thoughts are too difficult to verbalise, the suggestion to write a letter may help.

 At the risk of stating the obvious, the simplest way to write an unsent letter is to follow the usual conventions of letter writing. Some people will not struggle to write their letter; what needs to be expressed may come out in a rush, following the river of the writer's thoughts. Others, though, may find it hard to begin. Structure and a starting place can help. For example:

- Begin with a clean page, either in your journal notebook or a piece of fresh writing paper.
- At the top of the page, write the date.
- Begin with 'Dear...'
- In the first line explain why you are writing this letter.
- Write a paragraph in which you focus on thoughts beginning with 'I have been thinking about...'
- Write a paragraph in which you focus on feelings beginning with 'When I think about this I feel...'
- Read what you have written back to yourself.
- End the letter by saying how you feel now, having written it.
- Sign off with love or whichever form of address is appropriate.

It can help further to focus on a theme:

Is there someone to whom you feel grateful? Write them an unsent letter.

Is there someone, or something, with whom you feel angry? Write them (or it) an unsent letter.

Is there something you wish you could say to someone? Write them an unsent letter.

Is there something you want to hear for yourself? Write yourself a letter.

Delia says:

> I wrote letters to Mum and Dad, telling them how grateful I was to them, to thank them, and to hope they were kept safe, happy and well cared for.

She went on to write letters to herself:

> ...from Mum and Dad, saying that they were OK and together and safe. That they thought that I had done the right thing. That I must now start thinking about 'me' and 'stop worrying!' (this was one of Mum's phrases and she always said it in a certain way).

Following the actual letters she had written to the hospital after her mother had died (in which she complained about the standard of care), Delia wrote letters to herself from the recipients, telling her that they were sorry. She also wrote a letter from a patient she remembered seeing on the ward, 'saying that he/she was OK, was comfortable and well cared for and that everyone was being kind, caring and nice to her and had time to chat to her.' Delia reflects that 'These letters helped in a number of ways. It is strange how you "do believe" in what you write to a degree, when you read it back. Just writing it makes you feel somewhat "better."'

---

## Greenbank group

Anna might write an unsent letter to Pat's family, telling them how hurt she feels that her importance in Pat's life was not properly recognised in the funeral arrangements. This might help her to rehearse for a real conversation with Pat's sister.

Riaz might write to his brother, asking him for advice about the family business, or to express his bewilderment about his brother's decision to end his life.

Michael might invite both to talk about their letters in the group or in one to one support.

---

## WHAT TO DO WITH AN UNSENT LETTER

In the context of bereavement, Thompson (2011) suggests:

> Some kinds of unsent letters can be ritually burnt in emulation of funerary rites or even placed in the coffin before cremation or internment. (Thompson 2011, p.145)

She observes that the act of sending a letter up in smoke can be 'part of a purification or purging ritual' (ibid, p.145). The choice of what to do with an unsent letter depends on the subject matter and the relationship with the addressee. Unsent letters need not be destroyed. Some prefer to keep them and add to them as an ongoing conversation with the person to whom they are directed.

Unsent letters to the deceased can be sealed and kept in a special place, torn up, buried in the garden, thrown to the wind from a favourite cliff top, floated on a balloon or sent out to sea in a bottle. If the intended recipient is alive and available, they can be a useful way to rehearse an actual letter which is eventually sent.

The unsent email, text message or even tweet may act as a form of containment for those who wish to say something succinct. For those who use social networking sites, this is an increasingly popular form of unsent messaging.

The forms offered by new technology are evolving all the time. As long as care is taken not to inadvertently hit 'send' to those who are living, they can be of help. The best advice I can offer is to leave the address box or phone number (for texting) blank.

## 2. Dialogue

Dialogue enables something to be said, or a conversation to be carried on or completed. When imagined and written down like a script, the conversation can take place between the bereaved person and the one who has died, or between the bereaved person and someone else in their life, such as family members, friends or colleagues.

Alternatively, it can represent different aspects of the bereaved person; for example, a conversation with the self before and after bereavement. Adams calls this the 'dialogue partner' and provides a structured way into the dialogue:

**Me:** Dialogue Partner, can I talk to you?

**DP:** Sure. Just ask me a question, or make a statement, and I'll respond.

**Me:** It feels a little silly.

**DP:** You'll get the hang of it more quickly that you might think!

(Adams 2002, p.37)

The dialogue can then proceed on the page, taking up to 30 minutes or longer if the writer wishes.

An entrance meditation provides the way into dialogue writing (Adams 1990, p.120). The writer is able to envisage or discover who the dialogue will be with (they may not know beforehand). With practice you can create your own entrance meditations to suit the individual or group, or encourage people to make their own.

At the end of the dialogue, the writer thanks the person with whom they have been in dialogue and asks them if they can talk again, if the need arises (Adams 1990, p.106). If the answer is no, this can signify a moving on or acceptance of the loss of the person represented by the dialogue partner.

---

## Greenbank group

Anna comments that she and Pat used to chatter constantly but now there is only half a conversation. The house is too quiet. Fiona suggests that she might write her conversation down, like a script. When Fiona leads the group in an entrance meditation, she describes a smooth flowing river. She invites everyone to imagine they are floating gently along on a raft. In the distance, they can see someone waiting on the river bank; someone they are glad to see. As the raft draws close to the bank, they can see who the waiting person is.

At this point Anna realises she is seeing her mother, who died when she was ten years old. She writes a conversation between them. When she reads this to the group she is tearful but smiling. She explains that she has made a connection between her feelings of guilt at having let Pat down, with her feelings as a little girl who wondered if her mother's death was her fault. Afterwards, Anna asks Michael if she can see him to talk about this further.

---

## 3. Captured moments

Four sessions into a writing group at Princess Alice Hospice, Teresa reported that, in the week since our last session in which I had introduced the technique of writing a 'captured moment' (Adams 1990, p.94), she had felt unlocked for the first time. She had been able to write a description of swans she had seen on the river early in the morning on her way to work. She described her feeling of relief at being able to write fluently.

### The Silvery Swan

*The silvery swan swims serenely in the soft mist on the river*
*Shy sun shining through gaps in the snowy cloud*
*Smiling sagely, sighing, sliding away*
*And I pass by, brash on my motorbike; chin cold, nose dripping,*
*Eyes running with tears from chill air*
*Or maybe from wonder, relief*
*Yes, life is worth living, there is hope*
*And still the swan serenely swims,*
*Regal and unperturbed.*

In bereavement, it is a common experience to find memories too painful to recall. People often say that they don't want to write about the one who has died, and yet every subject seems to lead back to them. Even happy memories make people flinch when grief is raw and present. Memories of happy times with the one who has died are compromised by awareness of the loss.

The captured moment is a *Journal to the Self* (Adams 1990) exercise in which the participant pictures and then describes a memory or a moment in time in closely detailed writing. It uses an 'entrance meditation' (ibid), to ease the writer into their subject. This has a calming effect and can enable unexpected (often pleasurable) memories to surface.

For John, this stimulated a childhood memory:

### Grandad – My Earliest Memories

I was five years old when my Grandad died on Christmas Eve. I remember helping him in the morning, as he cut off overhanging privet in the yard outside, which collected the snow.

Every time we went 'down the yard' to the outside loo, you got showered with snow!

I remember too, the broth on the old black-iron grate, when we eventually came in out of the cold, which was so nice and warming.

Sadly, by nightfall, my dear Grandad, who I knew loved me, died (a few minutes before Midnight on Christmas Eve).

More than once he had bundled me out, back home next door, when he had had enough of me, as I was always next door with him.

That Christmas, 1935, the bottom fell out of my small world.

John's expression of the love between him and his grandad ('who I knew loved me') was so touchingly expressed with the evocation of snow and the family home, that the group responded very warmly to the description of this captured moment which, although sad, is full of fondness.

 In this exercise I draw on the inspiration of both Adams (1990) and Thompson (2011).

Begin with an entrance meditation.

- Close your eyes and take three deep breaths in and out again.

- Allow your mind to clear and let your shoulders relax.

- In your mind's eye, picture a blank page, pure white and smooth as snow. Let this fill your mind so there is room for nothing else.

- As you gaze at the page, images start to appear... photographs and snap shots, some in colour, some in black and white.

- As you look at the images you can see faces you recognise and scenes you remember. You can hear laughter and conversation; the sound of people enjoying themselves. You can hear your own laughter among them. Perhaps you can hear music and other familiar sounds.

- As you look at the images on the page, you start to concentrate closely on one of them; something that draws you to it.

- As you look closer at this image you can hear the sounds coming from it. You can see what the people in it are wearing, and you can see what they are doing.

- You can smell flowers or someone's scent, or perhaps the sea, or the aroma of food.

- As you look at the scene, allow yourself to experience the feelings and sensations you associate with the people in the picture and the occasion it represents. Let yourself stay there for as long as you like, experiencing it and enjoying the details.

- When you are ready, open your eyes, take up your pen and write about this moment.

The writing that ensues makes use of all the senses and the meditation allows the mind's eye to act as a filter. For people who find looking through the photograph album too painful, this offers an alternative way in to recalling positive memories of family life and other past experiences.

The writing may produce emotion, happy or sad, but the resulting sense of release and the satisfaction of having been able to write about something hitherto inaccessible, is likely to be a positive experience. Janet wrote this captured moment in the weeks after her brother's death:

### My Brother II

I admired his pullover. Hand-knitted by his wife, intricate cable stitches in beautiful wool. 'Be careful of that', I said, 'for heaven's sake don't spill your coffee on it. That pullover should be in a glass case.' He laughed, proud of his wife's skill and the care she had taken to make it for him.

We went for a little walk by the green, looking for ducks in the pond, strolling gently so that he did not get too tired. The sun was out, shining on fresh green leaves and there was that fresh spring smell in the air that tells you winter is truly gone and summer coming. Green shoots everywhere, all fresh and clean to start the year. Friendly neighbours nodded and smiled a 'good morning' greeting that added to our pleasure, each with the other, arm in arm and in no hurry. We were just enjoying each other's company, no need for much talk because we knew each other too well.

We paused to admire the neighbours' little front gardens. All different. All with the same function, to hide the road ten feet away but act as a necklace for each little house, laid in front of the windows for all to see. Our walk took all of half an hour taking the air and inspecting the neighbourhood, then we decided that all was well and came home for coffee.

My brother has died but yesterday I remembered that day and something else as well. I checked through my photographs and sure enough there he was. Standing in the front doorway, happy contented smile, wearing the pullover.

## 4. Visual imagery

Some may struggle to fill the blank page in their imaginations. Visual imagery from photographs and other sources can provide an alternative stimulus for captured moments.

### PHOTOGRAPHS

The experience of looking at photographs of the deceased, especially in the early days of grief, can be too distressing. Some people turn framed photographs to the wall, put them away or even destroy them. But as time moves on, photographs can be a source of solace and provide the trigger for writing about better times, about the life of the deceased and about family history.

The process of sorting through someone's personal belongings after a death can unearth photographs long forgotten and often accompanied by letters, postcards and personal ephemera. Reading through these brings the subject back as a strong presence and can stir up forgotten memories and feelings. Writing can enable such reactions to be contained and processed, as in this exercise:

- Choose a photograph which awakens a strong positive memory.
- In your journal, address the person or people in the photograph as if you were writing a letter to them or speaking to them.
- Note what they are wearing, where they are and what they are doing. Write a description, including the mood or atmosphere the photograph portrays; for example, celebratory, relaxed or formal.
- Using the following prompts, address the people in the photo and reflect on your own feelings:
  - In this photograph I can see that you are...
  - I remember that when this was taken we...
  - Seeing you like this now makes me think about...
  - Seeing you like this now makes me feel...

This provides opportunities to reflect on the viewer's own memories as well as enabling them to reflect on the feelings and thoughts evoked in the present. Maggie used this exercise to recall early memories of travelling with Dusan, her husband to be:

**Figure 3.1** Maggie's photo

### *A Photo*

We are in Devon. I told my father we are youth hostelling but we are staying in a B&B. I can't remember where; I only know that it is called St Anne's, that the sun is shining and we spend a lot of time on the beach. My mother's engagement ring is on my finger and I've turned it round to look like a wedding ring for in 1950 respectable establishments will not allow unmarrieds to share a room.

We had hitch-hiked from London having been picked up by a portly, middle-aged balding man in a Jaguar. He insisted that I take the passenger seat beside him and spent much of the journey with his hand on my thigh. I was too naïve to do anything about it and Dusan in the back seat was completely unaware of what was going on.

This photo was taken by a lurking street photographer so it is spontaneous and captures us at a moment when we are happy and carefree. I don't think it is possible to date as shorts and shirts have not changed much over the years and hair-styles don't give much away but I notice that I already have a penchant for wearing a scarf and slinging my handbag over my shoulder.

I love this photo; he with a thatch of dark hair which in later years he grew on his chin, my hair very fair. We both look slim and energetic as we stride along and it occurs to me that we resemble each other with the same sort of smile. Does this indicate a certain sort of compatibility?

We are joined together, my arm through his. We are in step and we stayed that way for 40 years.

## 5. Lists
The list is a useful tool in journal writing.

 Offer these as starting points and encourage people to make up their own ten things:

- about me
- I would like to say

- I feel sad about
- I would like to change
- I am coping with
- I am not coping with
- I have achieved
- that are helping me
- that are different compared to last year/month/week.

The trick is to write quickly, getting as much down on the page as possible in, say, two minutes (be sure to keep time). Invite the writer to read their list back to themselves and choose something to write about for a more extended bout of up to ten minutes.

If a list of ten is too long, try five or three. The limit can be exceeded within reason; it is there as a guide to enable the writer to focus.

Be alert to the clues a list may throw up as to the writer's current thoughts and feelings. For example, a list of 'things I am not coping with' can bring anything from not being able to face the gardening, or knowing how to change a plug, to feeling bereft in the company of friends whose spouses are very much alive. Such insights can open up discussion of ways to seek help. A further list might consist of 'three people I could ask for support', which in turn can lead to reflection about family members, friends or colleagues, who might offer support if they knew what was needed. This can enable the writer to achieve a sense of balance. Perhaps there is more support available than they have realised.

The outcomes of list writing can include:

- surprising insights, if something that was not uppermost in the writer's thoughts is expressed
- a step towards accepting something
- a step towards recognising what is important
- a step towards acknowledging that something is not important (if it has been left off the list)
- a step towards realising what might help

- a step towards making a decision

- a step towards feeling less chaotic.

Some people find lists oppressive ('I never seem to be able to cross anything out...', as one participant said to me). If this is the case, suggest a retrospective list of things that have been achieved:

  - five things I have achieved since yesterday/last week/ last month

  - five reasons to feel proud of myself

  - five things/people I have found helpful recently.

Looking back over achievements helps to balance feelings of helplessness and enables progress to be acknowledged.

## *6. Time perspectives*

The desire to put the clock back to an earlier happier time, or to stop it before a difficult anniversary, can be strong. In a painful contradiction the bereaved may also want to fast-forward to a better time when they no longer feel so bereft. At the same time, it can feel impossible to imagine such a different state of feeling.

In this difficult context, reflections on the past, present and future, and on the passage of time more generally, can be a source of comfort and relief in bereavement, if handled with sensitivity.

 A DAY IN THE LIFE

This is a form of diary writing, capturing thoughts and feelings in the moment on the day they happen. For someone wishing to capture their experience on paper but unable to think back or far ahead, the containing format of a worksheet with prompts and boxes can be liberating.

Think of something you've done today and write a description of what happened.

_____

_____

_____

Before I did this I was thinking…

_____

_____

_____

Before I did this I was feeling…

_____

_____

_____

Afterwards I thought…

_____

_____

_____

Afterwards I felt…

_____

_____

_____

*Note:* This worksheet is available from the JKP website, at www.jkp.com at www.jkp.com/catalogue/book/9781849052122/resources

The balance of thoughts and feelings can bring a sense of order in confusion.

 ## TIME CAPSULE

The time capsule enables the writer to reflect on a longer passage of time, perhaps a week or a month. Adams notes that it can 'capture the essence of your life as it was being lived at a given moment' (Adams 1990, p.159). Here I offer some structured formats for expressing a moment in time and reflecting on thoughts and feelings.

The month of _____ in the year 20___ Today's date____

The word or phrase that best describes this month is…

_____

A significant event in the past month was…

_____

_____

My most significant achievement in the past month was…

_____

_____

My mood in the past month has been…

_____

_____

When I think back over the last month, what stands out for me most is…

_____

_____

_____

This form of worksheet, with defined prompts as a starting point for writing, helps the writer get started. As confidence in the writing grows, people will begin (or can be encouraged to begin) to provide their own prompts and pose their own questions and topics.

*Note:* This worksheet is available from the JKP website, at www.jkp.com at www.jkp.com/catalogue/book/9781849052122/resources

 ONE YEAR ON

This can be used to prepare for the potentially difficult time of the anniversary of the bereavement, religious holidays (when the loss is keenly felt), or the deceased person's birthday. Someone stuck in their grief process, or at a still early stage, may not be able to imagine a different way of feeling, but the focus on the natural movement of the calendar may help to unblock them.

Today's date_____ Next year's date_____

One year from today I hope I will be…

_____

_____

I will have sorted out…

_____

_____

I can imagine myself…

_____

_____

*Note:* This worksheet is available from the JKP website, at www.jkp.com at www.jkp.com/catalogue/book/9781849052122/resources

This approach enables a shift in perspective. The structure can help the writer envisage a different situation for themselves, with a degree of control over what may happen next.

Liz, widowed in the previous year, could imagine herself visiting New York to see her late husband's relatives and extended family. She imagined making this trip on her own or with her grown up children.

Dave, in the same group, imagined having sorted through his garage, which was full of family items including old cine film canisters. He brought regular updates on his progress to the group until one day he announced that he had cleared the final boxes and redistributed their contents among the family. He wrote about this with an air of triumph, which the group literally cheered (see p.205). Liz reflected that she still felt unable to go through her husband's cupboards and drawers, but recognised that she would eventually tackle the task, in her own time.

## 7. Expressing gratitude

For people feeling overwhelmed by sadness the invitation to focus on gratitude can offer respite. A quick exercise for the evening or bedtime, it enables the writer to reflect on small acts of kindness and the people and things that have helped them through the day.

Delia found comfort in writing about gratitude:

> The journal helped me to look more positively at life. It made me focus on all my daily achievements and it even inspired me to achieve more, so that I had more to write about each evening (consequently the busier you are, the less time you have to focus on the sadness). It made me more grateful for even the smallest 'nice' thing that happened in the day.

 Write for five minutes from any of these prompts:

- Today I was helped by…
- Today I feel thankful for…
- Today I appreciated X helping me to do Y…

---

### Greenbank group

Cynthia might write: 'Today my assistant at work noticed I was struggling with my PowerPoint© presentation. She offered to help me with it in a way that didn't make me feel like a failure. She pointed out what was already good about it and asked me if she could make a few suggestions.'

When Michael asks Cynthia further about what made her colleague's approach so helpful, she reflects that she is very sensitive to criticism at the moment because she feels she has to be perfect and keep going. This leads to further conversation with Riaz who agrees that he feels the pressure of having to do everything to keep his business afloat without his brother. Fiona suggests they use their journals to write lists of 'what I need right now' and people they feel comfortable asking for help, and how they might engage with them.

---

# Journal writing for the host and facilitator

Listening to people while they write and talk about their grief and sadness can be emotionally draining. People's distress and its physical expression through crying can awaken sorrow in the listener, often out of empathy but also because it can trigger sadness of their own including realisations of unresolved grief in themselves. Awareness of boundaries of course helps, but it is a strong listener indeed who can get to the end of a tough session feeling unmoved.

As well as the lighter activities that provide distraction following a heavy session, the journal can be a listening friend as you reflect on what you have heard and offload anything that troubles you. Supervision is the place to take difficult issues, but the page offers a space to express thoughts and feelings while they are fresh, or to rehearse things you might wish to talk about.

Sometimes a client's attitudes, values and behaviour will present a challenge to the provider of bereavement support. In Chapter 2, p.51, I offered a warm up exercise in which the writers describe their shoes and how it feels to stand in them. Here is a variation on that exercise, in which the one offering bereavement support explores how it might feel to stand in their client's shoes; a powerful exercise in restoring empathy where it flags.

 STAND IN THESE SHOES

- Begin by picturing your client's shoes.
- Look closely at them. Study how they look, their texture, colour and condition. Are they sturdy or flimsy? Are they polished or rough? Are they new and smart or old and worn? Have a good look at these shoes.
- Now notice what they are standing on. Is the ground solid? Is it level? Is it at the top or the bottom of a slope? Are they on soft grass or rough stone?
- When you have observed the shoes and where they stand, look up and see the person standing in them.
- What is the look on her face? Is he making any sound? Is she upright or slouched? What is she carrying? Who is with him? What are they doing? What can you observe? When you are ready, write from the prompt: 'How does it feel to stand in these shoes?'
- Write as much or as little as you need to.

- When you have finished writing, read back to yourself what you have written.
- Underline anything that seems significant or that you find yourself surprised to have written.
- If you wish, write further about these insights before reflecting on them further or talking about them in supervision.
- Finally, ask yourself what difference this exercise has made to your feelings.

Beverly, a bereavement counsellor, offers an example of how this can work in practice:

I have chosen two clients with whom I had difficulty empathising with at first.

One client was a young man who lost his father. He never held a job for any length of time, nor did either of his parents. His father was an alcoholic and his childhood years were spent living in his grandmother's home with his mother. This client was late to sessions and often did not turn up without cancelling. I found it difficult not to tell him to go out and get any job available. I also found myself very frustrated with his issues around coming to the sessions.

When I wrote about his shoes I described his trainers. They always looked shiny and new. As I continued to write I began to focus on his shoelaces and imagined them to be pulled very tight, so tight that his feet were constricted and he felt immobile. Doing anything active gave him pain.

Another client was a middle-aged woman who was a recovering drug addict. Her husband asked her to leave, as her behaviour was threatening and dangerous to the children. She was homeless for a while and then entered the 12-Step Programme. She attended counselling sessions regularly and was always on time. I was fearful of her physically and found it hard to listen to her stories of violence towards her family. I started to write about her shoes. They were slip on shoes, ballet shoes that were scuffed. I imagined them to be comfortable but capable of falling off her feet easily. I wrote that she was careless with her shoes and often lost them. The soles of her feet were bloody and bruised.

Doing these exercises gave me back the unconditional positive regard and empathy required to be an effective therapist. I found myself considering my first client's pain in his state of stuckness and developed a deep respect for my second client's commitment to recovery. I appreciated how vulnerable they both were despite the difficult behaviour they exhibited as a result of their histories.

By taking off my own shoes and putting on those of my clients I was able to explore feelings that impeded the therapeutic relationship. (Moss in Neimeyer, 2012, pp.362–364)

---

## Greenbank group

Fiona and Michael encourage members of the group to keep journals in between meetings. In suggesting journal writing techniques, Fiona considers these questions:

- Who in the group already keeps a diary or journal?

- How can they be encouraged to talk about this and reflect on its value, with the rest of the group (mindful that journals are personal to the writer)?

- How can the group meetings be structured so there is time each week to introduce a journal writing technique, and time to share and reflect?

- Are any specific techniques likely to be of benefit to certain members of the group?

- How can they be encouraged to bring these into their one to one bereavement support meetings?

- How can she and Michael use journaling to reflect on their experience of the group?

---

# CHAPTER 4

# Working with Form

It is common for the bereaved to feel unable to settle to a task, read for more than a few sentences, or focus on what is being said. The Dual Process model (Strobe and Schut 2005) suggests that there are times when it is possible to get on with something approximating normal daily life. At other times, the loss and its attendant symptoms can feel as fresh and immediate as in the very early days following a death. It can be reassuring to be told this is normal; not everyone realises that they are not alone in feeling adrift.

I have often heard people who come to writing groups express their frustration at being unable to focus for long on reading, or to string more than a few words together when they try to write.

In this chapter I suggest ways to bring order to chaotic feelings and thoughts, through the containment of writing in form. Field (Field in Bolton, Field and Thompson 2006, pp.123–138) provides a valuable introduction to ways in which certain literary forms – in both prose and poetry – can enable people who struggle to focus, or who feel very stressed, to find a way into writing (Field in Bolton, Field and Thompson 2006, pp.123–138). If a writer knows she or he is aiming for 17 syllables (a haiku), or six words (a six-word story), there is something to aim for, and a certain relief in knowing they are not expected to write more.

In most groups, especially in the first few meetings, there will be one person who compares themselves to the others. He or she may say things like, 'I'm no good at this', or 'Look, they're all writing more than me,' and feel that they are somehow inferior in the way they express themselves.

Such participants may lack confidence or feel less experienced in writing; feelings they may have carried with them since school days. Form can help to reassure these hesitant writers that they are not in competition. Instead, the invitation to write to a given pattern or structure can present an enjoyable challenge in which they become absorbed.

Form provides the writer with boundaries and the sense of knowing *how* to write. In poetry the haiku, haibun, alpha poem, acrostic and sonnet offer the containment of form. In prose we talk about the short story, flash or nano fiction (very short stories), and the novel. Life writing embraces biography, autobiography and memoire. By form, writers, especially poets, mean the pattern in which they choose to write. In this chapter I shall show how some of these can enable people to write in a controlled and structured way, and how this can result in intense expressions, insights and a sense of release. Sometimes, order can be brought to chaos on the page.

How to write is one thing; *what* to write about is another, but here form can also help. The sense of absorption in form can have a therapeutic effect. Jan, who spent an hour writing haiku in a peaceful hospice garden on a summer evening, commented that she had lost track of time. It was her first experience of this minimalist Japanese form of poetry and after spending some time observing the flowers, listening to the wind in the foliage and looking closely at the activity of insects and birds, Jan wrote about her mother, who had died in one of the hospice rooms beside the garden:

> *Some white feather found*
> *Sending a sign from my Mum*
> *She is still around.*

Sharing this with the group, Jan explained that the white feather was a sign, to her, of her mother's continued presence around her; she often noticed feathers and they seemed to carry this meaning for her.

Form helps to overcome first sentence nerves. There is a pattern or a set of rules to be followed. Structure provides reassurance about how to start, how much is expected of the writer and when it is alright to stop. The closest analogy I can offer is to sculpture, where the stone is chipped away to reveal the final shape.

# Poetry

Poetry, perhaps more than any other literary form, offers choices of form for the newcomer as well as the more experienced writer. Many people read poetry for comfort and contemplation in times of sadness; some will also find solace and satisfaction in writing their own.

Here are some examples that can enable even the most hesitant to begin to express themselves through poetry.

## Acrostics

Acrostics are poems that use a word or a name as their starting point by building it into their structure. The first letter of each line, read down the page, spells out a word. The last letters of each line can also make a word, or a word can flow through the centre. They can be as simple or as complex as the writer chooses to make them.

The acrostic can give rise to moving personal insight. One especially moving example arose when participants were invited to introduce themselves to the group through an acrostic which summarised some aspect of their character or experience. The writer in this case had had the experience of caring for her late mother who had died following a long illness.

For her acrostic, she wrote:

> *Love*
> *Is*
> *Never*
> *Dying*
> *Alone.*

This enabled her to reflect on the care she had given to her mother. Although she had felt, at the time, that she was not doing enough, she could acknowledge now that she had supported her mother well and had been with her when she died. Her feelings of guilt shifted a little (Moss in Neimeyer 2012, pp.220–222).

As well as names, acrostics can explore and contain the difficult feelings and themes which can arise in bereavement; anger or guilt for example.

## Greenbank group

Bobbie, struggling to put her anger into words, is invited to choose a word and make an acrostic. She writes:

*Unless they can tell me honestly how he died, I will*
*Never get over this. He was so*
*Far away and in*
*Another country fighting*
*In a war that isn't mine. It makes me feel*
*Rage at everything and everyone.*

Too distressed to read it out herself, she asks Fiona to share it with the group. Hearing what she has written, Bobbie says this is the first time she has admitted her true feelings about the war in which her grandson died. She explains, tearfully, that she cannot say this to anyone else among her friends, many of whom are army families. She says she feels guilty because it seems like a betrayal of her grandson's dedication to the army. Michael suggests that it is important that she is able to express her own feelings. Around the room, heads nod in sympathy.

---

In these and other examples you may discover for yourself, the acrostic enables sad and difficult thoughts and feelings to be expressed with economy and clarity.

## *Alpha poems*

Rather like acrostics, alpha poems provide a simple structure. Letters of the alphabet provide the prompt at the start of each line. A prompt question such as, 'How was your day?', or 'How are you feeling this week?' might be hard to answer in free form, but the alphabet structure provides a signpost to the next line or word.

## Greenbank group

Ros, the quietest member of the group, makes an alpha poem on her mobile phone:

**A**lone with the baby in the day
**B**ereft in the evening
**C**rying all night
**D**ead tired in the morning.

When she reads this, Fiona admires the way Ros has managed to contain the whole 24 hour cycle of morning, daytime, evening and night in four short lines.

---

## *Haiku*

As Jan's example above shows, these short poems are the answer to anyone who says 'but I can't possibly write a poem.' The classic haiku contains 17 syllables arranged in three lines of five, seven and five syllables each. The words at the end of lines do not rhyme.

Traditionally, the haiku describes something that is taking place in nature, within a specific season. It provides a snap shot in close up of something the writer has observed, with the attendant feeling or sensation that accompanies the visual experience; for example, the sound of a leaf fluttering from a branch.

 If location and weather allow, invite the group to get up from their usual place (in the group's meeting room or at home by themselves) and go outside or at least move to a position where they can see a garden or the surroundings. Even a glimpse of trees over roof tops can be enough, or a vase of flowers in the room. The focus on the natural and external world lifts the writers from their physical and mental space into a new place where observation and sensory response are the focus.

Set a time limit, say 30 minutes, and invite participants to look around them, sniff the flowers, touch the leaves, observe birds and other wildlife, hear the sounds and feel the air. Invite them to explore and note what they see, hear, smell, feel and even taste, before spending a further 15–20 minutes writing their haiku. The time limit helps focus attention.

Participants may return to the meeting room to write, or
they may prefer to stay outside or at the window. Suggest
that they write as many or as few haiku as they wish. Some will
carefully craft a single three-line poem; others may produce
pages. Provide a gentle prompt when there is five minutes
remaining.

When everyone is seated back at the table, invite
participants to reflect on how easy or otherwise they have found
the haiku, and invite them to share what they have written.

If the haiku writing goes well and participants express pleasure in the
activity, suggest they try writing a daily haiku between now and the next
time you meet as a group. The haiku can be a soothing daily reflective
journal writing exercise. Delia commented on what she described as the
benefits of daily haiku writing:

> This activity requires keen observation. I also had to find
> the concise vocabulary which would both describe exactly
> what I meant and fit into the brief and precise verse plan.
> Consequently, for the length of the activity, life and its
> problems faded from the foreground. After the first draft I
> would keep returning to it and would be thinking during the
> day to see if I could find 'better' words for descriptions.

Delia's haiku focused keenly on details of nature:

> *Silver trail on stone*
> *At the end, under a leaf,*
> *Snail asleep in shell.*
>
> *Stillness, reflections*
> *Carp glides from beneath lily*
> *Ripples. Still again.*
>
> *Wasp lands on bird bath*
> *Dips forward to sip water*
> *Flies away. Refreshed.*

If haiku writing appeals, you might suggest the tanka. This is an extension
of the haiku, with the three lines of five, seven and five syllables followed
by a further two lines (a couplet) of seven syllables each.

While the haiku classically expresses the experience of nature, the subject matter of tanka can include love and loss (Sansom 2007, p.109). For people wishing to explore those themes in their writing, these short formal poems can be an ideal form of containment.

Having said that, haiku and tanka poems can be about anything. Their value lies in the structure and the calm feelings they can evoke in the writer. Here is a seasonal tanka by Rowena, a participant at Princess Alice Hospice.

### Winter Haikai

*Feathery snowflakes*
*Dropping from a cold white sky*
*Gently to the ground*

*Cold icing sugar*
*Sprinkled on every surface*
*Like a ghostly cloak*

*Tiny little birds*
*Small bundles of feathered warmth*
*Flitting through the trees*

*Finding sustenance*
*In the bitter cold landscape*
*Despite all the odds*

*Delighting all my sense*
*With the magic of winter.*

## Haibun

For haiku and tanka converts, the haibun offers a further variant. The haibun comprises a short, contemplative piece of prose which ends with a haiku, or a number of short prose pieces interspersed with haiku. The prose tells a story in short paragraphs or passages of 100 words or fewer. The haiku punctuates the story with moments of contemplation in between the passages of prose. Rosen and Weishaus's *The Healing Spirit of Haiku* (2004) is essentially a collection of haibun. As with the haiku, the aim is to capture an observation from the natural world or an event in life as it happens, and to express it in a way that conveys the thoughts and feelings induced in the writer as they experience it.

In the following example, Helen remembers an unsettling experience.

### Brother Haibun

My older brother sent me a draft of some writing he'd done. Is it a stylized autobiographical piece? Or is it just lightly based on events of his life and largely fictional? Only the writer knows. But I recognize parts of it. The boy's day trip set in Malaysia. The man's rather different way of thinking. And the woman: she's an amalgamation of two of his early girlfriends, Norma and Maria – small, pretty and dark-haired.

> Leaping, angry dog
> Careering towards the man
> Holding the shotgun.

He relates the stress and confusion, the ferocious yet slow-motion attack, caused by the pregnant dog's anxiety and hunger and fear. He heaves its body, using a Heath Robinson leverage contraption, into the boot of the car. She takes it to the vet for them to dispose of.

> She crumples up in
> Tears, fears her baby hopes are
> Gone again blood stains.

Skipping back in time to an excitable, semi-ADD, maybe dyslexic childhood (before those definitions were popular or fashionable), he writes of having the 'bestest little sister in the whole wide world,' as he gazes unobstructedly out at the many massive bridge supports struts. He counts them as the car whizzes by.

> Grateful boy looks through
> The window vacated by
> Her vomit-bent head.

## *Other poetic forms*

If a group or individuals respond enthusiastically to writing in form, it is worth offering some of the more elaborate structures. A participant who enjoys reading published poetry may feel inspired to attempt their own (or may of course already be practised in them; memories of being introduced to literary form at school can be a positive spur).

### VILLANELLE

The villanelle sounds more complex than it is. Some find its use of repeated lines in a pattern a helpful form of containment. As one participant said to me 'at least I know where I'm going with this one!'

Villanelles tend to express strong emotion. Their repetitive refrain acts as a kind of holding mechanism to drive the point home. One of the most famous villanelles in English is Dylan Thomas's *Do Not Go Gentle into That Good Night* (Thomas in Longley ed. 2010, p.184), familiar to many through its popularity as a reading at funeral services. Another one to consider is Elizabeth Bishop's *One Art*, although this is written in a different spirit, about the end of a relationship (Bishop 2004, p.178).

Here is one example in which the pattern over 19 lines can be seen.

### *The House on the Hill*

*They are all gone away,*
*The House is shut and still,*
*There is nothing more to say.*

*Through broken walls and gray*
*The winds blow bleak and shrill.*
*They are all gone away.*

*Nor is there one to-day*
*To speak them good or ill:*
*There is nothing more to say.*

*Why is it then we stray*
*Around the sunken sill?*
*They are all gone away,*

*And our poor fancy-play*
*For them is wasted skill:*
*There is nothing more to say.*

*There is ruin and decay*
*In the House on the Hill:*
*They are all gone away,*
*There is nothing more to say.*

(Robinson 2007)

As this demonstrates, the villanelle has only one rhyme, in the first and third lines. These are simply repeated alternately as the middle line of the next three verses (or stanzas), before meeting again in the final two lines of the concluding four lines.

## SONNET

Many will be familiar with the sonnet from memories of school exercises and readings from Shakespeare, perhaps with mixed feelings. Consequently, some may be daunted by the sonnet, but in its contemporary manifestation it can be a playful and accessible form in which rules are treated with flexibility.

The sonnet is a poem of 14 lines. The Shakespearean or English sonnet has a rhyme scheme which runs:

ABAB

CDCD

EFEF

GG

The Petrarchan or Italian sonnet goes as follows:

ABBA

ABBA

CDE

CDE

The rhythm of the lines is iambic pentameter: de dum de dum de dum de dum de dum which, as you can hear if you say it out loud, is the natural rhythm of English speech. Try saying 'I think I'd like to have a cup of tea' out loud. This is perfect iambic pentameter. For a thorough explanation and 101 diverse examples, see *101 Sonnets* (Paterson 1999). Contemporary writers treat the form with a lightness and flexibility which may encourage people to give it a try.

People sometimes express a desire to write poetry for inclusion in a memory box, or to be read at the funeral or printed on a memorial card (the Irish tradition of sending a card to family and friends on the first anniversary of the death, with photographs of the deceased and appropriate words). As with the other structured forms described here, the absorption in writing to a pattern can be liberating as well as containing.

# Prose

## Short prose

Poetry is not everyone's cup of tea. Those for whom prose flows more naturally may respond to some of the shorter prose forms to contain their expression. Here are some examples of short forms of prose to use with a group or with individuals who wish to tell a story.

## Six-word stories

Ernest Hemingway's example has already been referred to (see p. 26). The six-word story is an effective form of containment for the expression of thoughts and feelings which could take up many thousands of words. If the subject is too painful, sad or overwhelming for lengthier expression, a six-word story can be all that is needed to convey the meaning.

---

### Greenbank group

Cynthia writes: 'Mother died. My life went too'.

In this succinct piece of autobiography, she sums up how her mother's death has altered her own way of life. Hearing this, Ros writes: 'After the game, life ended,' which captures her own sense of normal life having stopped with her husband's death after a rugby match.

A week after hearing these, Riaz mentions that he has started writing six-word stories as well. He says he likes the challenge of making something fit.

---

## Nano fiction and flash fiction

Very short stories can pack an emotional punch. They provide the reader with a moment of intensity in which large events are summed up in a few words. These can be an effective way to capture intense feelings or moments of realisation. They may be fictional or autobiographical, as in this example by Derek from a Princess Alice Hospice group:

**Sorrel Point, Jersey**
**(A sense of achievement, though not entirely our own.)**

Sorrel Point is by the sea, so it's pretty. Being the most Northerly point on the island of Jersey, it was about as far as we could go from the house where we were staying: there was a sense of achievement just for getting there. A rugged place; no sand in sight. The whole of Jersey's North coast is rugged actually but Sorrel Point is less pretty than average due to the quarry, producing the warm red granite for which Jersey is deservedly famous. There are earthmoving vehicles, lorries, bulldozers and JCBs. We hear the whining of distant engines, the grinding of heavy iron on rock and the clatter of stones in giant metal scoops as the vehicles carrying them bounce along rough tracks. Closer to hand, and much louder, the screeching of the gulls that swoop and circle round us. Seaside sound! Holiday sound!

There are no seats – it's not really a tourist spot – so we are sitting on a handrail, eating sandwiches, relaxing. It's bright, although not full sun. We are raising our voices to hear each other speak over the noise of the wind.

Such a sense of achievement. We've been married nine months now and I'm daring to believe that this marriage thing might actually work. More relaxed now than when we were on honeymoon; more comfortable with each other. Beginning to believe that this is the start of something that really will last; the beginning of the rest of our lives. It's going to be good. Pregnant too – even more to look forward to.

This was the beginning of our holiday and there was a sense of achievement at just getting away successfully. Boosting the achievement sensation still higher, our best friends got married yesterday and were now on their honeymoon. The journey from England, the party, introductions to so many new friends, the bustle and busyness of the wedding, the last-minute preparations before it, the reception and the send-off at Jersey airport...now, today, for the first time, Sue and I plus our new, as yet unborn, family member are truly alone, by choice, on this remote point with two weeks of the same stuff stretching ahead of us. This feels more of a 'real' honeymoon for us than our 'official' one in Canterbury last year.

We'd made it!

Brilliant!

We'd all made it!

Revisiting this piece, and others that he wrote in a writing group at Princess Alice Hospice, Derek reflected:

Interesting how many of them are so directly about Sue [Derek's wife], and came so easily yet, had you said, 'write about Sue under the headings: (a) early hopes; (b) influence; (c) regrets', I would never have got started.

 The stimulus for Derek's piece came from a guided meditation which invited the group to remember a place of special meaning for them. Here is a similar exercise that can give rise to short prose pieces which include narrative as well as description:

- Invite the writers to close their eyes and let their minds clear.

- Take some deep breaths and feel the shoulders rising up and down, up and down.

- Let your mind settle on a scene with which you are familiar; somewhere you like to be or perhaps somewhere you remember from the past.

- Allow yourself to feel what it would be like to be there now; breath in the air, enjoy the feeling of the ground under your feet, notice any sounds or colours.

- Imagine who might be there with you; someone you know well or who you remember being in this place with you.

- Go for a short walk with them.

- See what happens next.

- When you are ready, write your short story about your encounter with this person in the place you are picturing.
- Try to contain your story on two pages of your notebook.

When the group shares the writing from this exercise, suggest that they take their stories away with them and work on them further, paying attention to sensory detail and working within the space limit. This will enable them to edit and draft, again becoming absorbed in the creative activity. Suggest to them that they aim to produce a short piece of up to 600 words (a couple of sides of A4 and a good length for reading back to the group).

## Folk tales and traditional stories

Whatever their cultural background, people have stories they can draw upon and adapt, whether from folk or fairy tales or stories handed down as fables and sermons or as part of oral tradition.

Such traditional stories can provide a narrative structure in which to re-imagine reality with a recognisable cast of characters and archetypes (princes and princesses, magical animals, monsters, giants and so forth).

A simple 'once upon a time' provides a way in for the writer to begin their story using archetypal characters and situations to illustrate their tale. Rowena's example that follows shows the power of the fairy tale to tell a story that was too difficult to write about directly. It tells a classic tale of disenfranchised grief.

### Once a Princess...

Once upon a time there was a princess. She didn't look much like a princess, being plain with red hair and freckles, and preferring making mud pies and digging tunnels to playing with dolls. Her family didn't think she was much of a princess either, telling her off for being so messy and untidy. Sometimes she even wondered whether she was in the right family, or had been swapped at birth – then she remembered her Grandad. Her Grandad *always* believed she was a princess – just the sort who got into trouble a lot. But as he seemed to get into trouble a lot too, that was OK, and the two of them used to run away in nature walks (and get into trouble for coming back dirty) or shut themselves away and draw and paint pictures (and get into trouble for that mess too!) or sit together and watch funny films instead of doing the serious stuff that members of royalty ought to do.

When the princess was old enough, she went out into the big wide world – she dug up the mysteries and secrets of the past – literally, with a nice little trowel just made for the job – but, yes, this was another messy thing that got her into trouble too. She travelled to foreign countries to see their marvels and had a wonderful time – although as she'd travelled *incognito* and without a bodyguard, she was told off for this too.

Well, this went on for some time – the princess grew up, followed her heart to the next exciting activity, and so invariably got into trouble that she forgot she was a princess. She began to wonder if that was just a story made up by a loving Grandad for his little girl, and that maybe there were no fairytales or Happy Ever Afters. As each prince she met turned out to have webbed feet after all, she thought maybe there was no Prince Charming for her at least.

So she married Prince Silly instead. He was much older than her, was a bit grumpy, but had a small castle of his own and made her laugh. Did I mention that laughing had always been one of the Princess's favourite things? So although people said 'What are you doing?', she ignored them, because she was so used to being in trouble anyway.

But this time it was big trouble. Not at first – at first, although Prince Silly wasn't much like the princess and didn't like doing the same things, they did have a very silly time together and laughed a lot. So the princess's family sighed a huge sigh of relief and thought, 'Thank goodness – no more trouble from her.'

But Prince Silly and the princess weren't as happy as they looked from the outside – especially the princess. Prince Silly gave her presents, but he didn't like doing the same things as her, and after a while he started saying he didn't really want to do very much with her at all. The princess was so unhappy, and so ashamed that Prince Silly didn't love her anymore, she didn't know what to do. She even forgot she was a princess, because after her beloved Grandad died, there was no one left to remind her.

Then suddenly, one day, out of the blue, she met Prince Charming. She couldn't believe it a first – there couldn't be a Prince Charming for her – and if there was, he must already have a Princess Charming of his own – and besides, she was already married to Prince Silly. So she said nothing about it.

But meanwhile, unbeknownst to her, Prince Charming *didn't* have a princess of his own because he had been waiting all his life for *her* – and as soon as he saw her, he realised that she was the princess he'd been searching for. But because she was married to Prince Silly, *he* said nothing either.

Eventually, someone who knew them both did say something about it – and met and talked and both said, 'You too?'

They both knew that this really *could* be big trouble, and what with the princess's experiences of princes turning out to have webbed feet, and the princess needing a lot of persuading that she really was a princess, not a worm, they took lots of time to get to know each other, and the more the princess got to know the prince, the less webbed his feet looked, and the more she was persuaded that maybe she wasn't a worm – more of a caterpillar, a sort of princess-in-waiting.

And so they decided to get into the biggest trouble of all and run away together, to a lovely little cottage on an island. And they were so excited – they loved doing the same (messy) things, and now they could do them together forever! They were both going to have the Happy Ever After they'd longed for, for so long.

And then, just as they were about to move into their cottage, Prince Charming died. Just like that. Just when everything was almost ready. And everybody who knew they were about to move into their cottage turned around and said it wasn't true, that the princess was making it all up and that she hadn't even loved Prince Charming anyway – *her* Prince Charming, who had been everything to her! The prince's family – who had wanted nothing to do with him when he was alive – turned up and took over his cottage, and his things, and locked the princess out. They wouldn't even tell her where they had buried him. The princess didn't know what to do – but she knew what the prince had wanted and what he would have done, and so she tried to do it for him. Even though her heart was broken, she fought back.

And she's still fighting. Even though this is the biggest trouble of all. Because she's a real princess now – and real princesses never give up.

This inspiring and defiant story would probably be untellable as a straightforward narrative. Rowena says, 'I think using the fairy story style to help tell a tough story is a really important message.' She thought long and hard before deciding whether to permit her name to appear with it, concluding in the end that if she chose to remain anonymous she would be further disenfranchising herself. I am grateful to Rowena for her decision and for allowing her story to be included here in full.

---

## Greenbank group

The forms described in this chapter offer vessels of containment. Fiona and Michael might offer these to specific members of the group:

- Acrostics and alpha poems can enable further group bonding to take place, and encourage those who write less, such as Roz and Riaz, to focus on a short structured writing activity.

- Alan and Roz, with young children, might consider writing short stories or poems to share with their children. These can become like games.

- Those who are stressed and tired, such as Cynthia, Marielle and Bobbie, might benefit from haiku and other forms of poetry. They may benefit from the calming nature of haiku and haibun writing, or find it enables them to encapsulate difficult emotions in a succinct form.

- Anna, who is experiencing disenfranchised and complex grief may use the fairy tale approach to distance herself from the events and feelings she finds hard to articulate. Perhaps she would cast herself as Cinderella in opposition to Pat's unsympathetic family.

---

CHAPTER 5

# Writing through Grief

Many of the changes we encounter through life have a positive forward momentum. Birth, falling in love, marrying, embarking on a new career, moving house; these carry the promise of the future. Bereavement, whether sudden or expected, is an end stop; a change imposed rather than planned and hoped for. The sense of powerlessness and finality can be such that it feels as if nothing will ever be right again.

Yet when a life ends, a different sort of journey begins for those who grieve. Some embark on it when they feel ready; others get stuck at the check-in desk. In this chapter I offer structured writing exercises which can enable people to explore where they are in that journey, to reflect on their past, present and future and to experiment with different kinds of writing to find their own unique perspective in the most confusing and difficult time of their lives.

These exercises take into account some of the common experiences of bereavement, including the emotional (finding it unbearable to think about the past or the future), and the practical (sorting through clothes in the wardrobe). They offer ways to explore the thoughts and feelings that arise from such situations in writing that can be simultaneously expressive and creative.

## Themes in grief work

The major themes of grief; numbness, anger and disbelief in the early stages, yearning, pain and despair in the middle stages, and acceptance and adaptation as we move on to the later stages, are all reflected in these exercises.

The writing themes offered here are universal. Themes such as going on journeys or travelling to new places can enable the imagination to explore different ideas about the future and the past. Writing about a possession or a personal item, such as a piece of clothing or jewellery, can provide a way into writing about loved ones. Writing about the senses, such as the taste of a favourite food, can enable the writer to tap into feelings about their current surroundings and situation.

It is impossible to predict how people in a group of mixed experience and at differing stages in their personal journeys through grief, will respond to these themes, but therein lies richness. When people share their writing and compare experiences, the comfort and reassurance of finding they are not alone can be a powerful element in enabling some to become less stuck, or to see how much further along they are in the journey, or how far it is possible to travel from their current state. Even contrasting experiences can enable someone to understand that there is more than one way of looking at their situation.

Always bear in mind that while some may wish to write directly about their bereavement, others may not. Themes and exercises should always be flexible enough for people to interpret and choose what they write about. This is equally the case for individuals' writing.

Another approach is to invite the group to decide where they would like the focus of their writing to lie; for example whether they would prefer to concentrate on exploring their creativity and experimenting with different styles and forms of poetry, or whether they would like to explore life writing. Most groups will favour a mix, but it is important to give everyone the opportunity to say what would be helpful to them (if they are able to pin point it), at the outset. Equally, it will help you as facilitator to check back with them from time to time, and seek their thoughts on whether and how they are benefiting from or enjoying what is offered.

## Theme: Going on a journey

The theme of going on a journey is not unusual in writing for therapeutic outcomes. In bereavement, the sense of a journey interrupted can be strong. It may seem as if the future as they had planned or envisaged it has been taken away.

This approach can work particularly well with younger bereaved people, such as those who have lost a partner or spouse at a time of life when they have plans for their future together, or for people who have lost a child, with the accompanying sense of a blank where their idea of the future used to be. Travel as a theme can enable the writer to imagine being somewhere else; somewhere other than where they are currently struggling.

 This exercise uses guided writing, lists and the unsent letter in the form of an invitation and a postcard. It can take around 45 minutes, depending on the size of your group, and is appropriate for people working through the acceptance and adjustment stages of grief. It can also assist with meaning reconstruction (Neimeyer 2007), for those who are adjusting to life without a person of significance to them. The ability to imagine arriving at a destination having chosen what to take and what to leave behind (in both the negative and positive senses), can enable a shift of perspective.

### WARM UP

Invite the group to describe their journey to the meeting today; the route they took and anything they noticed on the way. This gets everyone talking and introduces the theme of travelling to a destination.

To set the scene, begin with a short reading from travel writing or a poem. I sometimes use a poem 'What if this Road' (Pugh in Astley 2002), or a short passage from Laurie Lee's As I Walked Out One Midsummer Morning in which the writer arrives in Spain for the first time (Lee 1971, pp.45–46).

### IMAGINE A PLACE...

- Invite the group to close their eyes and picture a place to which they would love to travel.

- It might be a destination they have been to before, an old holiday favourite perhaps, or a special place from childhood. It could be as simple as the journey home, or as exciting as somewhere they have always dreamed of visiting.

- Invite them to open their eyes and write a brief description of that place.

- Next, invite them to write a few lines or sentences explaining why they would like to go there. What appeals to them about it?
- If they were about to set off there now, how would they feel?

## TIME TO PACK

- Announce the good news that the tickets have arrived and they can set off. First, they have to pack.
- Invite them to write a list of five items to take with them. This can include people, pets and something about themselves such as a sense of humour, as well as the camera, passport and so forth.
- When they have written their lists, let them know that there is a baggage restriction. They must choose just one essential item to take on the journey; the one thing they cannot do without.
- When they have made their choice, invite them to write an invitation explaining where they are going and why they would like it (or them) to come on the journey.

## LEFT LUGGAGE

- Next, ask the group to consider something they would not want to take on the journey. This will be placed in left luggage (they could use post-it notes on a white board or space on the wall under the heading Left Luggage).
- As with the list of things to pack, encourage people to consider non-material items such as responsibilities, moods, or feelings such as seasickness or fear of flying. Be prepared for disclosures; addiction or difficult relationships can be mentioned as things to leave behind. Such disclosures may require further reflection in one to one bereavement support or referral.

## ARRIVAL

- Invite the group to close their eyes again and imagine they have just arrived.
- Invite them to take a few moments to look around.
- What can they see? What can they smell or touch? What can they taste or hear?

- How are they feeling physically? Are they warm or cool?
- How are they feeling emotionally? Are they excited or calm?
- What is the first thing they do?
- Invite the group to open their eyes and write about their destination and how it feels to be there.

### SEND A POSTCARD

- Invite the group to write a postcard to whoever or whatever they decided to leave in left luggage (I sometimes offer 'weather lovely, glad you're not here!' as a prompt).

Finally, invite the group to share their writing.

In one example of this exercise, Karen wrote about a trip to New York which she had planned to make with her daughters, one of whom had recently died while still in her 20s. She imagined shopping at Macy's, having cocktails, seeing the sights and living the 'Sex and the City' lifestyle. She reflected that this was a journey she would still like to make, and that she hoped to do it with her remaining daughter. She said they would do it together in memory of the daughter who had died, in the knowledge that she would enjoy the thought of her mum and sister realising their dream. Although tearful, Karen smiled as she read her description to the group. Others in the group agreed that it would be a fitting way to celebrate her daughter's life.

## Theme: Remembering through personal items

This is suitable for those who have had the experience of, or are in the process of, sorting through the personal belongings of someone who has died. This taxing task can entail full scale house clearance, or inheriting personal items such as jewellery, books, household goods and furniture. Some may even inherit pets. Difficult choices sometimes have to be made. Family members may fall out over who gets what. The experience of opening a wardrobe and catching the distinctive personal scent of someone who has died, or the emotional impact of opening drawers to find lovingly stored baby clothes, a mother's wedding dress, or old letters and photographs can be overwhelming.

For those who embark on the task, there are bound to be surprises and poignant discoveries, sometimes made all the more poignant for raising questions that can no longer be answered. Why was this item or that one kept? The person who knew the answers has gone.

There may be the sense that one is invading privacy and discovering secrets that were not mean for your eyes. In Hardy's novel *The Mayor of Casterbridge*, the death of the Mayor's wronged wife prompts a village elder to say:

> Well, poor soul; she's helpless to hinder that or anything now...
> All her shining keys will be took from her, and her cupboards opened; and little things a' didn't wish seen, anybody will see; and her wishes and ways will all be as nothing. (Hardy 2003 [1886], p.155)

It is a poignant time.

This exercise can begin with the stimulus of a poem, 'Handbag' by Ruth Fainlight (Astley 2002) which provides the starting point for verbal and written reminiscence and guided writing. You might also use 'Piano' by D. H. Lawrence (in Longley 2010, p.55), or Joan Didion's comment about feeling unable to give away her husband's shoes: 'he would need shoes if he was to return' (Didion 2005, pp.36–37). All suggest the strong sense of presence that can emanate from inanimate objects and personal possessions.

 As a way into this exercise you can invite members of the group to bring an item which reminds them of someone; whether the person whose loss they are grieving, or someone else of significance in their lives; the choice is theirs. It is important to offer people this choice; remember that not everyone will wish to write directly about their grief. Those who are struggling to begin the task of going through personal possessions may find this too raw to attempt, or may opt to write about something that reminds them of other associations.

### WARM UP

Provide a handout with the reading you have selected. Read it to the group and invite the group to talk about the reading. What has it stirred in them in terms of thoughts, feelings and memories?

1. Invite the group to think about an object they associate with someone; perhaps the person who has died, or someone else who has been important in their life. The object might be something they themselves now wear or use, or something they keep about the house.

2. Write about the item using these prompts:

   - Write a few lines to describe this item.
   - Is it heavy or light?
   - What colour is it?
   - Does it have scent?
   - What does it feel like to touch or hold?
   - Who did it belong to?
   - Does it have a use, or is it decorative?
   - Where do you keep it now?
   - When you look at it or hold it, what do you think about? What do you feel?
   - For a further ten minutes, write about a memory you have of the person you associate with this object.

This can result in short prose pieces, stories or poems which enable the group to share memories and insights. The strong sense of the characters evoked by the writing is likely to be palpable in the room by the end of this exercise.

By the end of this exercise even those who write least are likely to have spoken about their items and the people they recall through them. There is likely to be empathy as people compare experiences. Someone who felt driven to dispose of household contents soon after the death might compare their experience with someone who is still unable to open their late wife's dressing table drawers or their husband's garden shed a year after they have died. There is no right or wrong way, but the comparison may stimulate people to think about their own responses and feel able to contemplate this aspect of grief work and acceptance of the bereavement.

Delia wrote about her mother's skill in elaborate cake icing. She brought her palette knife and a set of icing cones from the 1930s and 1940s to show the group and talked about the prize winning wedding and anniversary cakes her mother had iced (she showed newspaper cuttings and photographs of the beautifully ornate cakes). She wrote about her mother:

In the early 1930s, Mum's older sister introduced her to work at MacFarlane Lang's, who were biscuit/cake manufacturers. At first she decorated biscuits but she must have shown some flair because mum was soon chosen to be a trainee large cake decorator. Then she was decorating their large tiered wedding and special occasion cakes.

In those days royal icing was always used and the cakes were decorated with very elaborate piping. A tiered wedding cake could take up to a week to complete.

Mum iced cakes for some prestigious people of the day and she was allowed time to decorate her own wedding cake as work too. But, as was the rule in those days, when a lady married she had to leave work.

When I was young, I remember mum icing and decorating special occasion cakes at home for various people (the word must have got around). I would always kneel on a chair at the table, help with the mixing, etc. and watch.

Our family Christmas and birthday cakes were always iced in this elaborate way too. Mum continued with this tradition right up until her late 80s when she realised that her grip was too weak.

Mum would use the palette knife to smooth the first layer of icing over the marzipan, first dipping it into a jug of water. Several days later, when it was dry, the decorative layer would be applied. This took a long time because it had to be perfect.

Mum used many different icing 'cones'. They were inserted into a hole cut into the point of a bag made from a triangle of greaseproof paper. Each pattern she made had a name – shells, stars, garlands, leaves, birds ropes, lady in prison!

If any icing was left in the bags I was able to practise my skills on a saucer or sometimes on a Rich Tea Biscuit. Sadly, I never really got the hang of it myself.

The palette knife had not been used for years – it is now going rusty – but I would never throw it away and it is still kept in the knife drawer. Whenever mum and I cleaned out the knife drawer, out it would come and I am sure that you can imagine the stories that would be told. Now I dream the stories. Such memories!

The photographs would be brought out when visitors came. They were very important to mum. Even in her last week of life she was showing them to the nurses although, by then, she could not tell the story. But she did smile.

Delia shared this with the group and later reflected: 'After writing the story down, it was easier to share "verbally" with the creative writing group. I had got to know these people and I felt comfortable with them. Even so, I would not have been able to tell the story if I hadn't written it first. Writing has been a great help to me.'

## Theme: What would Superman do?

This exercise engages the imagination in creating a powerful figure – a superhero – who has important advice to offer. It enables a form of self-help and can assist those who are feeling overwhelmed in their bereavement. It can enable those who are struggling with feelings of guilt to find a more balanced viewpoint.

 WARM UP

Invite the group to describe a practical problem or a dilemma they have. When the group is ready (this may take time if people need to off-load their frustrations), suggest the idea of a superhero who could solve these difficulties.

Ask some questions about an imaginary superhero:

1. What special powers would your superhero have?

For example:

- X-ray vision
- the ability to fly
- the ability to predict the future
- the gift of immortality
- the ability to understand every language
- the ability to turn back time.

2. Invite each member of the group to think of a name for their own personal superhero and write it down.

3. Invite them to write a description of their superhero including what they wear and what they can achieve with their special power. Invite them to think about the benefits of having their special power, and whether there might be any drawbacks. Suggest they write their description for ten minutes.

4. Invite the group to imagine a situation their superheroes could tackle. How might they use their special power? Offer another ten minutes for them to write about this.

5. Finally, invite each member of the group to write a piece of advice to themselves in the voice of their superhero (another five minutes).

This exercise can produce powerful expressions, especially in the final part when the advice is written. Here is Derek's example:

### Mr Ifonly: Notes on a Superhero's Character

Mr Ifonly is a time traveller who lives in the present day but can pop back to earlier times to make tiny tweaks which will influence for the better the lives of people in the present day. Trouble is, many would-be tweaks require extra super-powers that Mr Ifonly doesn't possess – like breaking into offices to change the wording of a document; or moving money from one fund to another. He has to rely on his powers of persuasion as he meets and just talks with the key players. He comes across as an authoritative father figure, old, wise, seen-a-lot-of-life, reflective, respectable and trustworthy. His conversation suggests that he has a good understanding of human nature and of cause, effect and consequence. To gain credibility he often has to demonstrate his power by making short-term predictions to the people he meets just about the next day in their lives.

An example would be persuading someone to get a mysterious mole checked out even when pressures of their job make time so precious while the mole looks so small.

Mr Ifonly wants to say this: 'With my unusual understanding of cause and effect, I see many actions that you are choosing to do now which, were they to be tweaked in any way, would have worse consequences rather than better consequences. Be assured that the majority of your choices now are in this latter category.'

In another example, Rowena imagines Ariel:

### Ariel

Small, light, quick.

Gossamer wings that tuck into her body and can be hidden when on the ground. A special insulated layer of skin to protect against the coldness of the air when flying at speed – or a furry flying suit to keep her warm as she swoops over fields and woods, taking the short cut to the seaside and at the press of a button instantly turns inside out to become the outfit she needs to wear to mingle with the crowds of ordinary mortals.

Just rising above the busy crowded real world and into a quiet peaceful place, having a new perspective on life, not having to follow existing paths, but just going where you want.

But you'd have to travel light! No room for clutter! And she doesn't have to worry about other vehicles – traffic jams or being knocked off her bike, although you'd have to watch out for birds and indeed aeroplanes, telegraph poles, pylons...

But just to be able to see your journey's end makes it worth it.

### Ariel's Advice

You don't have to be able to fly to not feel so earthbound, so trapped in crowds and busy-ness. You don't need to be a superhero to mentally rise above the botherations of the real world. You don't need to be able to see where the journey ends, but just keep going – although maybe rest a little more by the wayside.

But it would be fun to pretend about the wings and sit in meetings and think, 'If only they knew my secret, *wouldn't* they be surprised?'

## Theme: Anniversaries

Nothing is more indicative of the progress of time in bereavement than the inevitable anniversaries brought around by the calendar. Birthdays, wedding anniversaries, religious festivals, the anniversary of a death; these take on a special weight in grief.

The sense of dread and inevitability which one date can carry was expressed by someone who had recently lost her husband, who brought an alarm clock to a writing session. The group had been asked to bring something that summed up their feelings as Christmas approached. As she planted the clock on the table she said, 'I just want time to stop.'

Around the room, heads nodded in sympathy. No one was looking forward to 25 December that year. Christmas, with its connotations of happy family gatherings and the rituals around present giving and meals carries special difficulty when someone is no longer there to participate.

 This exercise uses the acrostic as containment for the complex and difficult feelings that arise around anniversaries. An alpha poem can serve equally well, or the acrostic can be adapted to describe whichever anniversary or religious or public holiday is at hand. In this example, I use Christmas.

When you prepare for this exercise, ask the group to bring an item which represents how they feel about the anniversary that is approaching. In the case of a wedding anniversary, birthday, or the anniversary of a death, the items may relate to those events; for example, photographs, birthday candles, or a memorial card. Prepare to be surprised by people's imaginative response to this invitation!

You will need an A4 sheet with the acrostic letters arranged down the left hand side of the page, with enough copies for everyone. If the acrostic's starting point is to be left up to individuals, bring a supply of blank A4 paper (not everyone's notebook may be large enough to accommodate the acrostic on one page). If you are using the word Christmas as your theme I suggest printing it on colourful paper rather than cold white.

## WARM UP

Choose a seasonal reading; perhaps an extract from Dickens, *The Snows of Christmas* (Mackay Brown 2002), or *Memories of Christmas* (Thomas 1955). These enable a tone of gentle nostalgia to be established, lifting the group out of the present time.

1. Reflect on the reading, then invite the group to share the objects they have brought and talk about what they represent.

2. When everyone has spoken about the items they have brought (allow about five minutes each), invite the group to write their acrostic, drawing on the memories and stories they have heard, and anything the reading has prompted. Allow 20 minutes for the writing, providing a prompt five minutes from the end.

3. Invite the group to share their writing. It is likely that some will have chosen not to follow the acrostic pattern, but most will have stuck to the theme.

In one example, Derek presented a tangled string of fairy lights. He explained that he had been trying to sort out the faulty bulbs. For him, this symbolised the amount of preparation which, he now realised, his wife Sue used to do in the run up to Christmas, and which he was now doing on his own. In Derek's own words:

> The lights symbolise for me how much more time trivial jobs take than expected following a bereavement and, looking back over what is now 18 months since Sue died, I can still think of no other activity that would symbolise this phenomenon more effectively than those darned Christmas lights.

He wrote:

> These lights were our newest and most sophisticated set of Christmas tree lights, with 80 lamps on a fairly thick chunky loom of wires and a fancy sequencer providing eight possible flashing patterns. I was certain it had been working perfectly when we put it all away the previous Christmas but, during

the year, some little elf in my loft had sabotaged the lot. Nothing worked.

Being out of work, I was reluctant to ditch the set and buy new but, had I known how much time they would consume, I might have decided differently. As they consumed more and more time, I just became more and more determined to make them work rather than admitting to wasting that time.

Now, unlike the Christmas lights I remember from childhood, today's sets are supposed to keep working when individual bulbs blow – you are supposed to simply spot any dead ones and replace them. Not this set though. So I had to work out how the wiring worked. I had to work out whether the wiring was bust, whether the sequencer was bust or whether the problem was just down to broken bulbs. I found that more than half of the bulbs had broken in a variety of ways. Shops don't stock spare bulbs in these sorts of numbers. I had to go to several shops to try to get enough replacements. I discovered that shops just put in one order for Christmas light sets; they might include a few packets of replacement bulbs but then that's it for the year I was told. I persuaded one shop to give me their importer's phone number but had to wait for ages while they phoned around to get it. So I even ordered additional bulbs directly from the importers. It was all simple stuff but it just took so much time.

OK, so I got my lights to work properly again – all eight flashing patterns – but they will remain forever my top symbol of trivial jobs taking far too long.

When Derek shared his thoughts about the lights with the group, and especially his point about the amount of work to do on his own now, there was widespread sympathy and agreement around the table.

In another moving example, Jean presented a beautiful glass bauble. She explained that she had felt unable to dress her Christmas tree in the years since her mum had died, but that this year her sister had given her the bauble, which was decorated with a message of memorial to her mum. She was determined to 'do Christmas' this year and to give the bauble pride of place on the tree.

# Theme: Making sense of change

This exercise enables people to access memories from the past, pause in the present to reflect, and move ahead to envisage the future. It uses a checking in technique at each of its three stages, in order for comparisons to be made. It makes use of guided imagery and aural and visual stimuli. It works best with an established group in a room with which people are familiar. It requires active, attentive listening.

 You will need a selection of picture cards showing a variety of beautiful and evocative landscapes; for example, mountains, a river, a garden, a walk through woods, a street, a road heading off into the distance, a beach and a blue sky.

### WARM UP

Ask the group to close their eyes and listen to the sounds in the room. What can they hear?

1. Into the past:
   - Still with eyes closed, invite the group to choose a memory from earlier in their lives; something enjoyable which gives them pleasure to think about.
   - Invite them to open their eyes and write quickly for five minutes. What happened? Who was there? Write about the memory.
   - Invite them to choose a word or phrase that sums up how they remember feeling at the time of this memory (not how they feel now, remembering it, but how they might have felt then), and to write it down.

2. Back to the present:
   - Invite the group back into the present, here in the room. Suggest they sit quietly and write about what they can see and hear as they sit together.
   - In their writing, ask them to describe how they feel in the present moment.

3. Pause:
   - Invite the group to share what they have written so far. What are the most important features of

these memories? Note what is said about feelings, both past and present. Are there any similarities or differences? There is no right or wrong answer to this, but pausing at this stage provides an opportunity for reflection and comparisons.

4. Into the future:

  - Offer the picture cards and invite everyone to select one that positively appeals to them. Ask them to make a note of the feeling it invokes in them.

  - Invite the group to imagine something in their future that is triggered by the image they have chosen and the associated feeling; perhaps next year, two years hence or five years.

  - They can write as much or as little as they need to (allow up to 15 minutes but be ready to stop sooner if the writing has naturally come to a stop).

5. Finally, share the writing and reflect on the different feelings expressed in thinking about past, present and future.

This exercise can produce surprising shifts in perspective. If a memory from the past has provided comfort, it may be replicated in thoughts about the future. Linda (the Linda of Love Is Never Dying Alone) chose the image of a sunflower. She wrote about her late husband's allotment, which she had not managed to maintain during the past year. She wrote that she could imagine being able to plant it next year and that there might be sunflowers growing in it a year from now (Moss 2010).

The shift in time perspective enables people to acknowledge that they may not always feel as they do now. It can enable them to feel calm and experience the group's support as they write.

In a typical group there will be a range of responses. Be alert for the participant who is unable to envisage the future at all or whose writing suggests they may be having suicidal thoughts. For some, the ability to envisage themselves in the future can be a breakthrough. For others, it may expose deeper difficulty.

# Theme: The open door

This exercise uses a poem, 'Open the Door' (Holub in Astley 2002). The poem invites the reader to risk opening a door to see what is on the other side.

For a group nearing the end of its work together, or as a way of marking a New Year or some other transition, this exercise enables people to explore possibilities, hopes and fears as they step into the unknown. It can enable some to recognise something they need to do, or a risk they need to consider taking. It produced a moment of catharsis for Jean (Chapter 3), who realised she needed to complete a conversation with her mother.

 You will need a hand out with the poem, if you are using it. As an alternative you could use a selection of images of doors taken from home interiors magazines or art cards.

1. Invite the group to describe their own front doors, from the inside and the outside.

   - What do they see when they open it to enter?
   - What do they see when they open it to leave?

2. Read the poem or share the pictures of doors.

3. Invite the group to picture a door in their mind's eye; perhaps a real one, or one they imagine. Look at the door in detail and write about its appearance and location. Perhaps it is somewhere familiar. Perhaps it is new.

4. Now imagine that they are about to open the door. They reach out but pause before turning the handle. How are they feeling?

5. Now open the door. What is on the other side?

6. They step through.

7. Invite them to write about what they find on the other side of the door, and what they do next.

This exercise can provide an imaginative route into memory or into the future. In writing about memory it can provide a portal into happy recollection, as in Sarah's example:

### The Door

The emerald green door looks at me in its old haggard state.

The once effective keyhole is now hollow from front to back, having no role in protecting what's inside. I know that upon opening the door it will creak and groan in protest, but the round plastic door knob will allow me to enter.

If I wanted to I could see inside the weakly guarded room without needing to offend the creaking door. Its lower panels don't quite reach the bricked steps which lead up to it, and mice, rats, even a small terrier could sneak inside for shelter and food.

And what food they would find. For this door protects the bounty beyond it. I remember this door. It is the old stubborn beast that I entered several times a day to get food from the food store when I worked on the farm.

At least I think it is.

But hang on – this door seems different. There is a bright fire-lit glow appearing through the broken keyhole.

I place my hand on the door knob and attempt to enter. It's as stubborn as I remember, but somehow it feels so different. Warm and welcoming. Not cold and dark and damp like before.

The door creaks familiarly as I gently tease it open, the bottom left corner still requiring a gentle nudge with my boot to get it moving.

As I peer inside, the old stagnant water tank which produced such a stench has been replaced by an open log fire which crackles and pops all the louder as the harsh cold draught rushes in through the door.

The corner, which once occupied hutches for sick animals, now sports an old fashioned dark wooden rocking chair, which appeals to me after a long hard day. The cushions, I recognise. They seem to be the same ones Mum used to have. And the blanket – is not that the one she crocheted?

The wicker basket in the corner is definitely recognisable. Benji wouldn't sleep in it, but he liked to store his toys in it all the same. His favourite toy was – hang on – there it is, his squeaky pencil.

What a door to come across. I can't wait to open it again to see what more this shrine has to offer.

Reading this to the group, Sarah was struck by the way the writing led her into a warm, comforting memory. Her initial recollection of the farm door evolved into a string of positive associations (the cushions, the blanket, the dog's basket and toy squeaky pencil), which she had not expected to express or describe in such detail.

Using the same exercise, Derek envisaged his own kitchen door:

### My Kitchen Door

If there is any wind at all, it will be moving at the north corner of my kitchen where the outside door is. I can stand on the doorstep and hear the wind of the footpaths around Land's End or of the north-coast walks of Jersey or the surfer-powering wind of St Ouen's beach. Warm wind, exciting wind, reminders of happy times with people I love.

I enjoy standing in the doorway with the door wide open when it is absolutely pelting with rain outside; warm, dry, protected, cheating the weather. I am safe.

The top half of my kitchen door is glazed – double glazed in fact, using white uPVC no less. The glass is mottled on the inside of the glazing unit so that both sides of the door present polishable glass surfaces. Some plastic (uPVC of course) corner pieces provide a pretty arched effect to the door.

The door's lower panel has a thick foam insert (I know from fitting the cat-flap) that changes the outdoor sounds when the door is shut – I can hear the real wind rustling leaves outside and sense the weather conditions without opening the door at all. So there are no surprises on opening it really (I can even see the outside temperature on a radio-thermometer). I just wonder if my neighbour John will be outside smoking, or might I smell what he is cooking? I can't spend too much attention on the garden really – I need to be alert to stop the kitten getting out – he's getting desperate now.

The door faces North-East, looking towards trees and large gardens of various neighbours. It is a lovely rural view – more rural than my suburban location would suggest. It will be good, when summer comes and the kitten is old enough to go outside, to leave the door open again.

Derek creates a sense of safety, hearing the wind outside and weaving together thoughts about places and 'people I love'. This sense is carried through to the end of the piece, with the idea of the door being open again providing a metaphor for the next stage of life.

---

## Greenbank group

Thinking about how to use some of the themes with the group, Fiona and Michael will consider:

- How to manage the expression of difficult thoughts or feelings when the writing is shared.

- Whether any of the themes or exercises are particularly appropriate to the group. Alan and Roz might find the journey exercise fruitful in terms of exploring a different future for themselves, having lost their partners at a young age. Cynthia, facing the overwhelming task of sorting through her mother's belongings, might find writing about personal items a helpful way to enable her to say goodbye to some of her mother's possessions.

- For Anna, facing retirement without her partner, the Past, Present and Future theme might be too difficult, although writing about the door might enable her to envisage moving forward.

- Riaz might respond to the superhero theme. He feels he is trying to do everything to keep the family business going without his brother. His superhero might have valuable advice for him.

---

# CHAPTER 6

# Life Writing in Bereavement

In the days and weeks after a death, family and friends gather. They tell stories about the life of the one who has died. Sometimes they compare different versions of the same stories. Sometimes they themselves feature in the stories, sometimes not.

Stories give rise to stories; family anecdotes are handed down, the older generation shares memories with the younger ones who in turn will tell their stories to the ones who come after them. Family narratives have a tendency to be organic. They develop with each retelling, as different members of the family embellish the tale with their own variations.

The rituals that take place around a death are fuelled by stories of the life that is being commemorated, and of those who have gone before. The traditional Irish wake provides a place both for celebration and reminiscence, for example. Obituaries and eulogies, done well, can conjure the person's character in an act of shared remembering (they can also be a source of distress if inadequately researched or delivered by someone who did not know the deceased). Funeral, shiva and memorial services are all occasions when stories swim to the surface. Stories are important as a means of sharing grief, celebrating the life that has ended, and enabling those present to say goodbye.

Those who are absent from the mourning rituals around the time of the funeral miss this aspect of early grieving. They may subsequently struggle with the sense that they have not been able to say goodbye. This can be a feature of cultures or faiths in which funeral rites take place immediately after death.

Over time, the reminiscences may continue and the stories resurface at family gatherings and around the time of anniversaries, birthdays and religious holidays. Often new versions of old stories emerge. New information comes to light or someone's version of an event is contradicted. Then again, people may not agree about different versions of stories that describe the life. Walter notes that:

> Members of the same family may grieve in different ways or at different rates, making communication very difficult and the creation of a shared understanding of the role of the deceased in the family almost impossible. (Walter 1996)

The retelling of stories can be a way to keep the memory of the person present, and a source of comfort to those who wish to talk about them and keep them in the collective memory. After a long illness or traumatic death, anecdotes that recall the deceased person in better health and in better times can help restore the memory of them as they were in life, rather than the reduced version they may have become through ill health or accident.

This chapter offers ways into writing about a life, whether as biography (writing about someone else), or as a way for the writer to record their own personal memories and impressions of the person who has died.

The caveat to this – and it is a big one – is that for some, memories are too painful to contemplate for some time after a death. It can seem as if the one who died has taken the good memories with them; thinking about them is simply too painful to contemplate. This can especially be the case in early grief, but the raw feelings can persist for years. If an individual or someone in a bereavement writing group finds themselves unable to contemplate memories of the one who has died, this should not be forced. Perhaps they may be able to write about other aspects of their lives or the lives of others, but no one should be expected to write about material which is too painful for them to access without distress.

Before starting, it is worth encouraging people to consider how they want their writing, whether biographical or autobiographical, to be shared. Do they even want it to be shared? In the case of biography and writing about other's lives, reasons for writing may include:

- to pass on to the children
- to share with siblings and other family members

- to share with friends

- to make public, in print or online

- as a form of memorial or lasting record of the life that was lived.

Some of these may apply to autobiography too, as a way to leave a legacy or share personal experiences. The writing can have another purpose; to relocate people in their own life narratives or to help them adapt to loss and move on. Chapter 7 considers this.

## Choice of form

As a genre, life writing embraces a range of different styles and forms (sub-genres, you might say). Biography, in which an account of a life is given with chronology, facts, names places and so forth, is the history of a life. Autobiography recounts the writer's own life in narrative form. Memoire is selective. It draws on incidents or a specific passage from a life, usually from the writer's point of view although not necessarily solely about them.

Prose might be the norm, but some might wish to use poetry in their descriptions of a life. The subject matter will generally suggest the most appropriate form, as will the writer's preferences. Encourage people to be creative in their choice of form and style. Life writing can be celebratory as well as documentary.

## Starting points

Anyone sitting down to write the story of a life is faced with the choice of where to start. In *David Copperfield*, Dickens borrowed heavily from his own young life to tell the story of his hero from the day of his birth (Dickens 1997 [1849]). In *Cider With Rosie*, Laurie Lee begins with his earliest memory of arriving in Slad, the Gloucestershire village where he grew up (Lee 2002 [1959]). Diana Athill begins her memoire *Somewhere Towards the End* from the perspective of her current age and a reflection on the limitations that advanced years bring (Athill 2008).

There are many starting points for writing about a life in biography and memoire. The guidance I offer here is adapted from life writing practice, with consideration given to techniques and themes that are appropriate to writing in bereavement.

## Time line

A time line is 'a simple chronologically structured way of recording major milestones and significant life events' (Gibson 2011, p.134).

 Invite your group or the individual you are supporting to draw a line on a sheet of paper. The line can be straight across the page, or it can be an arc or a curve. When they have drawn their line, invite them to mark it with the decades of the life they wish to write about; alternatively intervals of five years or a year. The choice of timescale depends on the length of the life; this may not be a suitable exercise for those whose lives have been very short (say less than ten years).

On one side of the line (or above it), write the main events of the life. Below the line, or on the other side, write any major historical or public events that occurred at the same time. This may require a little research or consultation with family members or friends.

This provides a rough chronology of someone's life on the page; the overall narrative punctuated by events. In a fictional story, the narrative would be punctuated by plot points (events that drive the story forward). The events recorded on a life line serve the same purpose; they tell us what has happened to shape and influence the life that is being described.

The life line helps the writer decide which aspects to write about, where to start, or perhaps which episode or incident to focus upon. The early years of birth and childhood may be uneventful (or less may be known about them), while later decades are packed with incident (leaving home, travel, work, family and so forth). This will give the writer a clue about which parts of the life story to focus upon.

## Research

Having looked at the whole life and decided which aspects to write about, the writer can do further research. Sources include:

- family anecdotes, written, spoken or recorded
- their own memories
- information found in letters, diaries and emails

- public records (such as birth and marriage certificates) and family archives

- photographs, film and video

- items found about the home of the person who has died. Souvenirs, clothes, tools, cooking utensils; these can all suggest stories about the person who used them

- research in books and online.

When enough information is gathered, encourage the writer to think about how to describe the person they are writing about.

##  WRITING ABOUT A LIFE

This exercise takes the writer through a number of themed steps that enable them to build a picture of a life. As few or as many of the steps can be taken as the writer wishes. They can also devise their own, from their knowledge and memories of the life they are describing.

### NAMES

Names are a good place to start. Read Wendy Cope's poem 'Names' (Cope in Astley 2004), about the different names by which her mother was known during her long life.

Follow this with the invitation to write about someone's name. Include anything that is known about how they came to have it, its meaning, where it came from, whether it was ever shortened or changed, whether there were any nicknames, and what the person preferred to be called.

This can give rise to a wealth of anecdote and detail about a person's life and background.

### SETTING

In life writing, the reader is drawn into a description of someone they did not know (but whom the writer knows very well and remembers), through close and often sensory detail. The effect can be rather like a zoom lens moving in on its subject.

Invite the group to write a description of a room in the home where the deceased person lived as a child (or at the time of life about which they have chosen to write). Ask them to picture that room in as much detail as possible, using imagination if necessary.

What scent does the room have? What colours and textures does it contain in fabrics, furnishings and on the walls and windows? What sounds does the room contain; for example is there a clock ticking, a fire crackling, or noise from a neighbouring room or the street outside?

This can be repeated with other settings; place of work, specific rooms in the house, the car or train, at sea, in the greenhouse, or wherever the person being described might regularly be found.

## OCCUPATION

Next, think about who is in the room (or another setting) and what they might be doing.

Write a description of them using as much physical and visual detail as possible. How are they dressed? How is their hair worn? What are they doing with their hands? Do they look comfortable in what they are wearing?

Now think more widely about this person. What are they doing at this time of day? What will they be doing later? How do they spend a typical Sunday? How and when do they relax?

These details, which require an equal amount of research, imagination and input from family and friends, can provide the basis from which to begin telling the story about the most significant or interesting part of someone's life. The setting can be home, work, leisure, travel or anything that is appropriate to the life being considered.

# Structure and theme

Before starting to write the story of a life, consider its structure. How long will the story be? Here are some of the ways in which the life can be framed:

- a day in the life

- a year in the life

- early years

- schooldays

- leaving home
- young adulthood
- falling in love
- family life
- working life
- middle years
- retirement.

These themes or segments provide structure and a way to organise material. The writer may provide their own theme if there is something they wish to describe and preserve. Trying to describe an entire life can be overwhelming for any writer; perhaps especially so in bereavement where memories are raw. Bite-sized chunks are more digestible.

The containment of a theme or the choice of a decade or time of life provides boundaries in which the writing can take place. Other forms of containment provide an even closer focus on a specific feature of a life or personality.

For example, try the following starting points:

- Describe someone's eyes. What can they see? What would it be like to look through them?

- Describe someone's hands. What work do they do? Who in the family has hands like theirs?

- Describe someone's voice. Was it soft or loud, high or low in tone, smooth or husky?

- Describe someone's laugh. Was it distinctive? Did they laugh easily?

- Describe someone's scent. Did their work mean they carried an odour of some kind?

These prompts and others can provide the way into describing a character and the life they led. They can also provide ways into reflective writing about the relationship between the writer and the person they are describing.

Here is one example using a technique I call 'Written on the Body' (Moss in Neimeyer 2012, pp.73–75):

Invite your participants to close their eyes and picture a pair of hands. Suggest that they are the hands of someone who has been dear to them; whether the person for whom they are now grieving or someone else who has been significant in their past. They might be the hands of an ancestor or someone from more recent family history.

Suggest they study the hands closely, observing their age and appearance, the shape of wrist and fingers, and any marks or scars. Consider whether the hands are soft or rough; the hands of someone who has known manual or domestic work, or who has enjoyed leisure. Hands often contain clues about a person's life and occupation.

Invite them to imagine what the hands are doing and where they are, whether at rest or at work, making something or holding something. Suggest they look at the rest of the person. Whose hands are these? In their mind's eye, they can continue to regard the owner of the hands and to enjoy a memory of them. Ideally they will be able to picture themselves with the person in this memory and be able to describe their feelings about them alongside their recollection. When they are ready, invite the group to open their eyes and begin writing the story of those hands and their memory of the person.

In one example of writing from this prompt, Judith wrote a close study of her mother's hands.

### Keepsake

*Small, cold and old the hand*
*was hers, that now I see is mine:*
*the nails are pale, gently smooth –*
*but I bite mine – the knuckles proud*
*and like their owner independent;*
*nimble and sure the fingers loop and twist,*
*knit up all inconsistencies from the past*
*in cosy cardigan, intricate shawl.*

*Veins – French navy or Payne's grey?*
*spread in a maze of rootlets*
*under transparent, thin layered*
*skin like parachute silk*
*from the airfield*

*still flecked with blood*
*to swell the tears:*
*we sewed soft knickers and slips.*

*I like to think myself more capable,*
*more worldly than she, and wiser,*
*yet called a true daughter of her mother.*
*At best spring follows winter*
*in spite of time's eccentricities*
*of melting hours, grey heads, imagined hurt,*
*and at least*
*we share*
*the vivacity of wrinkles.*

Sharing this with the group, Judith reflected that the poem served two purposes. The image of the hands provided a metaphor for the relationship between mother and daughter, and it enabled her to write about her mother while also reflecting on her own life and the passage of time.

## Letters and diaries

Letters and diaries offer a mine of information, although some may feel uncomfortable reading words that were not intended for their eyes. Personal writing such as letter and diaries should be treated with special caution for this reason. If in doubt, do not read it.

Postcards and cards for birthdays and other celebrations are different; their open-sided nature makes them somehow more public, as if the message was intended to be shared. Like letters, they can be a rich source of insight in life writing, providing the unique perspective of the person who wrote them, information about their travels and tastes, and the kind of incidents that might be forgotten had they not been posted home. These hand written messages bring back the voice of the writer, capturing the quirks and mannerisms of speech that remain long after the voice has gone.

---

## Greenbank group

Sorting through his desk, Marielle has found that her husband kept every letter and postcard they ever wrote to each other; also a great deal of travel ephemera in the form of tickets, baggage labels, itineraries and maps from their travels. She has his leather case, plastered with stickers from airlines and cruise liners. There is so much material she does not know where to start and feels anxious about it. Fiona suggests she begins by organising some of the items into chronological order, then writing the story of the trunk.

This provides Marielle with a way into her material and a means of writing about her husband's travels that is less direct. She finds the trunk an intriguing subject and starts to write about it as if it has a character of its own.

---

## *Photographs*

In Chapter 3 we saw one way of using photographs as a prompt for journal writing (p. 81). The family photograph album, Facebook account, hard drive and smart phone may be full of images of groups, events, occasions involving family and friends, from the special to the everyday. It may be a while before some of these can be looked through without distress, but in time the urge to go through such material and record or identify who was there and the spirit of the event can be strong.

Anyone who has ever inherited an album of sepia, black and white and early colour images will know the frustration of not knowing who is in the picture beyond the familiar faces of grandparents and other close family. In future, with tagging and digital archives perhaps this will change; but certainly there is a need among many to record names, dates and places before it is too late.

## IN THIS PHOTOGRAPH I RECOGNISE...

Make a catalogue of photographs and images. Create a simple form to record the details you know about:

In this photograph I recognise...

> *The place is...*
>
> *The date is roughly...*
>
> *The occasion is...*

Then reflect on the image:

> *When I look at this image I think about...*
>
> *When I look at this image I remember...*
>
> *When I look at this image I feel...*

Even if factual details are scant, these prompts enable the writer to capture the available information and their own reflections on the image before them. The details can provide raw material for writing about the lives shown in the photograph – a holiday or day out, a special occasion, scenes from family life or work – and a way into capturing their meaning and importance to the writer.

Sometimes a random image or picture will spark a memory or a reflection about a life. Roger's poem was inspired by a picture of the river Thames.

### The Thames from Chiswick Reach

*In June*
*For a sunny month or so*
*He turned back to music,*
*Friends' chatter, laughter*
*Colour and poetry:*
*He was composing again –*
*No curlicues.*
*Only essential, stripped-down stuff*
*Minimalist – 'Just like me now!', he'd smiled.*

*If he were here now*
*With the curlews*

*He'd make music*
*Of quiet smudges in the river mist:*
*Slate sky, mud*
*Old boats, islets*
*And the other bank.*

*Come Spring*
*There'll be colour and sun again*
*I know...*

*But no John.*

## Self-care in life writing

It is important to exercise self-care when approaching life writing in bereavement. The time spent immersed in the detail of someone's life can be pleasurable, but it can also be physically and emotionally tiring.

Encourage people to emerge from their writing at intervals and give themselves time to reflect on the discoveries they make as they write. Suggest that they share and talk about the discoveries they make as they sift through letters, diaries, photographs and artefacts. Even if the writing is to remain private, the experiences and memories it captures may be valuable as part of an individual's and their wider family's collective adjustment to a loss.

---

### Greenbank group

Fiona and Michael discuss the use of life writing techniques with the group. They ask themselves:

- Who has talked about wanting to write about their family history or the life story of someone who has died? Marielle has said she wants to write about her husband's life and their travels together. Anna realises she has some early memories of her mother that have never been properly recorded.

- Who has children or wider family to share the writing with? What sort of record do they want to make? Perhaps Alan and Ros might write the story of their partner's lives as a record for their young children. They could involve the grandparents in writing down stories about Ali and Dan as children.

- Who in the group might find this difficult? Cynthia, an only child, might wonder who she is writing family stories for. Riaz might find references to childhood with his late twin brother too painful to contemplate. He might, on the other hand, find it easier to write about his own childhood memories, and embrace this as a way to describe his brother to younger members of the family.

---

# CHAPTER 7

Reflecting on Change

When someone close dies, the bereaved one's life story also changes. The very words that they and others use to describe them can feel strange and inappropriate as they struggle to adjust. A bereaved parent may wonder if they can still call themselves 'Mum' or 'Dad'. A wife may reject the term 'widow' but cast around in vain to find a word to describe her single-yet-married status. A sister whose sibling has died may struggle to think of herself as an only child. When the familiar structures of close family and friendship are changed, how do we reposition ourselves as single, parentless, childless, or missing one of the group that has defined us since birth?

Bowman notes that when we listen in bereavement support, we often hear people struggle to find language to express the experience of their loss and the difference it is making to them:

> Bereaved people want to have their stories heard... They seem to be searching for language to describe more than death and the accompanying bereavement – their words and our responses are not yet as 'suitable' for habitation. (Bowman 2000)

This chapter considers some of the ways in which a bereaved person can explore their own sense of self; the self they were before their loss and the self they are evolving into as they work through their grief.

We all grow up as the products of our social background, context and life experience. Most of us, from quite a young age, develop an expectation of how life is going to be. This is based on the social norms of the environment in which we are brought up; norms that include a path through education (going to school, college, university or straight into work or some other path), leaving home, forming friendships and close bonds, relationships, marriage, children, making a home, and progressing in line with one's peers.

When bereavement occurs, these norms are broken, The expected pattern of life is interrupted. Someone married in their 20s will have reasonably looked forward to a long life ahead with their spouse. By the same token, a parent does not expect to outlive their child, no matter what the child's age. Someone who takes early retirement with their partner does not expect to face old age alone.

These are just a few examples. When someone dies, the person who is left behind can feel that they have lost their life as well. The life they had is no longer available to them.

## Personal life narrative

Neimeyer has written compellingly about this experience, noting 'the extent to which our most intimate sense of self is rooted (and uprooted) in our shifting relationships with others' (Neimeyer 2007, p.261). Walter expresses the sense of reinvention and readjustment that takes place in grieving;

> Bereavement is part of the never-ending and reflexive conversation with self and others through which the late-modern person makes sense of their existence. In other words, bereavement is part of the process of (auto)biography, and the biographical imperative – the need to make sense of self and others in a continuing narrative – is the motor that drives bereavement behaviour. (Walter 1996, pp.7–25)

Questions such as 'who am I now?', 'who was I then?' and 'who am I becoming?' are too blunt for those in a state of confused transition after loss. To enable someone to check in with themselves and focus on specific thoughts and feelings, the containment of hands, with a visual diagram, can enable expression, as in this exercise:

## TAKE YOURSELF BY THE HAND

Invite the writer to draw an outline of their hand on the page.

- Invite them to think of five words to describe themselves; the first five that come to mind (try to be quick and not over-think the response). These are attributes, traits of character or perhaps words to describe their current state.

- Write the words on the five fingers of the hand; one for each finger and one for the thumb.

- Ask them to think of one phrase or expression which someone else might use to describe them – either someone who knows them well (a friend or family member), or superficial (a neighbour or a colleague). Write this in the palm of the hand.

- Invite them to reflect on the words they have chosen and to write further about those that seem significant or that offer insight into feelings and their current situation. If they wish, they can write a short story about themselves to illustrate the attributes they have chosen, or they may choose to write further about the way they may be perceived by others.

This provides containment and enables people to summarise themselves succinctly. For those struggling to express themselves in more than a few words it provides the safety of a pattern. The writer only has to come up with five words and one further word or expression.

---

## Greenbank group

Alan draws his hand and writes these words on the fingers and thumb:

*Father*

*Exhausted*

*Angry*

*Proud*

*Heartbroken*

In the palm of his hand he writes 'Coping'.

Michael encourages him to say more about his sense of coping. He asks him if he thinks this is the impression others have of him. Alan says it is, but that he is not coping. He says he keeps it to himself because of pride. He does not want to let his children down or be seen by others to be failing in some way. He says he has written 'proud' on one of the fingers because he feels proud of his children for the way they are coping, but he does not feel proud of himself.

This is a powerful realisation for Alan. As Michael and others have observed, he has been throwing himself into activity and is appearing to be in control, but feels the opposite is true. After the group session Michael invites him to talk further about his feelings in a one to one session, and to explore other kinds of support that will help him. Alan agrees and says he has been holding a lot inside. Writing it down clearly on the page has helped him admit this to himself and others.

---

If this exercise proves helpful, suggest the writer uses it to describe others too. The hand can be anyone's; the person for whom they are grieving, to capture their qualities and personality, or someone else of significance whom they wish to describe.

## Who am I?

The question 'who am I now?' goes to the heart of the bereaved person's sense of self. The exercise that follows can be used to enable a bereaved person or a group to look across the events and influences of their whole lives, not just the impact of loss.

 I often introduce this exercise by reading a poem or a short piece of autobiographical prose. 'I come from' (Seatter 2006) works well. This poem is in the accessible form of a list, in which the poet recounts his suburban background and reflects on formative experiences.

### WARM UP

Begin by inviting the group to say where they lived in their early years. This is gentler than asking where they were actually born; someone who was adopted may not be able to answer that question easily. Spend about ten minutes sharing and reflecting together, then provide a handout of the poem and read it with the group. I sometimes invite a male group member to read it for us.

I Come From
*By Robert Seatter*

*I come from a suburb waiting forever*
*for the train for London,*
*from smashed windows, graffiti,*
*fog on the platform,*
*skinheads and fights*
*if you look the wrong way*
*I come from clean handkerchiefs,*
*dinner money, God,*
*please and sorry one hundred times over,*
*draft excluders and double glazing*
*I come from Chambers Etymological Dictionary,*
*maths tables, 11+, Look & Learn,*
*an almost complete set of Observer I-spy books,*
*from a family of teachers and yet more teachers,*
*an Orkney grandfather, a Shropshire grandma,*
*from no accent at all*
*I come from kindness*
*I come from doh-re-me: The Sound of Music,*
*recorder, clarinets, a pianola*
*all the way from Scotland*
*I come from sin and masturbation,*
*rats behind the garage,*
*and a man who followed me*
*back from the library*
*I come from silence*
*I come from a garden*
*from my father mowing the lawn into the dark,*
*from fences, walls, gates and hedges,*
*Cuthbert's seed packets, The Perfect Small Garden,*
*from the sound through the night*
*of trains, trains, trains*

*(Seatter 2006)*

Invite the group to read the poem again to themselves, underlining or noting anything that strikes them as familiar or which reminds them of – or contrasts with – their own background. This allows for a diversity of experience.

Invite the group to talk about the poem. What do they like about it? What do they dislike? How effective is the use of the list structure? The group may comment on the image of trains which begins and ends the poem. They may notice the sparse punctuation and the way the poem is open ended with no full stop.

Sometimes, a group will comment on the poem's dark centre with 'the man who followed me home from the library'. A life story can contain dark moments as well as lighter ones.

## WRITING

Invite the group to take ten minutes to make their own list of 'where I come from'.

Suggest they shape their list into a poem (up to 40 lines) or a piece of short prose (around 300 words) that describes their backgrounds. Invite them to spend a further 20–30 minutes working on this.

When most people have finished, give a minute's prompt to enable the others to complete their writing. Invite people to share their writing and reflect on what has emerged from their memory lists.

I find that this poem works well as a prompt for mixed gender groups. The male perspective engages the men and encourages them to explore their own experiences. Everyone can relate to the detail of family background and household ephemera. Some may choose to tell the story of their lives in one complete piece, while others focus on their early life or a single formative moment. This provides scope for further exploration in writing or in bereavement support.

Derek produced this moving example:

### I Was
### (Not for sympathy)

I was the little boy
    who sat on the sidelines;
I was the little boy
    who listened to others' conversation, if they let me, but so often was
    unable to join in;
I was the little boy
    who never worked out what to say, or what strategies to play against
    the bullies;
I was the little boy
    who found it so hard to work out what was going on;
I was the little boy
    who seemed to be the butt of everyone else's jokes;

*I was the little boy*
> *who chickened-out of going fishing that first morning and never got*
> *invited again;*

*I was the little boy*
> *who chickened-out of going to cubs that first afternoon and never got*
> *the opportunity again;*

*I was the little boy*
> *who retained no friends from school days;*

*I was the little boy*
> *whose only brother, being five years younger, was too far removed to be*
> *a close playmate;*

*I was the little boy*
> *who had to make do with his own company.*

*But then, I met Sue.*
> *I am not who I was.*
> *I am not going back.*

The way this poem closes on a note of vehemence, 'I am not going back', was appreciated by the group as a strong personal statement and a tribute to the very positive difference his wife had made to Derek's life. Derek had worked on the piece in between two meetings of the group. It is a deeply felt piece.


## What am I like?

This next exercise uses metaphor to explore thoughts and feelings that are difficult to express in plainer language.

 You will need a selection of postcards or photographs of animals, birds, fish and perhaps insects: for example, a lion, bear, dog, stag, eagle, butterfly, dolphin, cat, peacock, blackbird, wren, hippopotamus, elephant, turtle, stick insect and so forth, to ensure a good spread of creatures with which a diverse group of people may identify.

The archetypes we associate with animals can work powerfully in writing. The lion's strength and pride, the bear cub's vulnerability, the bird's ability to soar above, the butterfly emerging from its cocoon, all can serve as metaphors for aspects of personality that have been subsumed by grief or which are emerging, slowly, from it.

## WARM UP

Offer the cards and invite participants to choose an animal that appeals to them.

## WRITING

- In a five minute sprint write, ask them to write a description of the animal in which they focus on its appearance, how it moves, any sound it makes, and the look of its skin, feathers or fur.
- Invite them to describe its habitat and anything they know or can imagine about how it eats or where it sleeps.
- In their writing, invite them to reflect on what they admire about this animal.
- Ask them to look closely into its eyes and to write about what they see in them.
- Ask them to imagine that they are looking through those eyes, back at themselves.
- Invite them to write about what the animal can see as it looks at them.
- Give a two minute prompt to enable those who are still writing to finish, then invite the group to share their writing.

Here is Derek's response to this exercise:

### The Deer

Gazing at a picture of an Alaskan Caribou, I see, in my mind's eye, a deer in Richmond Park (where my younger daughter Rachel first learned to ride her bike without outriders).

Motionless, it gazes forwards, deep in thought, apparently weighed down by its responsibilities. Its grand, magnificent antlers convey great maturity but not age. It is in its prime. Its coat is healthy so it must be doing well, able to cope with life's necessities. While I am not afraid of it, I certainly respect it; I recognise its authority and responsibility and neither want nor would dare to interfere. It seems to need its space.

We share the same ponderousness, the need to reflect on everything and the resistance to being rushed. It looks like a leader – is it one? How did it get to be the responsible one – did it fight for the position – did it volunteer – did it just find itself with the role thrust upon it? Would it swap the role if it could find another responsible deer? How far would it go to protect its co-travellers? Could it ever just shed its responsibilities and abandon its companions?

Oops – I've got too close. Just a look tells me that much. No sudden moves. I look away and slowly turn maybe 45°. His head keeps pointing straight at me but he has not yet moved. I hope he doesn't do the bellow that I have heard other deer do because people will start looking at me then. Slowly, trying to look disinterested, I take a few sidesteps, breathing more easily as the distance between us increases. His head turns away. He has lost interest in me. Suits me just fine.

Respect.

In another example, from a participant in the same group, a captured moment of empathy between woman and wild bird emerges. This is by Sarah, whose green farm door featured in Chapter 5.

### The Quizzical Puffin

The quizzical Puffin catches my gaze and the look turns to fear.

I stand still and relax resting quietly on the grassy knoll, never taking my eyes off the beautiful bird before me.

Her silvery catch hangs greedily out either side of her magnificent beak and she leaves me watching as she empties her load in her carefully dug burrow in the hillside.

I wait in silence for her to re-emerge and it's not long until she rewards my patience.

Puffins fly in overhead, but they are just a number. She knows I am there and recognises my friendship.

As she waddles towards me her wings open up and her graceful flight takes her over my head, back out to sea.

For Sarah, this contemplative piece enabled her to reflect on a less stressed version of herself. It captured a memory with a distinctive feeling. The combination reminded her that she could feel more connected to real life, in better, calmer times.

Sometimes an exercise like this will have an unexpected outcome for the writer. Teresa, grieving for her mother and frustrated in her attempts to express herself in anything other than blunt language, chose a picture of a large tabby cat. Several days after the exercise she found a half full milk bottle on her front step and milk splashed around the front door. This led her to ruminate on the activities of her own cats while she was out of the house. For the first time, she felt able to write about something light hearted and imaginative. She produced this story which, she reflected later, seemed to signify a turning point in her overall mood and adjustment to her loss. We enjoyed hearing it when Teresa read it to us at the Princess Alice Hospice writing group and the surreal story generated much laughter and speculation; an example of laughter being shared to everyone's benefit.

### The Curious Incident of the Half Full Milk Bottle

'I'm bored,' says Horatio. 'Mummy T has gone out and I've had enough sleeping, sleeping, sleeping all day. I can't tell you how many mice I've caught in my dreams. The disappointment when I wake up hungry...'

'Fat cat, fat cat, fat cat. You always think about food,' says Tiggy.

'Who's for adventure?' says Horatio, ignoring Tiggy's remark.

'OK,' she agrees, 'as long as I can run and hide if something frightens me.'

'Scaredy cat,' says Horatio.

'Don't be rude to your aunt,' says Foggy. 'As the oldest cat here, and your grandmother, I shall keep watch and sit very still.'

'Sleep more likely,' says Tiggy.

'Let's go then! Follow me,' and so they do, out through the cat-flap and across the patio.

'Tiggy, save your energy for our adventure, not for chasing that know-it-all squirrel and the fat, blobby pigeons. And don't try rolling in the cat-nip.'

'I can smell something in the front garden. My purring has started. Keep your cat's-eyes peeled.'

'What's this on the doorstep? She has forgotten to take in the milk. Here's our adventure. But how to get to it? Grandma Foggy, you know.'

'Just let me get comfortable in this nice flowerpot; such lovely soft earth to lie on. Do I look like the cat's whiskers here?'

'Tiggy, stop jumping about like a cat on a hot tin roof. I can't think.'

'Try tipping the bottle; the milk will run out.'

'Let me, I'm the strongest,' says Horatio.

'The heaviest, you mean,' says Tiggy.

'...and I've had lots of practice at pushing over tins of cat food,' continues Horatio, pretending not to hear what Tiggy said.

'Heave Ho. Watch out Tiggy, that's another of your nine cats' lives gone. Good thing it ran over your tail, not your body.'

'Ow, Ow,' howls Tiggy, 'this must be what a whipping with a cat-o-nine-tails feels like.'

'Children, children,' says Foggy from her comfortable flowerpot, 'that milk bottle has rolled away down the drive and you'll never push it back up. There's only one more bottle. You'll have to think of another way to get to the milk.'

'I've got it!' cries Horatio, 'we punch the lid in,' and his white paw swiftly pushes the shiny bottle top in. Delicious white creamy milk slops over the top. Pink tongues are busy and the purring is very loud.

'Whose tongue is the longest?'

'Mine!'

'No, mine!'

'Look, mine sticks out as far as my whiskers!'

'See here. This is even better. I can get my paw in and scoop out the milk.'

'Let me have a go.'

'Where can we hide the rest of the milk for later? No good trying to roll the bottle to the kitchen. You'd have no lives left, Tiggy.'

'Let me think,' says Foggy. 'I've seen the paper and letters pushed through there and Mummy T collects them from the inside. Perhaps we could do the same with the milk.'

'What a good idea! We can make a tower. Foggy, you sit here and Tiggy, you climb up on her. You know how clever you are at climbing up chairs. I'm the best at jumping and the strongest, so I'll jump up with the bottle, land on you, Tiggy, and pour the milk through the letterbox here.'

'Oh dear, some has spilt outside but at least I can hear it splashing on the floor inside.'

'Quick, round the back, and into the house to find the milk and hide it.'

Later, Mummy T asks, 'Do any of you cats know how the milk came to be splashed all over the inside and outside of the front door, the door mat, the paper and the letters?'

'Remember what I said,' mutters Horatio, 'mum's the word.'

## Themes for personal life narratives

Certain themes provide a way in to writing about personal history and experiences. For example:

- first day at school

- starting a new job

- going on holiday

- moving home

- learning to drive.

For some these will draw on memory. For others, they offer scope and containment in which to reflect on transitions and changes in their circumstances. The husband whose wife always did the cooking may now be learning to cook for himself. The partner who never learnt to drive may be starting driving lessons. Family holidays take on a new poignancy as well as practical challenges for the newly single parent or someone without a holiday companion. There may be issues around moving home or adjusting to having the house or flat to oneself.

Themes offer flexibility. Someone who does not want to consider their current living situation (or with the dilemma of whether or not to move house following their bereavement), can find that by remembering past moves, the possibilities become easier to contemplate. The choice of how to explore the theme is the writers', always.

Topics such as music, dancing, sport or food can provide structure. Food writers and recipe books provide rich stimulus for reminiscence-based writing around the theme of food and meals, as in the exercise that follows.

# Theme: Food for thought

 WARM UP

- Select a passage from a food writer or recipe book. I often draw on Nigel Slater's collection of short essays *Eating for England*. His description of Marmite (Slater 2007, p.250) captures the sense of 'love it or hate it' and gets people comparing their culinary likes and dislikes. An alternative would be to invite people to bring a sample of a favourite food to the session or to pass around a plate onto which imaginary food can be placed (Schweitzer 2004, p.74).

- Invite the group to talk about their memories of favourite foods, family meal times or occasions in which food features: school dinners, birthday parties, picnics and so forth.

### WRITING PROMPTS

- Invite the group to write about a memorable meal or food that they have enjoyed.

- Describe the food, who cooked it and, if they can recall it, the ingredients and recipe.

- Suggest they continue writing about an occasion on which they ate this food: a picnic, school dinner, Sunday lunch or a special feast day.

- Next, invite them to describe a food they did not like.

- In their writing, describe the taste, texture, look and smell of the food; encourage them to go over the top in their descriptions and why they disliked it so much.

- Invite them to write about an occasion when they remember eating this food; who was there and what happened?

This can give rise to comic writing and sharing of experiences about food. Dave, whose wife Jenny used to do the cooking, found himself learning to cook after her death. He wrote an ode to an invaluable cooking aid:

### To Mr Foreman

*Thank you George for inventing this.*
*It makes cooking almost seem like bliss.*
*Although it doesn't give me the biggest thrill,*
*I really like my electric grill.*
*It frazzles my bacon, cremates my chop,*
*Scorches my steak, makes my sausages pop,*
*And just to make sure I come to no harm*
*It even sets off my smoke alarm.*
*But sometimes I wonder why I'm so keen*
*cause it's really a bugger to keep it clean.*

Be aware that for some the topic of food may awaken difficult memories of being made to eat something they did not like, or of difficult social or family occasions. Be alert for someone for whom eating disorders in themselves or others (including, perhaps, the deceased) may make this an unsuitable or difficult topic.

For some, food, dining out and the associations with special occasions can provide a breakthrough into a positive memory. Sara, who attended a writing group at Princess Alice Hospice, was finding life very difficult since her husband Martin's death three years earlier. Martin was 56 when he died and his illness was short and unexpected. As Sara says, he was 'only ill for eleven weeks from his first symptom to his death.' The invitation to recall a memorable meal took Sara unexpectedly to Cadiz in southern Spain, where she and Martin had spent part of a cruise holiday. She wrote:

Cadiz was where we spent our 30th anniversary day. We walked around, and in the evening booked a table in the Steak Room. I had managed to get balloons put up on the table as a surprise for Martin. As we sat down, the ship left harbour, the sun was setting, it had been a magical day. My present from Martin was a china couple surrounded by a heart, which was a lovely surprise. My present to him was a medal. For a long time I had told him he deserved a medal for putting up with me, and so was able to get one specially made and inscribed. It really surprised Martin and he was very pleased with it.

A trolley was brought to our table with all the precooked steaks for us to choose from. It really took our breath away. When the steak arrived it was cooked to perfection, a wonderful meal to end a perfect day. A small cake arrived, totally unexpected, with a sugar rose which I still have.

Looking back tonight, for the first time in detail, not knowing how quickly my life would change, makes it even more special and treasured, but also sad.

Sara felt unable to read her piece out loud but she was keen to share her story with the rest of the group. I read it for her and she was able to experience the group's pleasure at hearing about her anniversary meal and the shared reflections it aroused around the table. Writing later, Sara commented that the writing group had resulted in her 'discovering an option to help deal with my grief I had never considered,' and that this exercise had led to her 'realising I have very happy memories that I can focus on – and can think about more'.

## Theme: Musical memoires

Music can be a powerful stimulus for memories; most of us can recall a favourite song or a piece of music we associate with events and people of significance to us. In bereavement, music can be especially emotive and, for some, too poignant to enjoy. Love songs on the radio, songs on the deceased's iPod or CD collection can simply be too painful to listen to. I have known people change the settings on the car radio to avoid listening to the radio station that was a favourite of the one who has died. Some, on the other hand, can find comfort in music. It can sooth as well as stir.

## Greenbank group

When the topic of music is raised in the group, Ros says she listens to her husband's iPod at night. She uses an ear piece in bed so she can hear the music quietly, on shuffle. She says it helps her go to sleep and comforts her if she wakes up.

Anna says she has been unable to listen to music since Pat died. Every time she hears the radio there seems to be a love song playing, which she finds painful.

 WARM UP

- Invite the group to share their feelings about listening to music. This may give rise to people discovering that they are not the only ones who find it hard to listen to music since their bereavement.

### PROMPTS

- Invite the group to think about a favourite song or piece of music. Ask them to write down its title, its first line or a line from the lyric.

- Invite them to make notes about their memories of hearing this song or piece of music. When and where did they first hear it? Do they associate it with a time of their life, an event or with someone of significance?

- When they have made their notes, invite them to use the title, or the first line or the lyric they have chosen as their starting point for a piece of writing.

An alternative is to prepare cards with well known song titles or lyrics. Invite the group to take one lucky-dip style and use it as the starting point for their own writing. It is best to avoid song titles containing direct references to love or loss, but to choose ones that are popular and therefore familiar. In a mixed age group, make sure you have a range of titles from appropriate decades, or ones that transcend specific age groups in terms of their popularity (a selection of Gershwin songs may not resonate with a group of 20 or 30-somethings although their titles may strike a chord).

Jenai's poignant example was triggered by a Beatles's song:

### I Want to Hold Your Hand

*I want to hold your hand.*
*I hesitate yet the yearning is so strong.*
*Scrubbed, white and yet unmistakeable.*
*Hands that have*
*nurtured, sewed, knitted, polished and cleaned*
*are now still and at rest.*
*They felt so cold and empty*
*Gone were the warm gentle hands of reassurance*
*that comforted childhood pains.*
*And the old frail clasped hands in mine that said*
*'Don't leave me here, take me home'*
*Now a cherished memory*
*I want to hold your hand.*

## Theme: Where were you when…?

Everyone can recall those 'Where were you when…?' moments when someone in the public eye dies unexpectedly or an event of historic significance take place: the moon landings, the death of the Princess of Wales, the end of the Second World War, 9/11 (the attack on the World Trade Centre) or 7/7 (the London Tube bombings) and so forth. Similarly, no one will ever forget where they were when they experienced or heard about the death of someone to whom they were close. It can be hard to draw directly on such memories and write about that experience (although some will, by choice), but an invitation to write about other such significant moments can offer a way into reflection on the experience of sudden loss.

 Use a time line to invite participants to write the significant public moments they can recall alongside the key events of their own lives. Suggest they pick one to write about (perhaps their earliest memory from the news), and create a written account of the memory, what it meant to them at the time and what they remember of the reactions of those around them.

The sharing of such memories can give rise to discussion about private and public grief, and about the way people behave around the bereaved.

---

# Greenbank group

- Working with metaphor can work well for someone like Riaz, who struggles to express his feelings in straightforward language, yet has mentioned his enjoyment of reading poetry.

- The hands exercise can enable someone like Alan to own his feelings about not coping as well as people perceive. Roz, who often writes short pieces including Facebook posts and texts, may also respond well to this contained style of writing.

- Anna might be encouraged to use the 'I come from' prompt to write about her own family. She is feeling distanced from her partner Pat's family, but her own background may now be a source of solace.

- The theme of food can bring back memories of childhood or of bringing up children and grandchildren, a powerful stimulus for Bobbie and perhaps Riaz, for whom eating has become complex with his need to balance the fasting of Ramadan with management of his diabetes. He might use this theme to reflect on his changing relationship with food and diet.

- Writing about music may be too emotive for some, but the realisation that they are not alone in their sensitivity can help to break down feelings of isolation.

- Bobbie might respond to writing about the death of public figures with her own reflections on the experience of hearing about the attack on her grandson's platoon on the news and the subsequent trauma of finding out about his actual death as (as she experienced it) an afterthought.

- Fiona and Michael will consider inviting the group to suggest their own themes around personal identity and how they see their roles shifting over time.

---

———————•◆•———————

# CHAPTER 8

# Writing for Memorial

The ways in which people choose to memorialise those who have died are many and various; among them are plaques, benches, memory boxes and written or inscribed tributes in private and public places. The range of options is huge; you can even sponsor a hedgehog box in someone's memory. In this century we are seeing new technologies adding to and taking over from traditional forms of memorial, while traditional forms are themselves adapting to modern usage.

Immediately after a death relatives and friends respond by laying flowers, teddy bears, cards and so forth at the graveside, or at or close to the actual scene of death (e.g. at the roadside). Such responses are to do with initial reactions and involve the placing of material items; what can be called 'the transient and temporary...a tool through which visitors could publically reveal their "movement" through grief' (Woodthorpe 2011). They may also flock to the Facebook wall or MySpace page, to post their reactions and send messages to the deceased as though continuing an unfinished conversation.

This handbook is concerned for the most part with writing in the traditional medium of pen and paper, with occasional forays into laptop and social media devices. In this chapter I want to look at some of the creative and innovative ways in which people make and share lasting memorials, from the multi-media tribute on a social networking site's wall, for instance, or the concise three line inscription on a memorial bench or plaque. Here are three diverse illustrations of memorials in the early 21st century.

In February 2009 a large rural area of Victoria in south Australia suffered what came quickly to be known as Black Saturday. The Australian Broadcasting Company's website gives a full account at www. abc.net.au/innovation/blacksaturday/#/stories/mosaic, with a mosaic of stories by people directly affected. A total of 173 people died and thousands were made homeless by bush fires that swept through the region leaving communities in ruins. Neighbours and families witnessed terrible scenes. Some only narrowly escaped the inferno themselves. The sense of shock was immense and the sights that greeted people when they tried to return to their homes were harrowing.

In the days and weeks that followed, residential areas were cordoned off by authorities who were still assessing the damage, endeavouring to make areas safe and beginning the painful and painstaking process of identification. The people returning to search for what was left of their homes were unable to enter.

At the edge of one village, a gum tree stood by the roadside. Charred and smoke damaged, it nonetheless had survived the worst of the firestorm. Slowly, as the days went by, pieces of paper began to appear pinned to the tree's bark. They grew like a new skin on the blackened trunk and sprouted from the branches like white leaves. The pieces of paper bore messages, poems, photographs and stories. They bore the expressions of the people who wanted to return home but, as yet, could not.

The tree became known as the poem tree and it sparked an idea; to recruit blacksmiths locally and from further afield to make a new tree on which people could hang leaves bearing messages of memorial for their community. A charity was formed and blacksmiths were invited to set up temporary forges around the site. People started to share news and send messages through Facebook. Soon the anvils were ringing with the sound of leaves being created with people's personal messages.

The poem tree grew into the Tree Project (www. treeproject.abavic. org.au), a symbol of the community's gradual renewal. It provides a moving and seemingly permanent memorial to those who died. Joji Mori of the University of Melbourne, has written a fascinating account of this act of spontaneous memorial which sprang from a community's need to express its collective and individual grief, and whose development through a website and the more traditional medium of blacksmithing brings together the modern and the ancient (Mori 2011).

Meanwhile, on the other side of the globe, in the garden of Princess Alice Hospice in Surrey, there is a poem tree. Those who wish to create a memorial to someone who has died in the hospice's care can have a leaf inscribed and hung upon the branches, in return for a donation. The idea is spreading.

More traditionally, in Kew Gardens there is a memorial bench (one of many), which bears an inscription to someone who 'loved this lake'. Because memorial benches are not fixed to the ground in Kew Gardens, the bench has moved some distance from the favourite spot, probably carried by picnickers. I hope the person who is memorialised by the bench enjoyed other parts of the gardens; perhaps his itinerant seat will travel back to the lakeside at some point. The moral of this story is to make sure your bench is fixed to the spot, or, failing that, to choose wording that fits the (possibly changeable) setting.

Somewhere between these two examples sits the idea of the memory box. Memory boxes can be made for the living or the departed. When a baby is born some will begin to keep a memory box so that when the child is older they will have keepsakes about grandparents and their family history. Others make a box after someone has died, to preserve stories and memories about their life, whether to share with the whole family and succeeding generations, or as a form of comfort and a way to make sense of the artefacts and fragments of a life. Some are shared, some are private to the person who creates the box. Charities including Winston's Wish (for bereaved children) and Macmillan Cancer Care promote the idea of memory boxes on their websites. If you search for 'memory box' online a long list of providers appears, many of them offering (and selling) personalised, decorated and bespoke boxes.

## Public memorials

Think about the public places where you might see a written memorial, or a memorial in which words feature prominently. They include:

- cemeteries

- public plaques

- memorial benches

- at a place of work

- public buildings or facilities endowed by a bequest from the deceased's estate

- roadside memorials
- social networking sites
- websites devoted to memorials.

These are public and on show. Even a tattoo can be a public way to memorialise the dead, if it is on show.

Walk through any park, on any beachside promenade or beauty spot in the UK and you are likely to find memorial benches or plaques. The Victorians began the tradition and it seems to show no signs of diminishing.

Memorial benches seem permanent but are in fact temporary. Most are leased from a local authority or landowner; the National Trust for example. Leases are taken for ten years or so before becoming renewable. The memorial bench is, in one sense, a form of sponsorship.

The guidelines for wording of bench plaques are often strict and do not allow space for much emotion or creativity; little more than a name and date in some cases. Some local authorities provide advice about the wording. Others leave the choice of words up to the client, although usually within a small word limit.

Within the narrow confines of ten words, how can a message carry sufficient weight to serve as a long-term memorial? Some of the forms of containment we have looked at can help focus ideas about what to say. Six-word stories (Chapter 4) and the hands exercise in Chapter 6 ('Written on the Body' example) could be adapted for this purpose. Acrostics and haiku might also be suitable, if space allows.

---

## Greenbank group

Anna wishes that Pat had had the woodland burial she knows she would have preferred, but sadly Pat's family did not consult her about the funeral arrangements. They used to go walking in the Peak District and there is a viewing point at which they loved to stop on their rambles. Anna makes enquiries about placing a bench at the site and writes a haiku with Pat's name and dates for the plaque.

Alan has an idea; he says he will make acrostics with the children, one spelling Alison (for him) and one using Mummy (for the children). He will suggest they plant spring bulbs in the back garden so that when spring comes they can have their own floral memorial to Ali, visible from the kitchen window.

---

## Online memorials

The technically-minded creators of the first social networking sites can surely not have envisaged their use as online memorials for the dead, yet that is what spaces offered by Facebook, MySpace, Flikr and a host of online networks and blogs have become in recent years.

The phenomenon shows no sign of abating. Almost every day new pages are created and people flock to post their messages and talk about (or to), the friend or relative who has died.

This is influencing the way young (and not so young) web-literate communities commemorate and communicate after a death. Eva Wiseman, a columnist in The Observer Magazine, reflected on her own use of the web after the death of a young friend in December 2010. She described the experience of looking at photos of him on his Flickr page 'where he still grins and grimaces...' (Wiseman 2010, p.5). Wiseman noted that, while Facebook used to delete the accounts of the deceased, now they leave them online so that friends and family can post messages. This effectively turns such media into high-tech burial sites where people can leave comments the way they would lay flowers. Wiseman observes:

> ...social networking has changed how we mourn. Instead of eulogies and plaques, today the dead are remembered through camera-phone photos of them in comedy glasses drunk at parties... (ibid)

The need to reflect on the death of a friend, and the desire to carry on a conversation with him or about him as part of the grief process is natural. Wiseman's perspective is that of a young adult, one who has grown up with and embraced the online age. Her friend's continuing presence on the web enables people to carry on a conversation with the person who has died (she gives one example in which someone's friend posted a message during the World Cup: 'Don't worry mate – you're not missing much' (ibid)). This may be helpful to some, in the way that writing an unsent letter or imagining a conversation may help, but Wiseman also wonders if her friend's continuing web presence will 'interfere with his family's efforts to move on from his sudden death' (ibid). How different is the creation of an online memorial to the creation of a headstone and a physical grave or plaque in a memorial garden, which can be visited? Perhaps the choice of which to service is generational. Increasingly, we mourn in public through these new media.

Whether such outpourings of online grief can be called genuine mourning is a moot point. The ways in which people choose to write about their perceived loss in such a public way, using poetry, stories and personal statements, are interesting. They are part of a social phenomenon that goes hand in hand with the tendency for the public to become active reporters of current events; the recordings of the last phone messages from those trapped in the Twin Towers on 9/11, or the ghostly images recorded by bomb victims in the London tube tunnels on 7/7, for example. People use new technology in ways that are constantly evolving. If it can be recorded and memorialised on line, perhaps grieving, to a younger generation, is no longer such a private experience, but something mediated through the collective use of technology.

As the technology rapidly develops, sites that are currently in use may soon be replaced by new online tools. Where does that leave the memorials that may be archived or inaccessible once the software no longer works? Looking through some of the sites it is clear that many are set up and tended to begin with, but after a while the updates peter out. Some are left untouched for years. This suggests to me that this form of writing has its use in bereavement for a time, just like other forms of journaling perhaps, but that people move on from them when they are ready as part of their natural progression through grief work. Perhaps head stones and rose bushes will endure, after all.

An increasing number of the many charities and voluntary organisations that provide bereavement support in the UK offer space on their websites for families and friends to post messages or contribute to blogs in memory of their loved ones. For some this is a free service, for others a donation to the charity is requested in return for hosting a page or maintaining the site's content.

www.muchloved.com was an early pioneer, established by Jonathan Davies in 1995 as a memorial to his brother and his mother, both of whom died within a couple of years of each other. It is run as a charity and offers ways to create a tribute using words, pictures and sound. The tributes can be viewed by closed groups and the creator of the tribute can control who sees it. Like a memorial bench, tributes are maintained on the site for ten years, with the option of continuing for longer (for a subscription), if the family wishes to.

Many users of this site and others like it return to it over time, adding messages and reflections in writing. The effect is a little like returning to tend a garden or visit a cemetery plot. Here is one example, in which the writer, Ray, reflects on the passage of time since his brother's death:

> *Happy birthday Malcolm,*
> *I can't believe how long it's been,*
> *since we sat in the garden*
> *and had a glass or two of gin,*
> *I hope you are sitting somewhere*
> *where the sun shines down on you,*
> *I hope you are allowed*
> *to have a glass or two,*
> *I will wish you happy birthday*
> *and say I miss you mate,*
> *a brother who was always there*
> *you are an all time great,*
> *Love you*
> *Ray*

The writing has the feeling of a conversation being continued, touchingly, between the two brothers.

Some sites, such as those maintained by charities catering for specific types of bereavement (for instance Babyloss, for bereaved parents of stillborn or miscarried babies, or those who do not survive to full-term), provide an online community or network of support as well as a place to post written messages and reflections. The quality and form of writing on such sites varies considerably, but is always moving to read and heartfelt in its expression. Some quote from well known and familiar texts; some write their own. For someone wishing to create such a tribute, or write a personal message to their unborn or stillborn child, an acrostic based on a name (if one was given), verses written in the style of a lullaby or nursery rhyme, or an unsent letter can be effective containments for expression.

## Memorial blogs

Some start their own. One example, www.merrywidow.me.uk, was started by Kate Boydell after the death of her husband Charlie, who was 38 years old. This lovely blog has grown into a resource for those who have lost their spouse or partner at a young age. It includes a diary, a guide, and links to sources of help and support, written in an entertaining, engaging and accessible style. The last posting was made in 2007. Kate's blog has now gone quiet as she gets on with her life and with raising her two daughters; but the blog remains online as a resource for people in her situation.

Setting up a blog need not be technologically challenging. www.wordpress.org provides step by step guidelines, and like a journal (although more public), the blog can be updated as frequently as the writer wishes. Forums, in which a community of people have an online conversation and support each other with information, answers to questions and discussion of shared themes can be useful in countering feelings of isolation. Some of the leading bereavement charities offer blogs and forums on their websites and, increasingly, provide links to Facebook, Flickr and Twitter. For those growing up in, or adopting, such social media tools, the move towards sharing thoughts and feelings with strangers online seems to be widely accepted.

## Online resources

If online memorials and bereavement blogs appeal to clients and groups, there are many to which you could refer them (or of which they will already be aware themselves). Here is a selection of the charities and bereavement support sites whose online pages include places to post writing and written memorials. You will find that most link to other social networking sites including Twitter and Facebook.

www.7julyassistance.org.uk
> For people bereaved by acts of terrorism, set up after the London 7 July 2005 bombings.

www.babyloss.com
> As the name implies, for people who have lost babies before or during childbirth, or shortly after.

www.crusebereavementcare.org.uk/Military.html
> Part of Cruse Bereavement Care's site, these pages are specifically for families and friends of those who die in military service.

www.dyingmatters.org
> A coalition of members dedicated to improving understanding and encouraging people to talk about bereavement and the end of life, including an annual awareness week and writing competition.

www.facebook.com/pages/Love-Goes-On-A-Bereavement-Support-Blog/209888215733892

A Facebook wall on which people blog communally about their loss.

www.friendsandrelations.com

A memorial site which enables people to post memorials of up to 1500 words and ten photos, free of charge, or with a donation to their chosen charity.

www.gonetoosoon.org

A not-for-profit memorial site for family and friends.

www.griefencounter.org.uk

A site aimed at children, with zones for adults, teens and young children.

www.memorial-gardens.org

A family-run website which invites people to use a range of media – poetry, video, photos and music – to create a memorial for their loved one.

www.merrywidow.me.uk

A blog describing the experience of a young widow, with information and advice and useful links.

www.muchloved.com

Referred to above, the site established by a family has now taken on its own life as a memorial site, run as a charity.

www.widows.uk.net

The website of the National Association of Widows, providing advice and support, a forum and a place for memorials to be posted.

www.onlinememorialbooks.com

Online memorial books collaborating with the RAF and other forces, charities to create memorials that have the appearance of real books on the screen.

www.rd4u.org.uk

Run by Cruse, this is for children and young people and includes interactive forums, poems and places for children to post their messages.

www.rememberlife.co.uk

> Online memorials, poems and tributes, with donations to the charity Tearfund for every memorial created.

www.remembranceonline.co.uk

> An online book of remembrance.

www.uk-sobs.org.uk

> For survivors of bereavement by suicide, with a page for users to post poetry and prose.

www.tcf.org.uk

> The website for The Compassionate Friends, the organisation supporting families after a child has died. The site includes a forum and a memories section.

www.wayfoundation.org.uk

> Support for people widowed under the age of 50, including an online memorial photo library and book loan service.

www.winstonswish.org.uk

> The UK charity for bereaved children, young people and their families. The site includes a graffiti wall and a skyscape on which young people can post messages.

*Note:* Websites have been accessed in February 2012

## Private memorials

Memory boxes, albums, scrapbooks and collections kept in the home serve as a more private memorial to the one who has died. The creation of a memory box provides a means of encapsulating memories through the choice of small personal items such as jewellery, letters, photographs and other keepsakes. Written messages in the form of unsent letters, postcards, stories and poems can complement such items and add a personal touch.

When someone is thinking about creating a memory box, the exercise that follows can enable the task of deciding what to include to become a creative activity in its own right.

 ## THE MAGIC MEMORY BOX

This creative writing exercise explores the idea of a magic box in which precious and unusual items can be kept safe. It makes use of a poem 'The Magic Box' (Wright 2009, p.91), which was written for children but which offers rich stimulation to the imagination, no matter what the age of the reader. Families might use this together to involve different generations in the creation of their own magic memory box.

You will need a handout with the poem, for each member of the group.

Begin by reading the poem together.

### The Magic Box

*I will put in my box*

*the swish of a silk sari on a summer night,*
*fire from the nostrils of a Chinese dragon,*
*the hidden pass that steals through the mountains.*

*I will put in the box*

*a snowman with a rumbling belly,*
*a sip of the bluest water from Lake Lucerne,*
*a leaping spark from an electric fish.*

*I will put in the box*

*three violet wishes spoken in Gujarati,*
*the last joke of an ancient uncle*
*and the first smile of a baby.*

*I will put in the box*

*a fifth season and a black sun,*
*a cowboy on a broomstick*
*and a witch on a white horse.*

*My box is fashioned from ice and gold and steel,*
*with stars on the lid and secrets in the corners.*
*Its hinges are the toe joints*
*of dinosaurs.*

*I shall surf on my box on the great*
*high-rolling breakers of the wild Atlantic,*
*then wash ashore on a yellow beach*
*the colour of the sun.*

(Wright 2009, p.91)

Invite the group to read the poem again for themselves, enjoying and speculating upon its rich and surprising imagery ('three violet wishes'). Invite discussion of the poem and encourage people to explore the strangeness of the language. The use of curious opposites – 'a cowboy on a broomstick/ and a witch on a white horse' – may resonate with people for whom, in bereavement, life is topsy-turvy.

For those nervous about writing poetry, it is worth pointing out that this poem is a list. When the group is ready, invite them to write their own list beginning with the prompt:

'I will put in the box...'

Invite them to write freely for ten minutes, then give a further prompt, asking them to describe their box, for a further ten minutes.

Finally, ask them to describe what they will do with their box, for a final ten minutes.

Invite the group to share their writing.

In this example, Sarah describes her box:

### My Box

*I will put in the box*
*The childhood memories which I hold so dear*
*The unconditional hug of my dedicated Mum*
*The comfort of our silences which still ring in my ears.*

*I will put in the box*
*A sixth sense which we so often shared*
*A scamper through the rain with a reluctant Benji in tow*
*A shore side stroll along Normans Bay, or a wade through the estuary at*
    *Wells-next-the-Sea.*

*I will put in the box*
*Happy shrieks of laughter of a private joke shared*
*The rib aching chuckles of a story well told*
*The uncontrollable hilarity felt by remembrance of a foolish act.*

*I will put in the box*
*My favourite photos from years gone by*
*Brightly coloured rosettes which never seem to fade*
*A perfect white orchid, as pure as can be.*

*I will put in the box*
*The snugly scent of Benji's popcorn paws*
*My mother's mellow murmuring voice deafening me through her chest*
  *wall*
*The taste of one last home cooked meal.*

*My box is not flash or showy*
*It does not attract attention, it is not meant to.*
*It remains untouched by all but me.*

*I will carry my box with me on life's journey, supporting me at every turn.*
*No key is needed to open or close my box.*
*Just a heart and a compassionate soul.*

Typically, participants find the imagery rich and strange. Some take the idea literally and begin to think about what they might place in a memory box. Others are more free with it and take the opportunity to think about experiences of their own they might want to preserve in an imaginary box. Jean, for whom journal writing had provide a powerful tool in her grief process, made her own list of experiences and memories, as well as starting to keep a literal memory box to share with younger members of her family so they could remember their Nana:

### I Will Put in the Box

*The clean fresh smell of the morning after a rainy night*
*The sound of friends laughing*
*The sound of children playing*
*My favourite song sung by my Goddaughter*
*Hugs from my Godson*
*Long summer days*
*The sound of Maddie giggling*
*Stephie-Lou dancing*
*Kyle singing*
*Frankie's energy and enthusiasm for life*
*Mum's smile*

*Dad's sense of humour, of fun*
*The smell of a bonfire on a winter's evening*
*Lunchtimes with Mum*
*A goodnight Kiss*
*Talking / long conversations with Mum*
*Spending time with my best friend*
*Talking on the phone on the way home*
*Swimming lessons*
*Night-time chats.*

 ## MEMORY BOX PROMPTS

What else might go into a memory box? Try these:

- An acrostic recording a name or aspect of the one who has died (perhaps taken from the hands exercise in Chapter 6).
- A relay poem in which members of the family or friends each write a line.
- A poem or story that takes its title or a line from a family favourite, or a favourite of the person who has died.
- Short stories written as 'captured moments' (Chapter 3) of a life or of the family's time together.
- Short stories to attach to photographs and small personal items (e.g. the story behind a piece of jewellery or a toy).
- Unsent letters and postcards, which may be added to over time.

The choice of what to include is, like the memories, personal. The box may be shared or kept by one person. The beauty of this kind of memorial lies in its flexibility.

---

## Greenbank group

Who in the group might seize on some of the uses of new technology and other forms of memorial in their grief work?

- Ros might communicate with her husband's friends through his Facebook wall and find comfort in the sense of community it provides.

- Bobbie might contribute to an online military forum where her grandson's former army colleagues are posting messages in memory of him and others in his platoon.

- Riaz, who has mentioned that he loved poetry when he and his brother were at school, could take the idea of The Magic Box and create his own poem around memories of their childhood.

- For Alan and Ros, the idea of making memory boxes with and for their small children can be a way for them to preserve stories about Ali and Dan. Alan's eldest child is old enough to write stories and draw pictures to include in the box.

- Marielle already has a suitcase full of her husband's memorabilia. She could arrange it into themes and begin to write a commentary.

- Cynthia is too busy at the moment to think about making a memorial to her late mother, but thinks she may do something in a year's time; perhaps a donation to the golf club where she played several times a week. Cynthia could write the wording for a dedication on a plaque or trophy.

CHAPTER 9

# Endings

Bereavement writing groups have a natural life cycle. Similarly, an individual will know when it is time for them to lay down the pen, close the laptop or change the subject of their writing. For every group, the series of writing sessions and the time spent together will come to an end. For people already dealing with the enforced change of bereavement, the matter of endings is sensitive.

When it is time to stop, it is important that the group draws to a satisfactory close and that the participants experience a good ending to the time they have spent together. Two exercises in Chapter 5, The open door and the Making sense of change technique, can be effective ways to draw a group to a close, both of them inviting the participants to focus on the future. Here I offer a further reflective way to bring a group to a close.

 PAUSING ON THE ROAD

This exercise engages every member of the group in the creation of a shared poem; a potentially revelatory experience for those who have never written poetry. It gives everyone around the table a voice, even those who have been habitually quiet. As an act of collaboration the making of a group poem both acknowledges and records the supportive way in which a group has worked together. It provides a concrete record and a souvenir for everyone to take away. The satisfaction of having made a piece of writing together provides a positive rounding off to the group experience.

For this exercise you need a handout with the poem 'Stopping By Woods on a Snowy Evening' (Frost in Astley 2002, p.73).

- Begin by reading the poem to the group or inviting one of the participants to read it.

- Invite the group to read it again for themselves and comment on its themes of pausing on a journey and finding the strength to continue ('for I have promises to keep...').

- Allocate a few words from a line of the poem to each member of the group, including yourself and any other facilitators present (this may be the one occasion in which the facilitators join in with the writing). Ideally there will be enough people for something from each line to be included.

- Invite everyone to make a new line of their own using the words they have been given. Up to ten words is a good guideline.

- When everyone has written their line (this should take no more than a few minutes – encourage spontaneity), invite the group to share their lines Quaker fashion with everyone sitting quietly until someone feels moved to speak.

- By listening to the line just spoken, members of the group may decide whether to speak their own line, if it seems to follow on well, or whether to wait until others have offered theirs.

- As facilitator, have a line up your sleeve in case no one speaks, but from experience I would say that this usually happens naturally. Do not be afraid to allow silence.

- When everyone has spoken, ask them to write their names on the piece of paper on which they have written their line, and to give it to you.

- Your task as facilitator is to take the pages away, write the poem in the order in which it has been spoken, with minimal editing, and to send it to members of the group as a thank you and a record of their time together.

The effect among people who, by now, trust each other and have empathy within the contained space of the group, can be extraordinarily moving and satisfying. This example arose from a group at Princess Alice Hospice:

### Stopping

*As the Circle Line train clatters*
*and lurches from the station*
*I become aware of other sounds*
*until one sound only remains;*
*a pigeon pecking at a dry crust*
*on the platform.*

*Like a feather on an easy wind,*
*I'm wrapped in the darkest evening.*
*Its heavy blanket surrounds me like a cloak.*

*I think I know, and yet I do not want to know;*
*If I was to ask a thousand questions*
*it would not be enough.*

*I think of my children and fill up*
*with smiling love; these promises*
*to keep us safe and protected*
*from the winds of change,*

*to stop without fear that I may get lost*
*and be snowed in and not be able*
*to find my way again –*
*I want the scary monsters to leave*
*before I go to sleep.*

*I'm stopping here to watch the swans glide*
*gracefully across the lake.*

This was written collectively by Derek, Sarah, Teresa, Rowena, Jean and others who prefer to be anonymous.

For Rowena, the group writing gave rise to a further piece of powerfully expressive and reflective writing. She had been given the line 'the darkest evening of the year' (Frost in Astley 2002, VI i), which prompted her own piece of writing after the group session:

> At first the darkness is so overwhelming, so frightening. You wake up in the dark in the middle of the night and the full horror of it hits you – he's dead, he's really dead – quickly, quickly, switch the light on...make it better, oh make it better please.
>
> And the dreams, the nightmares that come with the dark... night after night, darkness falls again, more dreams and waking and blurring of life and death. Scared of the dark for so long... and then, quite suddenly, you start seeing things in the dark. You pause to look more closely, not seeking to chase it away...and there are little gleams of beauty, not the great shining gold and diamond brilliant jewels of when he was alive, but tiny dusty little pearls, each one worth picking up and looking at closely, until slowly, gradually, you have a tiny little string, just enough for a bracelet to see you through the yet more dark days still to come, a tiny reassuring little gleam on your wrist as you trudge the remaining miles before sleep.

No one who has lain awake in the small hours, conscious of the space beside them in the dark, can fail to recognise the truth of Rowena's metaphor; a final and fitting example of something that is deeply felt, hard to verbalise, but uniquely expressible on the page.

CHAPTER 10

# Reflection and Feedback

It feels natural for me to want to know whether certain writing techniques are effective and, by extension, how I (as facilitator) can improve or adjust them. This practitioner research is part of my own development and an important element in offering a service to others. If the techniques I offer are of benefit to participants, I want to understand how and why. By the same token, if they are not (for some perhaps, rather than others), I also want to understand why.

In this chapter I suggest ways of engaging participants in the process of understanding how writing can benefit people (or not) as part of bereavement support.

There are three questions I would pose:

1. What are the most effective approaches when using writing in the context of bereavement support?

2. What are the outcomes and benefits of these approaches?

3. How do we know?

Those of us who promote writing in the field of health and well-being can point to many instances of the benefits of expressive and creative writing, but how do we really *know*? Our clients, the people whose writing we facilitate and support, tell us about the positive difference writing can make to them; sometimes they also tell us what does not work. In bereavement this can include certain sensitive subject matter. If someone is not ready to express themselves about an offered theme or topic, they will instinctively (and literally) flinch from it. The thoughts and feelings triggered by the theme are simply too raw to be touched.

In feedback, you are likely to hear people typically describing themselves as feeling lighter and less burdened or pressured. They will express surprise at the pleasure they have gained from writing about a fond memory; surprised because pleasure and enjoyment are the last emotions they might expect to feel in their sad state. They may remark on the value of being suddenly able to name a strong feeling and write about in their own clear voice, or in being able to rediscover some fluency of expression through their writing. They may cite the enjoyment of trying a new activity or making something, as a sign that they are ready and able to move on from the worst effects of their loss.

I would say that for some, the benefits of writing can be felt at the early as well as the later stages of grieving. Everyone is different and that is what makes the business of understanding the value of writing in bereavement so tantalisingly difficult in research terms. The anecdotes suggest that writing can be a source of pleasure and relief. It can provide respite from intense distress, or it can enable the writer to confront that distress head on, if they wish. It can provide purpose (writing about a life, to create a memorial or to capture memories), and it can provide routine and structure (writing a journal or attending a weekly group session). Participants in writing groups are, to a large extent, self-selecting, but experience has shown me that it is extremely rare to find someone who does not benefit in some way from writing. In the very few cases where people do not, timing seems to be a factor. Some people rush to embark on new activities following a loss (instrumental grievers, perhaps), but writing requires a willingness to express thoughts and feelings. For some this can be simply too raw to contemplate. By writing it down, the experiences can become all too real, as if in describing their grief they make it unavoidable. This is why I would never insist that people write directly about their loss.

How do we know what works and how do we know *how* it works? Pennebaker (1990) is the authority in terms of clinical evidence around emotional and physical health, but when we look specifically at bereavement the evidence is less clear. As Neimeyer and van Dyke have observed: 'To date evidence is inconsistent that expressive writing is beneficial in helping people deal with the death of a loved one' (Neimeyer, van Dyke and Pennebaker 2008, p.454).

There is a unique problem in relation to carrying out clinical research involving bereaved people; it is that they are bereaved. McGuinness and Finucane (2011), have pinpointed the difficulty of carrying out evaluation in a formal research context with control groups of bereaved people: 'The demands of robust quantitative methods may place too great a burden both on the participants and on the bereavement service' (ibid, p.39). Their study does identify three ways to evaluate a creative arts activity group in the context of bereavement support, by using three groups of informants:

1.  The participants, to discover whether they believed the group helped them with their grief, and, if so, how.

2.  The hospice service, to find out if the intervention should be resourced and become part of ongoing service provision.

3.  The facilitators – to find out what aspects they considered to be helpful and what improvements needed to be made (ibid, p.39).

I do not believe we can understand the value and effectiveness of writing in bereavement support by observation alone. We must engage the participants in a way that is sensitive and appropriate to their experience and needs as they grieve, making feedback an active and reflexive part of the writing experience. I have developed my own approach, drawing on techniques of feedback, self-assessment (by the participants) and reflexive learning (for myself as a practitioner who wishes to continually improve and develop her own practice).

I suggest three approaches to assessing the effectiveness of writing in bereavement:

1.  a before and after snapshot by the participants

2.  check in and feedback techniques during a series of writing sessions

3.  reflexive journaling by the facilitator.

## Before and after

In Chapter 1, I suggested a form of brief questionnaire (see pp.48–49) to enable the facilitator to gauge a group or individual's expectations of writing, what sort of activities and what they might enjoy or appreciate, and they might hope to gain from it. Put in the broadest terms, a semi-open question like 'How do you hope writing might help you in your current situation?' can elicit a diverse range of answers which will be unique to the individual. Typical answers range from the practical: 'It will help me get out of the house', or 'It will give me something to do in the evenings', to the personal, 'It will take my mind off what has happened,' or 'It will help me to remember the good times'.

At the conclusion of a series of writing sessions, repeat the exercise with a further form inviting participants to record their feedback and reflect on the experience of writing. I use a form along these lines, although you may devise your own:

 QUESTIONNAIRE

Please complete this short questionnaire to tell us what you have gained from these writing sessions. Your feedback will help us plan future writing activities and understand which themes and exercises are most effective in a group like this one.

Thank you for taking part. Your comments will be shared between [the facilitators] but are otherwise confidential.

Name: _____

(If you would rather remain anonymous, feel free to leave your name blank)

1. What would you say you have gained from participating in this group?

    _____

    _____

2. How would you say writing in this group has helped you?

    _____

    _____

3. Which themes or exercises have you enjoyed or found most useful?

    _____

    _____

4.  If you have kept a journal, how has this helped you?

    _____

    _____

5.  Is there anything you have not enjoyed about the writing group?

    _____

    _____

6.  Do you have any suggestions about how we could improve these writing groups?

    _____

    _____

7.  Do you plan to carry on with your writing?

    _____

    _____

Thank you. I hope you will continue to write.

*Note:* This questionnaire is available from the JKP website, at www.jkp.com/catalogue/book/9781849052122/resources

Responses to this type of questionnaire typically yield the following responses (these are not verbatim or attributable to named individuals, but indicative of generic responses):

- being able to lose myself in the writing

- respite from sad thoughts

- the enjoyment of sharing in the group

- being able to access happy memories

- feeling safe to explore and express sadness in a sympathetic environment

- feeling inspired to write about memories and experiences which had not been foremost in my thoughts

- feeling better or in some way 'lighter' at the end of a session, compared to the start

- feeling calmer after writing

- being able to go to sleep

- being able to laugh together and have fun; an unexpected experience

- gaining insight into personal thoughts and feelings

- gaining clarity by seeing something written down rather than carrying it in my head

- finding that others shared similar experiences, thoughts and feelings. I'm not the only one.

One participant, Delia, had a particular reason for wanting to write:

> Previously, I had been through a very difficult time; not only the loss of my dear mother, but I had also been very unhappy at the care and treatment mum had had in our local hospital ward. Consequently I had had to do a lot of unhappy writing and thinking. Mum did have three wonderful last days at the PAH [Princess Alice Hospice], for which I shall be so grateful for the rest of my life.
>
> The creative writing group has come just at the right time for me. I had just got to the end of this unhappy writing and the hospital had promised to make changes and improvements.
>
> I then needed to be able to mourn properly for dear Mum who I was very close to. Also I needed to be able to start to leave behind the bad memories and think more about the millions of happy memories. I was so grateful for the writing course opportunity.
>
> Also, I was unable to talk about things. Everything was just too raw. It was easiest for me to work through things in writing.

Delia took to writing regularly in a journal for which she bought a special folder:

> The journal helped me to look more positively at life. It made me focus on all my daily achievements and it even inspired me to achieve more, so that I had more to write about each evening (consequently the busier you are, the less time you have to focus on the sadness).

It made me more grateful for even the smallest 'nice' thing that happened in the day. I was able to use the journal as a way of recording happy memories. As things occurred each day, they may have reminded me of happy memories of the past. So I then recorded them in my journal too. I would also record Mum's little 'phrases' – how I know she would have reacted to the day's happenings.

I would also record worries and concerns, people and actions I was angry with, and things that had gone wrong. Being able to put these into the written word was a way of coming to terms and also solving problems and getting things 'off your chest'.

I still write in my journal each day and find it useful.

Delia describes her experiences of becoming engrossed in writing haiku poems:

This activity requires keen observation. I also had to find the concise vocabulary which would both describe exactly what I meant and fit into the brief and precise verse plan. Consequently, for the length of the activity, life and its problems faded from the foreground. After the first draft I would keep returning to it and would be thinking during the day to see if I could find 'better' words for descriptions.

Delia's haiku shows the outcome of this reflective work:

*Silver trail on stone*
*At the end, under a leaf,*
*Snail asleep in shell.*

*Stillness, reflections*
*Carp glides from beneath lily*
*Ripples. Still again.*

*Wasp lands on bird bath*
*Dips forward to sip water*
*Flies away. Refreshed.*

For Delia, writing has become a regular and valued part of her creative life post-bereavement.

Over time the perceived changes in mood and thought that can be experienced by reflecting on the page may translate into a sense of progression through the stages or tasks of grieving, of being in a different place emotionally and of being able to look back with hindsight and see the progress that time and other activities have wrought. Writing can both aid this process and capture it on record.

When Jean, whose journal writing proved so powerful, read her writing out loud to me almost a year after it had been written, she found herself reflecting on the extent to which she had moved on:

> It has helped us all to talk through our feelings again and I am beginning to see how far I have come, through the writing of both my journal and my creative writing.

Members of her family have also benefited from reading Jean's writing; sharing it has enabled them to talk about their loss together and articulate thoughts and feelings about their mother which they struggled to talk freely about.

Talking about her piece 'The Door' (pp.67–69), Jeans says:

> I see it as a positive piece of work, uplifting and it does give me a sense of peace and a sense of hope for the future. Others have told me that I should take this piece of writing as a sign that Mum is at peace and that I have nothing to beat myself up about as Mum knows I did my best. I'm still not fully there yet but I do think I'm in a much better place than I was this time last year.

Jean's strength of assertion that writing has helped her, and her ability to see and feel those benefits with hindsight suggest that a person-centred approach is an important component in understanding the value of writing in bereavement.

The ability to see change over a period of time, and to be able to look back and understand or accept something through having recorded it when it happened, is important. The sense of not being judged is highly valued, too, in individual's writing, perhaps even more so than in group writing, which carries the risk of not being understood, or that someone may disagree with you when writing is shared. The experience of finding comfort in the written word is shared in common between individuals and group writers.

From the responses you will be able to discern individual aims. Over time, you will be able to assess how these aims are being met from your observations of the writing taking place. You will be able to invite individual members of the group to reflect on their own progress and how their aims are being met. Like grief, it is a process that takes time.

Having said that, it is worth sounding a note of caution here about what can be assessed in terms of people's well-being. I stress that I am not an academic researcher; I am a writer in bereavement support undertaking practitioner research to observe and try to understand what participants tell me in feedback. As we have seen in the models and theories of grief discussed in Chapter 1, people's journey through grief is not necessarily linear. The Dual Process model (Stroebe and Schut 1999) and Tonkin's model of bereavement (Tonkin 1996) are important reminders of the difficulty of tracking people's progress through grief in a straightforward narrative way. Someone who feels able to cope one day may feel desolate the next. Only over a period of several weeks or months will people be able to see the bigger picture of progress and articulate it, whether verbally or in their writing.

## Measures of success

Who is measuring what in practitioner research? I suggest the following as measures to be aware of:

For the individuals and those writing in a group, measures of success might include:

- starting a journal or diary and maintaining it over a period of time
- learning techniques to express thoughts and feelings in prose or poetry
- using techniques for self-expression such as the unsent letter
- writing a memoire about their own life experience
- creating a piece of writing about family history to share with others
- starting a piece of life writing to record family history
- completing a finished piece of writing.

For the writer-facilitator measures of success include:

- everyone in the group writes something (no matter how short or rough) during each session

- everyone contributes by sharing their writing, ideally within each session but, if not, over the course of a series of sessions

- attendance is maintained with members returning each week

- sessions run to time with adequate opportunity for writing to be shared and for the group to share and reflect on the writing produced

- a high level of positive feedback reported at the conclusion to the series

- the ability to capture learning about what works, or not, with different groups.

## Check-in feedback

The nature of writing as a creative and expressive medium enables the facilitator to build writing into the process of checking in and feeding back. For example:

 Invite the group to check in at the start of a writing session with some creative prompts:

- Give us an alliterative descriptor alongside your name to express how you are. Examples from the Greenbank group might include Ragged Ros, Addled Alan and Miserable Marielle.

- Choose a colour to describe your mood today.

- What is your personal weather forecast today?

- Describe the day you have had today as a kind of race. Has it been a sprint, a marathon or the hurdles, for instance?

At the session's close, invite the group to revisit their descriptions and provide new ones. Any change they can articulate in this way will be revealing of a shift that has taken place as a result of the writing activity (although be sure to verify this with them. There may be other reasons for a change of mood, such as the relaxation of not being in work, or enjoying the change of scene).

This technique and others you may devise with the group are a useful way to assess the group's changing and fluctuating mood as a series of writing sessions progresses. At the very least, use this technique at the start, midway and end points of a series.

## Journaling in evaluation

The journal can be a valuable tool for self-assessment and comparative assessment for the facilitator. This can work in three ways:

1. for the writer-facilitator's own reflection as the group develops

2. for self-care, as a means of reflecting on, working through and off-loading difficult thoughts or feelings that are triggered by sad material shared by others in the group

3. as a means of comparison, where other members of the group have maintained journals which are then shared with the facilitator.

Many of the journaling techniques described in Chapter 3 are appropriate for this purpose. If the kind of comparison outlined in point 3 above is to be undertaken there needs to be a clear understanding from all parties at the outset that they will be invited to share their journals for evaluation purposes. There should always be a choice to opt out of this, or to offer only selective parts if people feel uncomfortable sharing what they have written. Alternatively, suggest that people keep a journal specifically for the purpose of evaluation; although this may be onerous for some.

## In the final meeting

Choose from these approaches:

- guided questioning

- written feedback

- verbal feedback through the bereavement support service

- follow-up letter and questionnaire from the facilitator.

# Following up

Some months, perhaps three, after the group's final meeting, send a written request for further feedback. This can be carried out by email or post, with an accompanying letter from the writer and bereavement support worker, delivered through the host organisation and returned to them.

## Questions to include

These are suggestions designed to elicit responses about the perceived benefits of the writing group, the participant's experience of writing since the group's last meeting, and their desire, or otherwise, to continue writing or take up other creative activities. There is also a marketing or recruitment element in terms of assessing demand for further writing groups.

You may wish to adapt these questions and add others that are relevant to the activity you offer. For example:

- Have you continued to write since our last group session?

- If yes, what sort of writing have you done?

- If no, are you able to say why you have not continued to write (e.g. you may have been too busy)?

- Have you taken part in any other creative activity such as painting or music?

- Have you taken part in any other new activity such as sport or volunteering?

- What would you say you have gained from these new activities?

- Looking back on our writing sessions, what would you say you enjoyed most about them?

- Can you put into words the difference that writing with the group made to you at the time?

- Can you say what difference, if any, writing has made to you since then?

- Is there anything else you would like to include in your feedback on the writing group?

- Would you like to be informed about future writing groups?

- What is the best way for us to contact you in future?

# In a retrospective focus group

These questions can form the basis of discussion with a group of writing group participants who are invited after the group has finished to reflect with the facilitators on the value of the writing experience; I call this a retrospective focus group.

In such a group it can be illuminating to include creative ways to elicit people's response, using the written word with open questions. For example:

 Looking back to the writing group experience, in a five minute sprint write, complete these sentences:

- The thing I enjoyed most about the writing group was…
- Something I enjoyed less was…
- The most important thing I discovered while writing was…
- Something that surprised me about writing in the group was…

Thinking about my writing now:

- When I write I feel…
- When I write I can say…
- When I write I think about…
- After I have written I usually feel…

Thinking of what I might write about in the future:

- I think would like to carry on writing because…
- I may stop writing because…
- I would like to write about…
- If I had to sum up the difference that writing makes to me I would say…

Allow time for free writing as well and invite participants to share their writing, with time for comparative reflection and discussion.

In Chapter 11, I offer an example from my own reflective journal as an indication of how this can aid the writer facilitator.

## Greenbank group

At the group's final meeting, Fiona invites everyone to write down one thing they will take away from the group. She provides each participant with a sheet of blank A4 paper, invites them to write anonymously, then pass the sheet to their neighbour. Then they write another thought, pass it on, and repeat the exercise until everyone's piece of paper has gone around the whole group.

Fiona invites them to pin their sheets up on the white board and read from them, so they can compare. The first sheet reads:

*Realising that I'm not the only one*

*Feeling peaceful when I write*

*Sleeping better after I've written in my journal*

*Staying in touch with Dan – feeling it's not wrong*

*Easier to write some things than talk about them*

*Rediscovering my love of poetry and that I can write my own*

*Brings me closer to Pat*

As the sheets are read out, some members of the group claim their own comments or remark on how similar they are to others'.

Fiona asks them to complete a feedback form as well; some choose to take these away with them to do at home, others fill them in straight away.

# CHAPTER 11

# A Facilitator's Journal

These extracts are from the journal I keep while running a writing group for the Macmillan Family Bereavement Service at Meadow House Hospice in the London Borough of Ealing. This is a small but enthusiastic group, comprising mostly women and (at the time of writing) one man. The group meets on a weekday evening.

The Meadow House group arose from an approach I made to Marianne Kolbuszevski, who leads the Macmillan team. Marianne was immediately enthusiastic and set about recruiting people. We had a couple of meetings to plan the group and identify an appropriate room, and Marianne introduced me to members of staff who are on duty when I arrive. Marianne and I usually meet briefly before or after the group, but Marianne is happy for me to facilitate the group by myself. Because of her support and availability for reflection, and my own training in bereavement support with Cruse, I feel comfortable doing this.

The journal illustrates the way sessions are planned, facilitated and reflected upon, and gives an impression of the realities of running a bereavement writing group. It is a mix of the practical and contemplative, which sums up my experience of Meadow House.

## Session 1

A chilly March evening. I approach the hospice through the back door which is beneath a grey concrete awning. The door glows with warm light from inside. The receptionist buzzes me in and I pad along the quiet ward corridor to fetch the key to our room. Our group is meeting in the education centre at the end of a corridor away from the ward; a helpful layout. Some members of the writing group are returning to the hospice for the first time since their loved one died here. It would be difficult for them to walk through the ward corridor.

On my way to the education centre I pass the patients in their rooms. Some are sleeping, some are sitting up reading, watching television or, in the case of one young woman, sewing. Beside her bed, a large teddy bear sits upright in an armchair. I notice the names on the doors, hand written in felt tip pen.

The education room is well-equipped with a large square table and chairs, and a kitchen next door. I pull back the blinds to let as much of the evening light in as possible and I prepare a tray of tea, biscuits and water from the kitchen. I have brought a box of tissues which I place on the chair beside me so it can be offered if needed. There is a photocopier close by, so I can make copies of handouts. It takes about ten minutes to get everything ready, then I wait for the participants to arrive. I always enjoy this quiet time before the group assembles.

The first meeting of any group is always exciting to me. Marianne has provided names and some basic information about the individuals, but I prefer to know little about them at the start beyond the nature of their bereavement and how recent it was. The rest will emerge as we get to know each other.

As people start to arrive I go to the door. I want to be able to welcome them and ask them to sign in before showing them to the room. As they enter, some are a little shaky. The return to the hospice is not easy for them. They are understandably nervous as well – one lady has brought a friend for moral support – and there is edgy laughter as we make our way to the room.

I pour the tea and invite everyone to sit, and we spend a few minutes getting settled. A couple of people mention how nervous they are feeling. I say that I am not surprised; this is new for all of us. I feel nervous as well but excited to meet them. Liz, who has brought her friend Valerie with her, says she is not sure this is for her. She may leave after ten minutes.

We begin with introductions and I invite everyone to say what has brought them here. We talk about writing and what sort of activities they might enjoy. Several mention diaries and journals. One, Dave, tells us he enjoys writing poetry. He mentions Clive James and Alan Sillitoe as two of his favourite writers. Everyone cites stories about their lives and family history as something they might be interested in. Two of the participants have Irish backgrounds. From this very early stage I can tell that this is going to be a lively group.

I start them on writing using lists (see p.56). The response tells me that they are not all habitual writers, but they seem happy to share stories and to talk and write together as an activity. Some have attended social groups at the hospice but want to try writing as a more focused way to express themselves; also to get them out of the house and kick start them into the next stage of life. Liz tells us she has an imminent writing task, to produce a memorial card for the first anniversary of her husband Dan's death. This is an Irish tradition. Words and images are arranged on a card which is sent to everyone who attended the funeral and the wider circle of family and friends. She says she is concerned to 'get it right'.

The writing and conversation covers a range of themes; everything from gardening (which some enjoy and some do not), to the need to learn new skills such as changing electric plugs and cooking. As they share their writing and compare experiences, I can sense the beginning of group bonding. They seem instinctively supportive of each other and looking to make connections.

By the end of the evening, there has been a mix of tears, laughter and animated conversation. The box of tissues has moved to the middle of the table. Liz has stayed beyond the first ten minutes and as she prepares to leave she says she has enjoyed herself even though she did not expect to. I thank them for coming and say I hope I will see them again next week. Heads nod enthusiastically. One lady offers another a lift home.

## Session 2

One lady does not return this week; the rest are all present and seem glad to see each other again. Some have been in touch with each other to arrange lifts. Connections are being made.

I have prepared for this evening by reflecting on what went well last week and my observation that this is a talkative group. I need to find ways to focus the writing and achieve a balance between writing and the enthusiastic conversations that arise when the writing is shared. One lady is a little hard of hearing so I must take that into account when I give prompts.

We write about colours to express mood, thoughts and feelings. Liz chooses red for pain, fire and strength. She tells us about her multiple sclerosis, which flares up from time to time. Her choice of red captures the fierceness of the pain and her defiance of it, she says.

We play the furniture game (Sansom 2007) (see p.52). I ask the group to choose a flower and Dave names the cowslip which he says, flowers and is beautiful, and then is gone, 'like her'. He is referring to his late wife Jenny; an affecting and beautiful image which we all appreciate.

In the second half of the session I invite the group to write about someone who has influenced them. This is a way into memories that can be affirming and comforting, taking them further back, I suggest, than their more recent experience of loss. Liz writes about a fat nun who taught at her convent school. Her account of bumping into her, literally, at Lourdes many years later has us all falling about. Valerie also writes about a nun, an inspirational teacher at her convent school. We reflect on the contrasting nun stories.

I have a sense that I will need to try more approaches before this group settles down. The key will be to find engaging subjects that can provide material for reminiscence and the comparing of experiences. I can elicit these from the group as well as devising my own. Without strong themes and a structure for containment there will be a tendency to go off on tangents (enjoyable and interesting though these are).

One participant finds her rhythm when she is interested in the theme for writing, but sometimes needs a little coaxing to find the relevance to her own experience. When I asked the group to write about someone from their past who had influenced them in a positive way in their early life, she said that she had had a difficult life and there was no one she could write about. I suggested she think about someone who was in her life now; a friend or someone who supports her perhaps. Immediately she brightened and wrote about her neighbour who helped her throughout her husband's illness and continues to be a supportive friend. She smiled as she read her writing back to us and we all agreed that friendships like these are important.

Liz closes her notebook when she has finished writing, as if to say 'that's what I have to say about that!' We use this as our cue to talk about journal writing and the way it can be private and secret, if the writer chooses.

During the evening, the topic of sorting through someone's possessions and clearing out wardrobes comes up. Dave is tackling his garage which contains boxes of cine film he has taken of the family over the years. Liz says she cannot yet face opening the cupboard containing her late husband's clothes.

This is a theme we can return to.

## Session 3

A smaller group this evening; one member is not able to attend at short notice and this makes a difference to the group dynamic, making it slightly more focused.

I have reflected since the last session and decided to take a more reminiscence-based approach, as the group often heads naturally in this direction. This enables us to write more as well as talk, and to achieve a balance between the two.

We revisit Liz's colour red. She says it has softened to a more pinkish glow. I ask the group to talk about their shoes (see p.51). Lots of stories flow. Valerie has difficulty finding shoes that fit, but she adapts her own by removing the toe caps with a Stanley knife. We admire the effect. Dave is wearing his son's Ted Baker shoes. Liz is wearing comfy blue suede loafers ('better not step on them!').

This leads to writing about how it feels to 'be standing in these shoes'. Liz and Valerie write immediately; Dave pauses, deep in thought. Valerie wishes she could still wear attractive shoes. She recalls a favourite pair she used to wear; grey T-bar shoes with stacked heals. This prompts Dave to talk about a pair of shoes he had when he was 11. He describes them as 'cool' and remembers being given them by his mother who was a softer touch than his father. He thinks he must have pestered her for them. Liz also reads out her piece. She does not close her book tonight when she has finished.

We move on with a brief discussion of the associations personal possessions can hold for us. We read Ruth Fainlight's 'Handbag' poem (Astley 2002) (see p.115), which they like, commenting on the sensory language. I have brought a little wooden box with me (a prop I sometimes use). Without showing them what it contains, I place it on the table and invite them to think about an object or personal item that carries strong associations for them. This time, everybody writes.

The writing includes an oak table with twisted legs and glass feet, which Liz's father bought in a fire sale with a dresser and matching chairs. In its time the table has served as the family kitchen table, for pastry making, cooking and eating, with everyone sitting round it.

Now it stands in her living room and holds her TV. If she had to move, it is probably the one thing she would make sure she had room for; an object rich in family associations and memories. This prompts Liz to wonder out loud whether she will move from her current home. She feels uncertain and we reassure her that this is normal in her situation. There is no need to make a decision until she feels ready.

Dave describes his collection of film which he took using one of the early portable video cameras. He is gradually transferring the reels onto DVD so they can be viewed by the family. He has a wonderful archive, including his wife, their children when young, family events and holidays. Valerie writes about her first watch, a gift from her father. It no longer works but she keeps it in a box in a drawer and will not part with it.

This exercise and the session as a whole has felt constructive and focused. There has been sustained concentration on the exercise and the discussion has given rise to some rich reminiscence and empathy in the group. Sadness has been expressed, but this has been held by the group and balanced by laughter and enjoyment as stories are shared.

Of course, they wanted to know what was in my little wooden box so I revealed its contents at the end: a set of alphabet letters carved by my great grandfather. I do not often disclose personal information, mindful of boundaries, but the contents of the box are appropriate to the writing activity so I explain their origin.

The learning I take from this evening is that a reminiscence-based approach works well with this group. They enjoyed the poem and it seemed to focus the writing.

## Session 4

We are back to our full number tonight. The group settles quickly into a writing exercise in which they each choose a card with images of scenery from seaside views to exotic beaches and snow capped mountains. The theme this evening is journeys.

The cards picked include a view of San Francisco, an aerial photograph of Cambridge, a colourful row of beach huts and a meadow with poppies. I invite the group to write about the associations the cards produce for them, including any memories or ideas they trigger. I ask them to look closely at the cards again and spot something they have not seen before. Finally, I ask them to imagine what is outside the picture and to write about the wider scene.

Valerie writes about Cambridge as somewhere she would like to visit. She speculates on a tiny red dot on top of one of the buildings. Is it an observatory? She imagines the river snaking up to Ely through the Fens.

Greta writes about a family day at the beach in Brighton. She imagines the promenade with people strolling and eating ice creams; a happy seaside scene and an enjoyable memory for her.

Dave, who has chosen the poppies, reflects ruefully on his own garden and his attempts to get it under control. This year he is hopeful that it will stay in good shape. He has planted seeds and flowers protected by chicken wire to keep the cats and foxes away.

Liz recalls holidays in California. She remembers noticing that people walk a lot in San Francisco, whereas in Los Angeles and San Diego everyone drives. She imagines the redwood trees in the national park across the bridge and Marin County beyond.

After the exercise with cards I guide the group through an exercise in which they imagine an ideal destination and decide what to take with them and what to leave behind (see p.29). The destinations they choose include China, Scotland, North Wales and Niagara Falls. The items to be taken on the journey include a best friend and a camera. Liz says she will leave behind her bad legs so she can walk around freely.

This exercise has produced gentle humour and the sharing of memories and impressions of places. The group has settled well and exercised imagination as well as description in the writing.


# Session 5

A quiet evening at Meadow House. As I walk along the corridor to collect the key I notice the ward rooms that are now empty. Each week or so the names written outside the doors change as new occupants arrive. Most of the doors are closed this evening.

In the education room we are in good spirits. I read an extract from Laurie Lee's *Cider With Rosie* in which he describes his very earliest memory of arriving in Slade, the Gloucestershire village in which he grew up (Lee 2002). We admire its effect.

I have brought worksheets to enable the group to draw their life lines, with happy or positive events above the line and less happy events below (see Time line p.133). Everybody populates their lines with events and memories. I notice that for one member of the group most of the writing is below the line.

This seems fruitful for Liz. She shares some vivid stories about experiences in her late teens and early 20s when she lived in Italy, working for a family who wanted an English companion for their daughter. She describes her arrival and the moment she realised that the family must be very wealthy. She was treated as one of their own and enjoyed every comfort during her time with them.

Liz goes on to talk about meeting Dan, her husband, in Ireland, having their family together and then, in her 30s, being diagnosed with MS. She is strong and optimistic in the face of her condition and her positive nature shines through. She has a wealth of stories to tell.

When I invite the group to write about the day they were born Greta tells us that she was adopted. She describes meeting some of her siblings later in life, which was a good experience. I had planned to conduct an exercise around stories about the day of people's birth, but instead I invite the group to choose something from their life line and write about it. This works. Greta writes clearly and factually about her background in Austria. In some short paragraphs she offers information which is intriguing and makes us all want to read on. She seems pleased by our response, as knowing where to start to tell her complex life story has been difficult for her.

Dave writes about the day his first daughter was born. He describes sitting in the car on his own just after her birth, smoking a cigarette and hearing 'Dancing Queen' (the Abba song) on the radio.

This has been another talkative session, but I reflect that when the group focuses on writing they always produce thoughtful and insightful material. The conversation seems to feed that. At the end of the session they all comment on how much they have enjoyed themselves. I ask them to say more about what they have enjoyed and they cite the ability to write about enjoyable memories and subject matter they have not thought about for a long time and to be taken out of the everyday.

# Session 6

This evening we talk about the life line exercise from last week and about big public events that can be added to our own (see p.133). The Royal Wedding and the death of Osama Bin Laden are in our minds and other examples of those 'where were you when...' moments are talked about; the assassinations of President Kennedy and John Lennon, the death of Princess Diana and the moon landings are among the memories the group has in common.

I read a short essay by Nigel Slater about Bisto (Slater 2007, p.213), the prelude for writing about food and memories of special occasions, recipes and meal times (see pp.155–156). Stories pour out from this.

Greta describes the Austrian potato salad she makes for family occasions and celebrations. It uses pumpkin oil, an ingredient which is popular in Austria (where Greta was born), but hard to find in the UK. Her grandchildren love it, she says.

Dave speculates about condensed milk. How would it taste now? We reminisce about milk jelly and Liz shares a recipe she remembers. She describes Spam fritters as a treat when there wasn't much meat after the war.

We laugh a lot this evening. The group has settled well and there is good listening between them. Greta offers to bring us some Austrian potato salad to try next week.

## Session 7

Note to self: try not to set off the burglar alarm again!

Unbeknownst to me, the education centre has an alarm which goes off when the outer door is unlocked. Usually, on the evenings when our group is due to meet, the alarm is not set but today it goes off like a banshee when I open the door. Fortunately a kind nurse is on hand to help me disarm it, but the experience of running quietly, along the ward corridor to fetch help, with the alarm piercing the hushed atmosphere, is not one I would care to repeat.

This evening we move swiftly through several short exercises. Acrostics are a hit and alpha poems produce lively writing from Liz and Dave.

Liz has said she is not a fan of poetry, but I introduce Kit Wright's poem 'The Magic Box' (Wright 2009) (see pp.171–172). Liz likes this very much and the group writes their own lists of treasures. We link this to discussion of memory boxes and other kinds of memorial. Liz is working on her memorial card for Dan. Dave is still sorting through his cine film and photographs.

As we are a small group tonight I find us moving quickly through the planned material. Perhaps a couple of new members could boost the group and (on a very practical note), provide more writing and feedback to be shared in the time. I shall ask Marianne if she is aware of anyone else who might like to join us. This might work best after a break for the summer holidays.

At the end, the group reflects again on what they are gaining from the writing sessions. The benefits, they all agree, are partly social, but they also mention the ease of being in a room with people of similar life experience in which they do not have to keep up a brave face. They can be themselves, laughing and crying, in the safety of our room.

## Session 8

This evening Marianne and I speak beforehand about the group's progress and whether to use the two week break we are about to have as an opportunity to invite more to join. I feel it would be a good idea, now that there is a regular core. The group seems to agree when I discuss it with them, although they would be happy to continue as they are if no one else joins.

We write about hands, drawing a hand on the page and writing the attributes of a personality on each finger, the thumb and in the palm of the hand (see p.145). This is a success. Liz writes and talks about her Aunty Vicky, a vibrant character who ran pubs in Hove, Victoria Street in central London, and Richmond. She had jet black hair piled on her head, wore striking colours and had three husbands and many boyfriends after the death of the third. Liz's written account is strongly descriptive of a vivid personality. Her written work stimulates further reminiscence on her own young life and her family.

Dave writes about his father, Lloyd. He died four years ago at the age of 95. In his youth he trained as an architect but had to give it up because of lack of funds. Instead, he went into building and eventually joined the police. He was passionate about gardening, which Dave has not inherited(!). Dave's description calls him a kind man. In hearing about him we have the impression of a gentleman, dedicated to his work and family, and to his garden.

For the first time, Valerie writes about her son who died four years ago at the age of 34, of Sudden Adult Death Syndrome. Valerie's loving description seems accepting of his loss. We reflect with her that he lived a full life; the life he wanted to live.

We talk further about the future of the group. Liz and Dave agree that they came to it at the right time. They are both approaching the first anniversary of their bereavements and, they both feel, could not have embarked on this kind of activity before now. Liz comments that in the early stages of bereavement, there is too much to do, not enough space for anything else and everything feels 'too raw'. Although sometimes tearful this evening, she is adamant about her enjoyment of the group. We also talk a little about Meadow House and what it means to them. They seem all to have positive associations, enhanced by their attendance at this group. They speak admiringly of the Macmillan team.

## Session 9

We are back after a two-week break. I have decided to try using more worksheets to help focus the writing. This evening's theme is diaries and time perspectives (see pp.85–86). I have chosen this mindful that two members of the group have had the first year anniversary of their bereavement during our break.

Liz and Valerie arrive first, full of enthusiasm, telling me how much they have been looking forward to resuming. Liz says she would never have expected to enjoy something like this. She calls it a 'course' and we discuss that. She can't think of a better word, although we agree that group or club might also apply. Whatever we call our writing group, Liz feels she is learning about herself and others.

There is a good balance tonight between writing and conversation arising from the writing. I use a lot of open questions and active listening to elicit expression. Although we are talking about sad events there is good camaraderie in the group and, as always, much laughter. Liz and Dave describe their two very different ways of marking their anniversaries. Liz held a Catholic mass, sent memorial cards and paid a visit to the cemetery to place a memorial hedgehog box (the first time I have heard of one of these!). Dave took himself off for the day on his own.

They agree that both days were appropriate and went as well as could be expected, although the run up to the day was unexpectedly hard. Everyone comments on the number of phone calls one receives at a time like this, while also noticing who has not called.

The worksheets seem to enable the group to settle and focus. Insights arise from the separation of thoughts and feelings. Liz expresses feelings of contentment. She did a good job arranging her husband's memorial. Valerie comments in her writing that she has not had time to read today and that has meant the day lacked something.

This has been a good session, perhaps our best yet in terms of focused writing and the way it has provided the trigger to talk about some difficult thoughts and feelings one year into bereavement in a contained way.

At the close we talk about the difference a new member may make to the group dynamic. Liz is concerned that it may be difficult for a new person to bond with the rest of the group; 'we might put them off!' We agree to hold a further six sessions before taking a summer break, then seek some new members to begin a new 'term' in September. This seems right.

## Session 10

Greta is with us again this evening, after a gap of several weeks. She has brought her potato salad for us to sample. I reflect on boundaries but feel this is such a kind gesture on Greta's part and our response (interest, pleasure, gratitude) is important to her. It is very tasty; piquant with peppers and a little onion, in a light dressing of the pumpkin oil.

The mood is upbeat this evening. Dave seems in good spirits, telling anecdotes and jokes which have us falling about. Greta's return makes the group feel complete again. I use hand out sheets to contain and generate writing.

'Today's news' works well as a form of checking in, especially as the group has not been together for a while. Liz and Valerie write about the sun coming out. They write headlines, a news story and a photo caption to describe something about themselves; their own 'news headlines'. Dave writes about having finally sorted out his collection of old coins in the garage and sold the half crowns (we cheer). He is going to buy items for the garden with the proceeds. This leads to discussion about clearing out old belongings. Liz mentions having opened her husband's cupboard a few times but shut it again. She has spoken about this before but seems to find it easier to talk about now. We reflect on how the time has to feel right before such things are tackled.

Tonight's session is a balance between reminiscence and writing. Lucille Clifton's poem 'Homage to My Hips' (Astley 2002) works well as a starting point for writing about aspects of themselves. Liz, who is adamant that she does not like poetry, likes this one. Greta produces a nice piece about how she has always been complimented on her legs and shapely ankles. She met her husband at a nurses' dance, she tells us, and she always loved to dance the English waltz, which is slower and more romantic that the Viennese version.

Next week, I have asked them to bring photographs of themselves to the session.

# Session 11

Everyone has brought a good selection of photographs. I invite them to choose one and write about it using a prompt sheet I have devised. This works well as structured containment for thoughts, feelings and memories (see pp.81–82). Everyone writes quickly and with enthusiasm for the task. When we hear the feedback it is rich in detail and reminiscence.

Valerie introduces us to herself, aged 12, as a school girl in pigtails. She remembers the school uniform and walking in a crocodile with 20 other borders at her convent. Her long hair was plaited and tied up in double rows, 'as they used to wear it in those days'. She describes how the photograph was taken at the police station for her visa when she first came to England. She says that these are happy memories.

Dave shows us a photograph of his wife Jenny and his father-in-law at the cottage in Hampshire where they lived. He talks about the place as somewhere they all loved. His father-in-law stands with his pipe in his hand. Again, these are good memories.

Greta proudly shows us a photograph of herself with her fellow nurses at the old Ealing Hospital. They wear smart uniforms with capes and starched white hats. Greta is very proud of having worked as a nurse in the NHS from its earliest days, doing a job she loved. We affirm this for her and she beams with pride. She shows us further photographs of her granddaughters, and of her and her husband dressed up for a dance in the early days of their marriage. They look very glamorous, in the style of the day, and we agree that they make a handsome couple.

Liz shows us a photograph of her aunt, Sister Bernadette, who lives in seclusion as a Carmelite nun. The photograph shows her behind bars. Liz describes her vibrant personality, despite the restrictions of her life.

We talk about how to keep these photographs and to ensure that others know the stories behind them. Writing about them like this helps others to know about them and prompts a stream of further stories, as this evening has shown.

This has been a happy session, full of laughter, a few tears, and rich reminiscence.

# Session 12

This is our penultimate session before taking a break for the summer. Tonight we read and talk more than write. I invite the group to write about their own perfect moment. This gives rise to reflection on the page and in conversation, with some interesting and moving insights.

Liz describes having time for herself now, doing what she wants to do when she wants to do it. She describes herself as feeling 'liberated', although missing her husband.

Valerie shares memories of her son when he was young. She tells us a story about two relatives who did not get on and the occasion when both of them gave him the same toy. She remembers how his eyes 'literally sparkled' with delight when he saw it; 'the only time I remember him looking like that'.

Dave describes quiet moments in the garden, around the house, collecting his granddaughter from school, and listening to the radio. He seems to be describing a kind of adjustment to his situation.

Next we read 'Ironing', a poem by Vicky Feaver (Feaver in Anderson 2006, p.172) and talk about our relationship with household chores. Dave's wife used to do all the ironing so now he relates to the line about 'converted to crumpledness'. Valerie likes the poem and likes ironing. Liz likes ironing but not the poem. This leads to more discussion of the things we learn to do after the one who used to do them has died, or which we don't bother with anymore. Greta says she has not cooked a full meal since her husband died.

# Session 13

Our final session before the break. We focus on two techniques.

The first, a journal writing prompt of 'what's going on?' yields a variety of expression. Liz is looking forward to going to New York to see her relatives. Dave is looking forward to a break in Hampshire. Valerie's attention has been caught by various stories in the news and Greta has a friend arriving shortly for a visit.

We move on to examine the contents of the treasure trove, a box of odd items which I have brought along. Val chooses a tiny music box which reminds her of one she had as a young girl. Dave picks a little handbell which reminds him of his Aunty Lil who had a similar one. We notice that it comes from Ostend. Perhaps it was a souvenir brought back from The Great War (I have never thought about this before). Greta also chooses the bell because it reminds her of an Austrian restaurant in London where the owner used to play traditional cowbells after dinner. She describes the beautiful sound of the chimes and the tunes he played.

As the session draws to a close I ask the group to complete a feedback form (see pp.183–184). This will help me plan our future sessions and reflect on what they have gained and enjoyed from our meetings so far, as part of my own practitioner research (see Chapter 10). As we prepare to leave, Greta says she is sad that she will not see us again until September. I suggest she comes along to the hospice's social group on Friday afternoons, so she can meet more people and talk to others.

Reflecting for myself, after this series of 12 meetings, 'what's going on'?

- I am learning more about the value of containment and how to bring focus to a talkative group, not all of whom are used to concentrating quietly on writing.

- I am learning to trust the process and let the conversation flow once a theme has triggered memories and associations.

- I am discovering the value of structure in the form of work sheets and guided exercises, especially for non-habitual writers.

- I am learning the value of sharing reminiscence and using this as stimulus for further themed writing.

- I am aware of boundaries, as the group gets to know each other well.

- I am pleased with the way the group has developed over the past few months; I can see (and they confirm for me in their feedback) that it is making a positive difference to them, by offering them a new activity and enabling them to reflect on their own lives and the lives of others in the safety of our space.

- I am grateful for the opportunity and the resources offered by the hospice and Marianne; generous hosts.

- I am grateful for regular contact with Marianne; although not formal supervision as such, it is useful to reflect together.

- I am conscious of the need to strike a balance between planning ahead and going with the flow.

- I shall think carefully about how to integrate new members into this well-bonded group.

- I am looking forward to resuming in September.

Thank you, Meadow House.

---

## Greenbank group

For Fiona and Michael, their own journals are a valuable way to enable them to note and reflect upon the group's progress. The journal is also a place in which they can record their own thoughts and feelings as part of self-development and self-care. The trust between them means they feel comfortable sharing parts of their journals together and they find it valuable to compare notes as part of their mutual learning.

For example, Fiona finds Riaz's silence and occasional absences a challenge, but Michael is able to reassure her that he can see Riaz making progress in his own way and at his own pace. Michael shares his journal reflection that Riaz seems more comfortable talking to him on his own (perhaps for gender or cultural reasons). This is reassuring for Fiona, who has also felt especially moved by the nature of Riaz's loss, having lost her best friend to suicide at a young age. She uses her journal to reflect on the feelings Riaz's situation has awakened in her, and she writes an unsent letter to her friend, which she finds comforting.

Michael finds himself using his journal to explore his own feelings about his mother's dementia. He finds that Cynthia's situation awakens fears in him that he will have to deal with his mother's death and consequent sorting out of belongings and property. He finds himself admiring Cynthia for the way she is tackling her own task, while acknowledging that he will have help from his partner and other close family, which Cynthia, an only child, does not appear to have.

# CHAPTER 12

# Resources for Establishing a Writing Group

When you set up a bereavement writing group, or introduce writing into bereavement support, there are practicalities to consider in terms of how to bring people together to write and the resources and skills you will need. This chapter provides guidance on how to get started.

Consider this scenario involving the fictional Greenbank group:

## Greenbank group

Imagine the group's first meeting. Several participants have child care considerations (Alan and Ros), and some (Cynthia and Riaz), are in full-time work. Fiona and Michael have decided to run the group in the evening towards the end of the week, in the hope that this might be easier for those who work, and that others will be able to make necessary arrangements with enough notice.

Michael introduces Fiona to the evening receptionist and ward staff, so they know who she is when she arrives to set up the room. For the first meeting, Fiona arrives early. She unlocks the room and makes sure the refreshments are ready. She makes tea and sets out a water jug and biscuits. The room is arranged so that everyone is sitting around the table with a view into the garden. Fiona positions herself and Michael at the end of the table where there is a view through glass doors back towards the ward. She has a hunch that many in the group will prefer not to have to look in that direction. Finally, Fiona pulls down some of the window blinds to make the space feel less public.

Michael greets the group members as they arrive at reception and guides them to the room. Many are nervous. Ros, the youngest, is quiet and tearful. Marielle, although lively and sociable, looks tired. Alan sits next to Riaz. Riaz is flustered when he finds he has not brought a pen, but Alan lends him his spare. Bobbie smiles but does not say very much. Cynthia places her phone on the table as if keeping an eye out for texts or emails from work. Anna fidgets in a small rucksack and takes out a pocket dictionary and a sandwich.

Fiona can see that some of them are stressed and anxious. Her first task is to bring them together as a group, reassure them about the activity they are about to embark upon, and enable them to begin writing.

Fiona does not yet know much about the group members' bereavements. That information is held by Michael. He has been seeing some of them as clients and knows the background to others through supervision group meetings with his team of volunteers. He is hopeful that Ros may benefit from the group as she has shared her diary with him in counselling. He hopes it may help Anna, who is stuck in her feelings of guilt, to find new ways to express herself. He has recently learned about her mother's early death and suspects that Anna may have delayed grief from that experience. He is aware that Bobbie is angry and her emotions are quite raw. Bobbie, like Anna, is nervous about her written English and being 'marked' for bad spelling. Michael has met Alan and Riaz in other groups run by the hospice; he is aware that Alan is throwing himself into a lot of activities, whereas Riaz is preoccupied by work and family. Michael has observed that Riaz tends to play down his own needs, so his attendance at this group may be a good sign that he is doing something for himself. Marielle, whom Michael has been seeing for the past six months, is lonely, and has been looking forward to the group as a means of meeting new people.

---

# Establishing a group

Most people who seek bereavement support do so after the early stages of grief; perhaps after several months to a year. People rally round in the early days after a death, but once family and friends return to regular routines and levels of contact, it can feel as if others are getting on with their lives and that there is no one to talk to. Regular meetings with a counsellor or bereavement support volunteer can offer a place to speak and be heard. Group meetings can further help to counter feelings of isolation. Many bereavement support services and charities offer social groups or group activities. Writing can fit easily into this category of regular weekly or fortnightly contact.

Meeting other bereaved people in a group enables individuals to understand that their loss is not unique. Over time, and as others join the group, they may see that they are making progress through their grieving compared to others whose loss is more recent or, perhaps, more complex. It is inevitable that people in a group will compare themselves with others.

Writing, too, is a solitary activity, yet many writers will acknowledge the value of having a group of fellow writers with whom to share their writing, reflect upon it and receive constructive feedback as it develops. When bereavement support and writing are brought together the result can be a close-knit group activity, with a creative focus and a strong bond of trust between its members. The activity may be new and daunting to some, but in bereavement almost everything is new and daunting. For the participants in a writing group, the mere act of signing up and attending each week can signify a positive step along the road through grief.

## The invitation

The invitation to join a writing group, whether verbal or written, should give participants an idea of what to expect. Participants may need to be coaxed; a written invitation or publicity from a trusted source, such as a counsellor, volunteer, pastor or GP, can be effective, especially if it is reinforced verbally.

Some participants will respond to un-targeted publicity (leaflets and posters displayed in appropriate places), if the style and content strikes the right chord and they feel ready to try something new. Most, however, will need a little persuasion. People who have never thought of themselves as writers, or who have never taken part in a writing group, may be put off if they think their writing will be criticised or that they will be expected to be creative on demand. Some will be comfortable with the prospect of writing about their bereavement, or about painful or sad subject matter; others will not. The suggestion that they will be expected to write directly about their loss can be offputting.

Aim to describe the activity on offer in a way that is reassuring and accessible, so that participants can decide whether it is right for them. Terms such as 'group', 'informal meeting' or 'gathering' are preferable to 'class' which suggests something like school. I always reassure people at the first meeting that spelling and punctuation will not be commented on. I am interested in how people express themselves, not whether they can produce pristine sentences. People will sometimes bring a dictionary with them. This may reassure them, but I have never seen one actually being used.

Be clear about the purpose and benefits of the writing group. A personal invitation, whether in writing or face-to-face, could say, 'I think you'd find it useful to meet people in a similar situation. You could support each other and enjoy writing creatively at the same time'. A piece of publicity that says 'come and read out your work' is offputting, whereas 'join us to hear each other's stories' is friendly and welcoming. This introduces the idea that writing will be read out and shared, but in an informal way.

## Whom to invite?

When thinking about whom to invite or encourage, consider any client who:

- mentions keeping a journal or diary
- naturally uses metaphor and imagery when they talk about their experiences
- seems blocked in their attempts to talk about difficult thoughts and feelings
- is stuck in their grieving process; a different form of communication or expression may help them
- responds well to the suggestion that they write an unsent letter
- mentions having enjoyed creative activities such as art, literature or music in the past
- expresses a desire to write about their family history or to write about memories of their life with the person who has died
- talks about feeling ready to try a new creative activity
- finds pleasure or comfort in reading poetry or fiction, or in being read to

- has attended social groups but is looking for something more structured and with fewer people (some can feel a bit lost in such larger gatherings).

The stress that this is a *writing* group is important. Someone for whom the bereavement is very recent (say up the first six months) may be reaching out for activities that get them out of the house and provide distraction. They may have a strong need to talk and to be in company. In a writing group there is likely to be a balance between writing and talking which arises from the content of the writing; someone who wants to talk rather than write might be better off seeking a social group. Be mindful as well that writing can stimulate powerful memories and emotions which may be too much for those in the early stages of grief. Perhaps you might suggest that they wait a while or join a talking group in the meantime.

I notice that people who have not written since they were at school, and who do not think of themselves as habitual writers, often express an interest in doing so after a significant loss. 'I've never written a thing in my life' should not necessarily be a barrier to participation in a writing group. A person's willingness to turn up in a room with a group of strangers and begin to share their writing, even brief sentences, can be a sign that that person is undergoing some sort of adjustment to their loss. Such people should be actively encouraged. They may emerge as the most enthusiastic participants.

## Size and composition

The facilitators should agree together the ideal number to aim for and have that in mind as they publicise and recruit. As a guide, any fewer than four may not be worth pursuing, while more than ten is a lot to handle. If you want everyone to be able to share their writing and reflect together, then a group of between six and eight is a comfortable number for a session lasting an hour and a half. With more, it is harder to include everyone and those who are quiet or shy may find it harder to join in.

Some may prefer an all women or all male group (perhaps for cultural reasons), or to be among others of similar age or bereavement (for instance, young widows seeking others in a similar situation). If you plan to run a group for men who have been widowed in their 30s, or women who have lost parents, for example, make this clear in your publicity and in your invitation.

Groups with a wide age range make for an interesting mix. A group containing people who have lost spouses at both ends of the age spectrum, for example, can lead to supportive alliances and shared insights across life experience.

Be alert for those experiencing disenfranchised grief; the woman left out of her married partner's funeral arrangements for example. The stories such people wish and need to tell may be difficult to articulate in a group alongside other married bereaved people. Someone who has lost a child may find it hard to be with those who talk or write about their living children. Consider the balance of a group and, if necessary, recommend to some potential participants that they join a different group.

## Open or closed groups?

Decide and make clear from the outset whether the group is to be closed to new members, or whether others will be joining as time goes on. A closed group can achieve a level of closeness and trust; new members can alter the dynamic. If you decide to invite newcomers to an established group, be sure that the other members are happy for this to be the case, and that the new member is prepared to be integrated into an already bonded group.

Ideally, the participants themselves should have the final say if they decide that the makeup of a group is not for them. Be prepared to talk it through if someone is having difficulty fitting in, or if their behaviour and attitudes are challenging for the rest of the group.

## Individuals

In identifying individual clients who may benefit from writing, look for those who seem blocked in their efforts to verbalise difficult thoughts and feelings. Writing a journal (Chapter 3), may provide them with a means of private expression which they could reflect upon and possibly share in one to one support. Look, also, for those who are casting about for new activities and who mention a love of books, stories and reading. They may not consider themselves writers, but the offer of a creative activity can be appealing as they begin to move forward in their grief work. This can be part of the meaning reconstruction defined by Neimeyer (2007) as they begin to make a new life for themselves.

# Resources

## The place

Ideally, the writing group will meet at a regular time in the same room. The room should be well lit and large enough to accommodate everyone comfortably around one table or in a circle with a firm surface to write on. The group should be able to face each other (rather than sitting in rows), and the facilitators should be able to see everyone. A flipchart or white board is useful.

The room should be quiet and private, rather than in an open plan or mixed-use space, or overlooked by other parts of the building. Open plan areas, although often light and spacious, can lack privacy. Time of day comes into play here: a daytime group is likely to overlap with the general life and daily buzz of the host organisation. In the evening venues tend to be quieter.

Whatever the setting for your group, try to ensure distractions are kept to a minimum. It is important for everyone to be able to concentrate and to feel relaxed and not on public display. An atmosphere of peace and quiet will enhance the experience for those who arrive feeling stressed. Privacy will be reassuring for those who are feeling emotional.

## The time

For most bereaved people, the rest of life does not stop. Family responsibilities continue, livings have to be earned, homes maintained and all the demands of daily life somehow met. It is no wonder that bereaved people can be feeling exhausted. Bear this in mind when planning when to hold your writing sessions.

The timing of your group will depend on a range of factors including the availability of a room and the facilitators, but it is important to consider whether a weekend, weekday or evening would be easier for your participants. Saturdays might provide respite from the busy week. Weekday evenings can be appropriate for those who work, although they may arrive stressed after a bad (or even just average) working day. Daytime brings considerations such as childcare, although those with children of school age may prefer day time during school hours. Anyone who finds the evenings lonely may prefer to come out at night. If you have flexibility and resources, offer a choice.

For the writing session itself, an hour and a half provides reasonable time for a variety of activities. You might organise the time like this:

| | |
|---|---|
| Welcome with tea and coffee | 10 minutes |
| Short writing exercises and games to warm up | 20 minutes |
| Introduce a theme or read a published text together | 10 minutes |
| Extended piece of writing around your theme, including time to share the writing | 45 minutes |
| Time for reflection and winding down | 15 minutes |

This is a flexible structure. Always be prepared to allow more time for a theme to be explored if the group is enjoying it, or be prepared to move on quickly if an exercise doesn't go quite as planned. Have some spare ideas for writing up your sleeve if the group does not respond as expected. If a theme or topic emerges through talking and it seems to strike a chord, incorporate it into the session or make a note to include it in a future exercise. Chapter 14 offers a selection of sample writing session plans as guidance.

## Frequency and duration of writing sessions

The frequency can vary according to the availability of resources and desires of the group. A one-off writing workshop of two hours or a half-day might provide a 'taster' for people considering whether they would like to join a longer term group; helpful for people deciding whether to try a new activity following bereavement. If you can offer a trial session to the bereavement support team this will gives volunteers and therapists a first-hand experience of what is being offered, so that they can describe it appropriately to their clients.

A series of weekly or fortnightly sessions might run over eight to ten weeks or longer if resources allow. If a group is to continue over an extended period (say six months or a year), consider dividing the sessions into series of eight to ten weeks. This enables the facilitators to have a break, which is necessary for self-care and to plan further writing activities.

A break also gives people the opportunity to bow out, if they feel the group has served its purpose for them. If this is the case, the opportunity to say goodbye and mark the moment with them is important.

## Attendance

For practical or emotional reasons participants may struggle to attend every session. Make sure everyone has a telephone number or email address for the host organisation so they can let the facilitators know if they are not able to attend.

If someone is absent without explanation, a representative of the host organisation should contact them to make sure they are alright and gently encourage them to return when they are ready. Reasons for non-attendance can include the practical (a change of shift at work, or a diary clash they had forgotten about), or the emotional (a sad anniversary, or just a bad day).

In bereavement even the smallest challenges can feel like mountains to climb. If you know the reason for someone's absence and they have given you permission to share it with the group, make sure the group's sympathy and good wishes are conveyed back to the absentee, if appropriate.

## Other resources to consider

Have a box of tissues in the room, discreetly. Tears are inevitable and one person's may set others off. Not every session will produce expressions of sadness, however; be ready for humour and laughter too, but if someone cries, let them recover in their own time. Others in the group may move to comfort them and this can be welcome, but may also be awkward before group members have got to know each other. As facilitator the tone you set – supportive but not invasive – will give a signal to others. If someone is very distressed, offer them the opportunity to step outside until they recover.

Tea, coffee and water are a welcome addition, with ten minutes or so at the start for the group to have refreshments together and chat or offload about the day or week they are having. This sociable time enables people to relax a little before focusing on writing.

If the organisation hosting the sessions is able to provide a notepad and pens for the group, that is a nice touch. If not, ask participants to bring their own but be ready with a few spares for those who forget or are unable to. The choice of notebook can be unexpectedly meaningful; one group member commented that the glossy black notebook provided was 'too funereal'. Another group, presented with a range of brightly coloured notepads with cartoon animals and flowery patterns, had fun choosing (there was a scramble amongst the men to choose the least floral). The good humoured conversations that resulted were almost as much an icebreaker as the subsequent writing exercises.

At the risk of being too obvious, think about what to wear. It is a personal choice, but I would not wear black to facilitate a bereavement writing group. Black is not the colour of mourning in all cultures, but it can be viewed as formal and impersonal. I prefer to wear warm or neutral colours for this work.

## Skills, roles and responsibilities

### The role of the facilitators

There are two kinds of facilitator referred to throughout this handbook:

1. the bereavement support specialist (whether a counsellor or trained volunteer)

2. the writer working in the context of bereavement counselling (also, ideally, trained in bereavement support or with awareness of the grief process).

Whether these roles are taken by two people working as a team, or are to be found in one person, they are complementary and often overlap. It is worth taking time to understand both.

### The skills of bereavement support

My summary of the skills of bereavement support is informed by the Cruse Bereavement Care training model (Cruse Bereavement Care 2007). Others may refer to their own training within the British Association for Counselling and Psychotherapy framework.

Carl Rogers describes the core conditions of person-centred therapy in the model known as CUE:

Congruence (realness, genuineness. Your body language reflects what you are saying.)

Unconditional Positive Regard (respect for the client. You hold the client in high regard at all times.)

Empathy (a complete understanding of the client's thoughts and feelings.)

(Rogers 1967)

No matter how difficult or challenging the subject matter, the bereavement counsellor shows acceptance and respect. In bereavement support, interpersonal skills are an important part of the supportive role. The person is likely to have sought support in their loss because they feel no one else is available to truly listen to them. The ability to be non-judging and fully attentive while someone pours out their grief is paramount.

Gerard Egan has identified three stages of the 'skilled-helper model' (Egan 1998, p.24) that one relevant to bereavement support. In stage 1 (Egan 1998, p.25) of the model the aim is to enable the client to understand their situation and problems. Stage 2 (ibid) enabled the client to consider what they want to change and what support or action they need in order to see an improvement. In Stage 3 (ibid) the client creates strategies to achieve what they need, with the counsellor's support. By now the client is able to make progress and move forward.

The ability to summarise is important: the bereavement counsellor listens, summarises what has been said and offers it back to the speaker to show they have been heard; also to seek clarification if anything is unclear or contradictory. The purpose is to provide positive support and affirmation of whatever the bereaved person has expressed, and to encourage them to explore difficult thoughts or feelings further.

Active listening is an essential skill. The listener is fully focused on the speaker and does not allow themselves to be distracted with their own thoughts. They must be seen to be listening, through body language, eye contact and the way they offer prompts to encourage the speaker ('yes, go on...' or 'can you say a little more about that?').

I like to think that the one offering bereavement support plays midwife to the story that needs to be told. Graves acknowledges the importance of story and narrative to bereaved people:

> The work of the therapist is to help the client rethink the characters in their story and their behaviours, to re-interpret their story and explore how they might write their future stories. (Graves 2009, pp.36–37)

In general conversation we have a tendency to break silence, interrupt and finish each other's sentences, but in bereavement support silence is a powerful tool. It enables the client to reflect on what has been said, to allow thoughts to form, and to feel unhurried as they express themselves. If a client becomes stuck, leading to a long silence which they seem to find uncomfortable, the one offering support may sometimes break the silence with a gentle prompt ('yes, go on...') enabling the client to continue.

These listening skills and the ability to receive and hear whatever is being expressed is equally important when the communication being shared is written rather than (or as well as) spoken. When writing is shared it should receive full attention.

## The skills of a writer

Writers too are listeners. They listen to themselves on the page and they listen to others, when they read or hear writing shared aloud. They are trained in (or have a natural aptitude for) the nuance of language and the subtle, sometimes hidden, meaning behind words.

Writers come in all shapes and sizes. Some are published, some are not (some mind about this, some do not). Some are skilled in enabling others to write, some focus on their own writing. Some are trained in psychodynamic counselling, adult education, facilitation of training and workshops, and working as writers in residence. Some focus solely on their own writing practice.

A writer entering into the field of bereavement support will ideally be able to offer the following:

- enthusiasm and commitment to enabling others to produce their own writing

- skills in facilitating writing with others, including occasional writers and those new to creative or expressive writing

- practice as a working writer in fiction, poetry, life writing or other genres

- knowledge of a wide range of literary forms and techniques

- skills in generating new writing (their own and others'), and in drafting and editing

- skills in facilitating the sharing of writing, feedback and critiquing
- skills in working with sensitive and personal material
- skills in active listening and interpersonal skills
- commitment to diversity and inclusivity
- strong interpersonal skills, with the ability to engage with people and put them at ease
- a track record of residencies or facilitation in health and social care settings
- awareness of bereavement support theory and practice
- understanding of the need to establish and maintain boundaries between client and bereavement supporter
- awareness of the need for self-care in the context of bereavement support
- commitment to partnership working
- commitment to personal and professional development
- awareness of good practice through membership of national networks such as Lapidus UK (see below), regional arts and health fora and the National Association for Writers in Education
- willingness to participate in CRB checking and to provide appropriate references and evidence of insurance (if required)
- willingness to participate in training and induction programmes for paid and voluntary staff at the host venue
- good organisational skills and commitment to good timekeeping.

As a further guide, Lapidus UK, the network for writers involved in reading and writing for health and well-being, recommends a set of core competencies (Flint, Hamilton and Williamson 2004).

The writer used to working in adult education will find that their skills in critiquing others' writing as part of a learning process, are not necessarily appropriate to bereavement writing. The difference lies chiefly in people's reasons for writing. In education, people come to learn and develop their writing. In the counselling room or group setting, bereaved people come to express themselves and share experiences through a creative activity. They may be taking their tentative first steps into a new life following significant loss. The last thing they need is to be told how to improve their grammar or spelling. Sharing stories and experiences and having them affirmed by the group is of far greater value.

This is not to suggest that writing of quality will not emerge in bereavement writing; it very likely will, but literary technique is not the most important part of the facilitator's role. The ability to enable people to write, and to listen and support them in drawing out the meaning of the writing, is more important.

The writer working in bereavement will ideally have awareness of current bereavement theory, although not necessarily to the degree of being an accredited counsellor. The level of understanding achieved through Cruse Bereavement Care's training for bereavement support volunteers is a good benchmark, as are the bespoke training programmes offered through charities, counselling teams and hospices. Willingness to undertake such training (if a writer does not already have it) should be a prerequisite of involvement in this field. I would strongly recommend that a writer who is not also trained in bereavement support always works in partnership with someone who is.

## Working together

The relationship between a counsellor, therapist or volunteer and a writer is crucial to the success of a writing group, or to supporting individuals through writing. Here are some questions to consider, as you clarify the respective roles:

- Who will lead the facilitation of a writing group?

- Who will be the first point of contact for the participants?

- Who will organise the practical arrangements (room, invitations and so forth)?

- What are the lines of communication between facilitator and organiser?

- Who will plan the content of group sessions?

- How many writing sessions will you run?

- What are the minimum and maximum numbers to aim for in your group?

- How much time do you have to give to the writing group and its organisation yourself?

- How will feedback be gathered?

The counsellor, trained therapist or volunteer may find themself in the position of host, employer or manager of the writer who comes into an organisation to deliver specific services for groups and clients. 'Host' is the most appropriate term for a relationship in which the skills of each party are complementary and mutually supportive, and in which one member effectively hosts the other.

If you invite a writer into your organisation, you should ensure that:

- the writer is well-supported in the setting in which they will be facilitating writing

- the space provided for writing is appropriate

- access to facilities such as photocopying, stationery, cloakroom and WC, parking (ideally free) on the premises or nearby, and refreshments for the group

- that the writer is introduced to other members of staff and that their role is explained

- that the writer has a second point of contact if you are unavailable

- that reception staff and others on duty are aware of group meetings, so that people can be welcomed appropriately

- that the writer is aware of ethical guidelines relevant to your organisation and those who work within it or provide services for it; for example, seeking permission to reproduce or quote written work in case studies or for publication and public display or performance

- that the writer is made aware of health and safety information (such as fire exits, alarms and drills)

- that you are available for consultation over the content of sessions (such as themes to be explored in writing exercises), and for reflection after the sessions and the end of a series.

If the writer has appropriate training in bereavement support or experience of conducting groups in the context of bereavement, then the host's attendance at the writing session may not be vital beyond the first session. This can depend on the size and nature of the group. A situation in which a participant becomes distressed and needs to step out of the room for a while is dealt with more easily with two facilitators present. If you are able to attend and work as a team, this can be the ideal arrangement.

If the host does not attend the group sessions they will ideally be available afterwards. Whereas a writer trained in bereavement support will have access to regular supervision, a visiting writer will not. It is important that you take time together to reflect on the group's progress.

## *Advice for writers working with a bereavement support host*

Bereavement brings with it its own themes and subject matter of which you will be aware from your understanding of the grief process. You will be prepared to meet people who are variously in a state of confusion, sorrow, despair, anger, guilt, exhaustion and frustration. They may or may not wish to write overtly about these feelings.

As a writer you bring literary and practical skills. You can enable participants to structure a narrative, draw convincing characters, deploy metaphor and imagery, write in different voices and from different points of view, and work with form in fiction, short story, poetry and memoire. You will be able to offer techniques to enable journal writing, writing for memorial, dialogue, and perhaps blogging and online writing. Working in collaboration, you will be part of a supportive partnership that allows for mutual care and reflection.

Not everything that is written about and shared among bereaved people in a writing group will be sad or distressing; indeed there is much scope for fun and enjoyment. People will quickly lose their embarrassment at crying in front of others (although they may express annoyance with themselves). Even if they spend much of their day at work or at home keeping a brave face, the feeling of safety and of being held in the group, and being free to write whatever they need to write, is among the most important things you can offer.

## *Advice for those who combine skills in writing and bereavement support*

I have said that the roles of writer and counsellor or bereavement support volunteer are separate but complementary. In some, they combine in the same person. If this is you, the following advice is worth bearing in mind:

- Exercise self-care. If you work alone, find someone who can coach or mentor you in the early stages of bereavement writing work.

- Maintain your own reflexive journal as a place to acknowledge the feelings which others' writing may awaken in you. Hearing about others' losses – whether verbally or on the page – can bring back memories of your own. You may find you have unfinished or unexpressed grief of your own to work through. The page can work for you as it does for those whose writing you facilitate.

- Maintain awareness of current and emerging thinking in bereavement theory. Be open to developing your knowledge and expertise.

- Do not take on too much. Bereavement work is enriching but can be tough and, if you practise alone, isolating. If you feel yourself flagging, take a break.

## *To write or not to write?*

The host and facilitator should decide whether or not to join in with the writing and whether and how to share the results. This raises questions of professional and personal boundaries.

Joining in can be appropriate in a smaller group. The sight of the host scribbling along with the rest of the group can enhance the sense of trust among the participants, but when (and if) you share your writing you may need to self-edit in order to preserve boundaries. Be prepared to step back into an observer role if someone in the group needs support.

The same can be said for the facilitating writer, who may decide to join in if the group dynamic suits. Above all the writer is there to facilitate, pay attention to timing, and ensure everyone is able to participate. There is a lot to listen to and observe whilst holding the space. As a writer working in bereavement support your role is to support others in their writing, although you may from time to time scribble something down in your notebook.

## Setting the tone

Although individuals will be experiencing their own sadness, as a group they will soon develop their own style of repartee as stories and common experiences are shared. A sympathetic and friendly tone from the facilitator, laced with gentle humour and a sense of structure, soon puts people at ease.

Show your pleasure and admiration at people's inventiveness with the written word. Even the simplest expressions can carry a weight of meaning. People may express things in their writing that they do not say outside the group. The affirmation they receive when they share their writing, especially when it is about a difficult subject, can be a major benefit.

## Ground rules

Ground rules are the guidelines a group sets for itself at the start of a series of writing sessions, so that everyone is clear about what to expect. Begin by eliciting these from the group. This will bring the group together and engender a sense of trust. They are important from an ethical point of view, particularly with regard to confidentiality.

A typical set of ground rules might include the following:

- In this group you will be encouraged to write and to share your writing. If you would sometimes prefer not to share what you have written, that is alright.

- If you would like the group to hear what you have written but find it hard to read out yourself, you can ask the facilitator to read it for you.

- If you feel upset, you can take time out until you feel ready to join in again.

- When we read our writing out to each other, everyone will be quiet and listen carefully.

- We will treat everyone's writing with respect.

- If someone feels distressed, we will support them by listening.

- Everything we write and say to each other remains confidential within this group.

- If we want to share our writing with others outside the group, that is alright, but we must seek permission before sharing anyone else's writing.

- We will start and finish on time.

- If we miss a session we will try to come to the next one.

## *Sharing writing outside the group*

After a while, it is likely that participants will have a body of work that can be shared more widely. For example, if the writing group has met regularly in a setting such as a hospice, counselling service or health or community centre, there may be opportunities to display some of the work, organise a reading, or produce a pamphlet. The choice of what to include should be up to the participants, but the facilitators can encourage work to be put forward and may offer to edit contributions or work with members of the group who wish to edit their own.

The experience of seeing their words in print can be very positive. For bereaved people, the production of a collection shows the passage of time and can be a powerful indication of progress made through grieving.

## *What does it cost?*

Much of the material offered in this handbook can be incorporated into the techniques used by counsellors, volunteers and others involved in bereavement support. It is worth considering, however, that writers with the appropriate training and skills increasingly make their living (or part of it) from this kind of activity. Some may do this on a voluntary basis, but for others it will be part of their livelihood. Their services as writers in residence, or to deliver a defined programme of work, are offered on a professional basis.

If you are making a funding application, Lapidus UK (www.lapidus. org.uk) offers guidance on writers' payments, which can help you plan and budget your project. Individual writers will have their own scales of payment including hourly rates and rates for multiple sessions; be sure to discuss these before you make an agreement.

Other potential costs include room hire, but this and items such as refreshments may be covered by your organisation as in-kind support.

Essential items to include in your cost breakdown are the writer-facilitator's fee and expenses, the room, coffee, tea and water, notepads and pens.

When you have all this in order, you are ready to begin.

---

## Greenbank group

Thinking about the practicalities of establishing the group, Fiona and Michael consider the following:

- How will the group be recruited? Who can Michael approach from his team's clients?

- Who writes and sends the invitations, and who follows up?

- What size of group are Fiona and Michael aiming for?

- What is the best time of day to host a mixed group in which some members work and others have children?

- Is the room sufficiently private and quiet? How can it be made more private?

- How can they reduce the potential for distress in members of the group returning to the place where their loved one may have died?

- Who will arrange coffee and tea, bring the box of tissues and provide notebooks for the first meeting?

- What are the roles on the first evening, in terms of meeting and greeting the participants and setting up the room?

---

# CHAPTER 13

# Useful Terms

This chapter lists some useful terms in expressive and creative writing which have been referred to in earlier chapters.

## ACROSTIC

A form of writing (poetry or prose), in which the first letter of each line down the left hand side of the page spells a name or word. This can be useful as a form of containment.

## ALPHA POEM

Similar to the acrostic, in the alpha poem each line begins with a letter of the alphabet, in sequence. These are a fun way to enable people to start writing poetry. They can use parts of the alphabet or can present the challenge of going all the way from A to Z (Butler in Bolton, Field and Thompson 2006, pp.46–50).

## DIALOGUE

Like the unsent letter and postcards, written dialogue enables the writer to express thoughts and feelings in conversational form. The dialogue can take place between the writer and someone with whom they feel a need to speak (whether the deceased or someone else in their lives), or with themselves (Adams 1990, pp.102–122).

## DIARY

A daily (or less frequent) account of the writer's life and experiences in which events are recorded and commented upon. In bereavement, a diary can provide daily routine and structure. Over time it can enable the writer to see that they are making progress through their grief. It can also be an aid to memory at a time when concentration and the ability to hold information are affected by the disorientating effect of grief. A diary can be an anchor in daily life.

## ENTRANCE MEDITATION

A way to clear the mind before starting to write, enabling the writer to access thoughts and feelings (Adams 1990, p.100).

## FORM

The term used by writers to describe the style in which they are writing; for example, short fiction or free verse (a poem without deliberate rhyme).

## FREE WRITING

Similar to sprint writing, this is the technique of starting to write with no particular theme or expectation in mind. The writer is simply invited to see what flows from the pen. Further writing can arise from reading back what has been produced, underlining anything surprising or significant to the writer (for instance something that has been repeated), and continuing to write about it. (Hilsdon in Bolton *et al.* 2004, pp.212–220). Sansom gives this heartening advice:

> Stress that they cannot get this wrong… If they get stuck they can write, 'I'm stuck, I'm stuck' over and over or note down things they see in the room, until the writing comes free again. (Sansom 2007, p.68)

## GUIDED WRITING

This is led by the facilitator who may use a series of images, prompts or a story to stimulate writing. The principle behind guided writing is that most people find it hard to begin, faced with a blank page and the instruction to write. The stimulus of being guided into the writing theme enables people to discover what they wish to write about. For bereaved writers, feeling blocked or uncertain what to address on the page, guided writing can enable subject matter to emerge gently.

## HAIBUN

A mix of prose and haiku poems in which short pieces of prose tell a story, interspersed with haiku poems that reflect on the feelings evoked by the story.

## HAIKU

Short blank verse poems of 17 syllables arranged in three lines of five, seven and five syllables. Derived in English from a classical Japanese form, they typically describe something happening in nature with reference to the seasons.

## JOURNAL

A journal is a flexible means to explore thoughts and feelings and to have a conversation with the self and others. The journal is less defined by days, weeks and months than a diary. It may take the form of a notebook, folder, secret box, or a loose collection of papers. It can be used whenever the mood takes the writer and can embrace a wide range of writing styles and forms.

## LIFE WRITING

Memoire, biography, autobiography and family history based on real life stories and memories. Life writing can be useful for those wishing to capture and record memories of someone who has died, either for their own benefit or to pass on to children and others among family and friends. It also has value for those writing about the profound change to their own life and adjusting to a new life narrative.

## LISTS

When asked what they write on a day-to-day basis, most people will mention lists; even a shopping list counts (in my book) as a daily writing activity. Lists offer both familiarity and containment. The invitation to write a list gets most pens flowing. Most lists contain at least one surprise for the writer.

## METAPHOR

A way to describe something in terms of something else. The invitation to describe, say, someone's mood in terms of weather can elicit anything from stormy skies to misty mornings. The choice of a calm clear day after a period of thunderstorms, as a descriptor of general spirits, can be symptomatic of a shift in the grief process. Someone may arrive at a writing group feeling like fog, but leave like a shaft of light breaking through cloud.

## NANO FICTION

Very short fiction including six-word stories or anything from 100 to 500 words. This is also called flash fiction; a short, intense story with the essential elements of character, plot and narrative.

## POETRY

Writing that captures human experience, observation and emotion in forms including free verse, rhyming verse, and forms such as haiku, sonnet and villanelle (these are explained further in Chapter 4). With their use of structure and form, poems offer containment for intense or specific thoughts and feelings. Poetry can induce a feeling of calm and release, to say nothing of the satisfaction that comes with having made something.

## POINT OF VIEW

A technique whereby the writer decides whose perspective they will write from in order to best express a story; for example I, you, or he or she. Changing the point of view in a written piece can be revelatory and enable people to empathise with others and address feelings of guilt and responsibility.

## POSTCARDS

Postcards provide containment for a brief message addressed to the writer themselves, or to someone else. It is worth considering other short forms such as the unsent text message, email or even tweet. These can contain big thoughts in small words.

## SIMILE

Similar to metaphor, the simile likens something to something else which expresses its qualities. It can be useful in unblocking someone who has difficulty explaining how they feel or describing their situation.

## SONNET

A 14-line poem that typically describes the experience of love and loss. See p.102 for an explanation of the different patterns in which a sonnet can rhyme.

## SPRINT WRITING

A quick burst of writing, timed for a minute or more (usually up to five). For people unsure how to begin, the five minute sprint provides a quick way in, without time to over-think or worry about spelling and punctuation. The only rule for a sprint write is to just let it flow. If you do not know what to write, simply start by writing 'I don't know what to write' several times. In the vast majority of cases, words will appear (Thompson in Bolton, Howlett, Lago and Wright 2004, p.76).

## STRUCTURE

Structure is the way in which a piece of writing is arranged. It can be told in a linear way, from start to finish, or it can be told in hindsight, starting at the end and looking back over events.

## TANKA

A haiku with a further two lines of seven syllables each.

## TENSE

Like point of view, the choice of tense in which to write can be revealing. A piece written in the past tense lends some distance to the events being described, whereas re-writing the same piece in the present tense makes it more immediate and produces insights into the lived experience.

## TIME LINE

A technique borrowed from life writing to set out the key events of a life or a period of time on the page. This can be used to express the passage of time both visually and in words and can enable the writer to understand a sequence of events or see an event in its wider context.

## UNSENT LETTER

The unsent letter enables the writer to say things to someone who cannot be spoken to directly. In bereavement this enables the grieving person to say things to the person who died, or to address others, such as family members, friends or health workers, to whom they feel a need to express difficult feelings such as anger. It can be used for positive reasons too, as a way of saying thank you or to complete a conversation, or to say goodbye.

## VILLANELLE

A 19-line poem in which two lines that rhyme are repeated in a pattern. See pp.101–102 for a fuller description and an example.

———•◆•———

# CHAPTER 14

# Sample Writing Sessions for Groups

These sample plans for writing sessions offer a model for you to follow as you start out on this work. The plans draw together some of the techniques and exercises described in the handbook and arrange them into themes with suggested warm up exercises and timings.

The structures provided here are intended as a guide. As you devise you own ways of working you will develop a feel for timing and the flow of a session and the timings will depend upon the numbers in your group. Try always to allow enough time for everyone to be heard. A balance of writing and talking through sharing the writing is ideal, although some groups may prefer to write more and talk less. Your ability to keep a watchful and sensitive eye on timekeeping will enable people to feel a sense of security and trust in the group. You may depart from the plan you have set yourself on the page, but having a plan at the outset will ensure that you retain some control even when the writing or the conversation goes off on a tangent. The sense of being anchored by a theme and structure will help you and the group.

*Note:* The sample plans in this chapter are available from the JKP website at www.jkp.com/catalogue/book/9781849052122/resources.

## TABLE 14.1 THE FIRST MEETING

| | | |
|---|---|---|
| Resources | Names of participants, name badges, notebooks (if you are providing these, or a spare pad of paper), spare pens. | |
| Room | Table around which everyone can sit and see each other in a quiet, well lit room. A box of tissues should be available. A white board or flipchart with pens is useful, also Post-it notes in bright colours. | |
| Refreshments | Tea, coffee, water (biscuits are a nice touch if you can provide them). | |
| Welcome | Facilitators welcome everyone and explain the purpose of the group. Run through housekeeping information (fire exits, location of WCs and so forth) and reiterate start and finish times for the sessions. Provide contact details for facilitators and request that participants to let you know if they are unable to attend. Mention ground rules and say writing will be shared, but only if and as far as participants feel comfortable doing so (this will be revisited and developed at the end of the session). | 10 minutes |
| Introductions | Work in pairs, threes or as a full group (depending on numbers). Introduce yourself by saying something about your name and its meaning. Share names with the whole group and reflect on the stories that have arisen from people's names. | 25 minutes |
| Start to write | Acrostics: invite the group to write an acrostic using their name, or a word they would use to describe themselves. Offer an example: **J**ust **A**bout to try a **N**ew writing **E**xercise. Be prepared to join in if that seems to encourage others to start writing. | 5 minutes writing, with a 1 minute prompt after 4 minutes; 10 minutes sharing |

*Cont.*

*Cont.*

| | | |
|---|---|---|
| More writing | The furniture game: offer the following prompts and invite the group to write short descriptions of themselves as a piece of furniture, a tree, an item of clothing, an animal, a kind of music or the weather. Invite them to share their lists and reflect on their choices and any insights that arise. | 10 minutes writing; 20 minutes sharing |
| Wind down | Invite the group to reflect on the session. What have they liked or enjoyed? Has it met their expectations? What would they like to do more of (they might say more about their reasons for coming to the group and how they see writing as an activity). Draw up ground rules based on their experience of the session. These can be revisited at the start of the next session. | 10 minutes |

## TABLE 14.2 THEME: JOURNEYS

| | | |
|---|---|---|
| Resources | Spare writing paper and pens. A selection of postcards. | |
| Room | As for Table 14.1. | |
| Refreshments | As for Table 14.1. | |
| Welcome | Welcome back. Invite the group to reflect on their experience of the first session and any thoughts or feelings that have arisen for them from the writing. Revisit the ground rules and invite people to add to them or refine them. | 15 minutes |
| Warm up | Invite people to write about what has brought them here today in literal terms (the bus, the car, the train), as well as motivational (what they hope to get from the session, or what mood they are in). Invite them to share what they have written and talk about their reasons. | 5 minutes writing with a 1 minute prompt at the end; 15 minutes to share |
| Exercise | A Journey (see pp.111–114): guide the group through the exercise. When you come to the part when they are invited to send a postcard home to their left luggage, offer them a selection of actual postcards to choose from. | 45 minutes including 30 minutes for writing and 15 for sharing |
| Wind down | Continue the sharing if more time is needed. Reflect on the theme and any memories or thoughts about the future it may have elicited. Finally, invite the group to say what they will do when they get home – the end of a different journey. | 10 minutes |

**TABLE 14.3 THEME: CAPTURING MEMORIES**

| | | |
|---|---|---|
| Resources | Spare writing paper and pens. | |
| Room | As for Table 14.1. | |
| Refreshments | As for Table 14.1. | |
| Welcome | Welcome everyone back. Ask if anyone has been writing since your last meeting and invite them to reflect on this or share anything they wish to with the group. | 10 minutes |
| Warm up | 1. Check in by inviting them to say one thing for which the past week has been memorable (such as a new experience they have had, or something they have done or enjoyed). This will help you assess the mood of the group and individuals and encourage sharing and comparison of experiences.<br><br>2. Invite them to think about their journey to the place where you are meeting. Have they noticed anything unusual along the way, or anything they have not noticed before on an otherwise familiar route? | 10 minutes;<br><br><br><br><br><br>10 minutes |
| Exercise | Write a captured moment: lead the group through the journal exercise in Chapter 3, pp.79–80, using an entrance meditation. Invite them to share their writing. | 45 minutes including 25 for the meditation and writing, with a 2 minute prompt before the end; 20 minutes for sharing and reflection |
| Wind down | Close by asking the group if anything else now comes to mind from the past week. The captured moment exercise may have brought other thoughts and images to mind. Encourage them to use this technique for themselves during the week and to bring their writing to the next session if they wish. | 15 minutes |

**TABLE 14.4 THEME: ANNIVERSARIES**

| | | |
|---|---|---|
| Resources | Spare paper and pens. In preparation for this session, ask the group to bring an item with them that sums up how they feel about an approaching date in the calendar, whether a personal anniversary such as the first year following their bereavement, or a shared moment like New Year or a religious holiday when they will be missing the one who has died. Prepare a handout with your chosen reading, if you are using one (see Chapter 5, pp.122–123 for examples of Christmas readings). <br><br> If you are using the same anniversary for everyone, prepare a handout of coloured paper with the structure of an acrostic: for example, Christmas, Birthday, The First Year. Otherwise, bring a supply of blank A4 coloured paper. | |
| Room | As for Table 14.1. | |
| Refreshments | As for Table 14.1. | |
| Welcome | Welcome everyone back. Invite the group to share any writing since the last meeting and to reflect on it. Check in by asking them for their own personal weather forecast. | 15 minutes |
| Warm up | Invite people to introduce the items they have brought with them, relating to an anniversary theme they all share. Spend time hearing people talk about these items and what they symbolise or signify. | 20 minutes |

*Cont.*

*Cont.*

| | | |
|---|---|---|
| Exercise | If you are using a reading, provide the hand out and read it to the group. Invite them to read it again to themselves and reflect on its meaning and the stories they have just shared about the items they have brought.<br><br>Hand out the coloured paper. Invite them to think as far back in time as they can to an example of the anniversary they have in mind; perhaps their first memory of Christmas. Invite them to write their memory using the acrostic form (they can use the one prepared around the theme or write their own). | 5 minutes for the reading; 20 minutes for the writing; 20 minutes for sharing |
| Wind down | Reflect on the exercise and check out by revisiting the weather forecasts. Reflect on any differences people have expressed. | 10 minutes |

## TABLE 14.5 THEME: AT THE TABLE

| | | |
|---|---|---|
| Resources | Spare paper and pens. Bring some food related items such as a jar of marmalade, Marmite, tea bags, Bisto or other well known brands. Alternatively, provide a handout with a reading from a food writer such as Nigel Slater (see Chapter 7, pp.155–156). | |
| Room | As for Table 14.1. | |
| Refreshments | As for Table 14.1. | |
| Welcome | Welcome everyone back. Check in by asking what is everyone's favourite meal of the day. It is possible that some will mention loss of appetite or the difficulty of cooking for one. Reflect on these comments before moving on. | 15 minutes |
| Warm up | Present the food items you have brought along. Go round the table and ask for 'one food I love' and 'one food I dislike'. Compare tastes and offer their own memories of well known brands from childhood. | 20 minutes |
| Exercise | Invite the group to think about a meal they remember from earlier in their life; one that stands out as truly memorable, perhaps because of a special occasion or because of who used to cook it, or because it was a favourite. Suggest that they recall a meal that was enjoyable and delicious. When they are ready, invite them to write the story of that memorable meal. Offer them a prompt to think about the smell, taste, look and texture of the food, any sounds they associate with it; chatter in the kitchen, the sound of soup bubbling on the stove, | 45 minutes, including 20 for writing and about 25 for sharing |

*Cont.*

*Cont.*

| | | |
|---|---|---|
| | conversation in the restaurant and so forth. After about 10 minutes ask them to pause and read back to themselves what has been written, underlining anything that strikes them as significant, or about which they could write more. Ask them to continue until they have written as full a description as possible, using all the senses. Finally, invite the group to share their writing. | |
| Wind down | Reflect on the memories this has produced. Ask them what they will eat or drink when they go home, as a treat to themselves and an exercise in self-care and nurturing. | 10 minutes |

## TABLE 14.6 THEME: SUITS AND BOOTS

| | | |
|---|---|---|
| Resources | Spare paper and pens. Bring a handout of a poem or reading such as those suggested in Chapter 5, pp.115–116. In preparation, ask the group to bring something with them that has a significant association with someone they would like to write about. | |
| Room | As for Table 14.1. | |
| Refreshments | As for Table 14.1. | |
| Welcome | Welcome everyone back. Invite people to place the items they have brought on the table in front of them. | 15 minutes |
| Warm up | Go round the table and ask people to comment on what they are wearing today, especially if they are wearing something they always have with them, such as a favourite tie or piece of jewellery. Reflect on the stories that will arise from this, about people who gave the items to them, or why they choose to wear certain things. | 20 minutes |
| Exercise | Read the poem, if you are using one. Having read it and reflected on the meaning and the sense in which it evokes a character through an inanimate object, invite the group to write freely about the item they have brought with them and associations it carries for them. After 5 minutes, ask them to focus on describing the person with whom they most closely associate the item, and a memory they have of them using it or wearing it. After a further 15 minutes ask them to read what they have written and then spend the final minutes adding anything else | 45 minutes, including 20 minutes for sharing |

*Cont.*

*Cont.*

| | | |
|---|---|---|
| | they want to say about them or to them. Invite them to show the object to the rest of the group and share their writing. | |
| Wind down | Reflect on the memories the writing has produced and the characters it has evoked. Ask them what they will do with the item when they get home. If it is usually kept hidden away perhaps they might leave it on display for a change. | 10 minutes |

# Postscript

In times of loss the pen, page and keyboard will always be present as a listening friend.

This handbook has set out to offer practical and creative techniques for counsellors, writers and others who provide support to people in bereavement. It has suggested a range of interventions, ways of talking, and of being listened to on the page and around what is written. Perhaps uniquely, the activity of writing enables people who are working through grief to talk and listen to themselves honestly on the page, speaking from the heart at those times when the head cannot make sense of experience.

More evaluation would be valuable to enable practitioners to understand more about the ways in which writing can enable people to work through complex or 'stuck' grief. I would argue also for more training and development opportunities to bring the disciplines of writing and bereavement support together.

I hope that others with capacity and resources in a clinical or academic research setting may take up this work. I hope that this book may be among the resources that can be drawn upon by those with an interest in taking the work forward.

I hope to be argued with and challenged, and I hope that what I have set out here can be a source of inspiration and ideas. I urge anyone interested in using writing in bereavement support to try these approaches, find out what works best in a range of situations and with diverse groups or individuals, and to share to your understanding with others.

Finally…

## Greenbank group

If we imagine the members of our fictional group sometime after their final meeting (six months to a year, perhaps), they might look like this:

*Cynthia* has taken a sabbatical from work, thanks to her sympathetic employer. She is making slow but steady progress through her mother's cluttered home. She writes in her journal most days and writes herself messages of encouragement which she places on Post-it notes around the house. She writes haiku and captured moments to reflect on her days. She finds these help her to feel calm and she enjoys reading back over them from time to time.

*Alan* is seeing Michael for one to one support and is continuing with the monthly drop-in group. He is making a memory box with his four-year-old and is writing stories about Ali which he hopes both the children will enjoy as they grow older. The memory box will contain photographs of Ali with the children, drawings, favourite songs and stories from their life together. Alan has also decided to write Ali an unsent letter on the children's birthdays. He feels he may do this for as long as feels necessary, as a way of letting her know about their progress.

*Bobbie* has started volunteering at one of the recovery centres for the charity Help for Heroes. She tweets about her work for the centre and she has set up a memorial page for her grandson on www.muchloved.com. She has invited her daughter and her grandson's fiancée to contribute to it with her. The family has pulled together around this idea and Bobbie feels more in touch with her daughters and grandchildren.

*Anna* is working on an unsent letter to her mother. She has realised she needs to write one to her father too, forgiving him for keeping the details of her mother's death from her as a ten-year-old. She has invited Pat's sister Joan to come and see the memorial bench she has had placed at the beauty spot in the Peak District where she and Pat used to go walking. She has written a haiku to be inscribed on the bench below Pat's name.

*Ros* is using Facebook to run a campaign to raise funds for Dan's rugby club. She no longer sends texts to his mobile phone but instead tweets about her progress with the fundraising (she helped Bobbie get started with her own tweeting). Ros has a wide following among Dan's rugby playing friends.

*Marielle* is enjoying writing about her husband's life and their married life together. While sorting through his papers she has come across letters they wrote to each other in the early days of their marriage, before she joined him abroad. These have brought her great pleasure, as well as some tears, and she is using details from them to flesh out her account of their travels. Her husband's eldest daughter is visiting her soon and she hopes to show her the life history so far. She has used his old suitcase to create a memory box.

*Riaz* is attending the monthly drop-in group with Alan. He has joined a local poetry group and is sharing his poems with his wife and sisters. His brother's son, Laith, has graduated from business school and is joining the family firm, taking some of the pressure from his uncle. Riaz still has conversations with his brother, but now he writes them down and uses them in his poems instead of replaying them in his head. He found it difficult to attend the group during Ramadan, when he had to manage his diet carefully while fasting, but his blood pressure is back to a healthy level and he is keeping a food diary in which he also reflects on his feelings.

*Fiona* has enjoyed working with this group. She has found Riaz's silence and occasional absences a challenge at times; also Bobbie's anger and Alan's tendency to talk rather than focus on writing, but she has learned from working with the group. In particular she has appreciated the value of trusting in the writing and in persevering until she was able to find the ways in which writing would help each of them. In the cases of Riaz and Bobbie, their eventual choices were a surprise to her and to them, but the outcome has been positive.

For *Michael* the group has confirmed for him the value of writing as part of the counselling service's bereavement support. He has noticed a positive change in all the participants and is keen to understand more about the specific benefits. He plans to invite Fiona to develop a training programme for the rest of his team, as well as running further groups with him and other volunteers. He is seeking funding for further collaboration, as he recognises that Fiona cannot continue on a volunteer basis. He has started to keep his own reflective journal and finds this a helpful way to achieve a better work-life balance and exercise self-care. He plans to invite Riaz to read some of his poems at the Hospice's next Light Up a Life Service.

---

This is an ideal outcome perhaps, but not untypical. As you embark upon this work, be prepared to be surprised, moved and challenged, but above all expect to feel privileged to see people move on in their journeys through grief, pen in hand.

APPENDIX

# *Writing Exercises and Prompts*

## CHAPTER 2 STARTING TO WRITE

## CHAPTER 3 KEEPING A JOURNAL

## CHAPTER 4 WORKING WITH FORM

## CHAPTER 5 WRITING THROUGH GRIEF

## CHAPTER 6 LIFE WRITING IN BEREAVEMENT

# References

Adams, K. (1990) *Journal to the Self*. New York, USA: Grand Central Publishing.

Adams, K. (2002) *Journal to the Self Workbook*. Lakewood (USA): The Center for Journal Therapy.

Astley, N. (ed.) (2002) *Staying Alive*. Tarset, Northumberland: Bloodaxe Books.

Athill, D. (2008) *Somewhere Towards the End*. London: Granta.

Bishop, E. (2004) *Elizabeth Bishop, Complete Poems*. London: Chatto and Windus.

Bolton, G. (1999) *The Therapeutic Potential of Creative Writing*. London: Jessica Kingsley Publishers.

Bolton, G. (2008) *Dying, Bereavement and the Healing Arts*. London: Jessica Kingsley Publishers.

Bolton, G., Field, V. and Thompson, K. (eds) (2006) *Writing Works*. London: Jessica Kingsley Publishers.

Bolton, G., Howlett, S., Lago, C. and Wright, J.K. (2004) (eds) *Writing Cures: An Introductory Handbook of Writing in Counselling and Psychology*. Hove, East Sussex: Routledge.

Bonnano, G. (1999) 'Laughter During Bereavement.' *Bereavement Care 18*, 2, 19–22.

Bowlby, J. (1998) *Attachment and Loss. Volume 3: Loss*. London: Random House.

Bowman, T. (2000) 'Bereavement and Shattered Dreams – Exploring the Connections.' *Bereavement Care 19*, 1.

Butler, L. In G. Bolton, V. Field and K. Thompson (eds) (2006) *Writing Works*. London: Jessica Kingsley Publishers.

Cameron, J. (1995) *The Artist's Way*. London: Random House.

Cameron, J. (2002) *Walking in this World*. London: Random House.

Clifton, L. (2002) 'Homage to My Hips.' In N. Astley (ed.) *Staying Alive*. Tarset, Northumberland: Bloodaxe Books, p.36.

Cope, W. (2004) In N. Astley (ed.) *Being Alive*. Tarset, Northumberland: Bloodaxe Books.

Cruse Bereavement Care (2007) *Awareness in Bereavement Care: The Cruse Foundation Course*. London: Cruse Bereavement Care.

Dickens, C. (1997 [1849]) *David Copperfield*. Oxford: Oxford University Press.

Didion, J. (2005) *The Year of Magical Thinking*. London: Fourth Estate.

Didion, J. (2011) *Blue Nights*. London: Fourth Estate.

Doka, K. and Martin, T. (2010) *Grieving Beyond Gender*. Abingdon: Routledge.

Egan, S. (1998) *The Skilled Helper: Models, Skills and Methods for Effective Helping*. Kentucky, USA: Brooks Cole.

Etherington, K. (2004) *Becoming a Reflexive Researcher*. London: Jessica Kingsley Publishers.

Fainlight, R. (2002) 'Handbag.' In N. Astley (ed.) *Staying Alive*. Tarset, Northumberland: Bloodaxe Books.

Feaver, V. In Anderson, L. (ed.) (2006) *Creative Writing; A Workbook with Readings*. Abingdon, Oxon: Routledge.

Field, V. (2006) In G. Bolton, V. Field and K. Thompson (eds) *Writing Works*. London: Jessica Kingsley Publishers.

Flint, R., Hamilton, F. and Williamson, C. (2004) *Core Competencies for Working with the Literary Arts for Personal Development, Health and Well-being*. www.lapidus.org.uk/resources/index.php, accessed 16 April 2012.

Frost, R. (1923) 'Stopping by Woods on a Snowy Evening.' In N. Astley (ed.) (2002) *Staying Alive*. Tarset, Northumberland: Bloodaxe Books.

Frydman, B. (2010) 'The Learning Journal.' *Lapidus Journal 5*, 2.

Gibson, F. (2011) *Reminiscence and Life Story Work, A Practical Guide*. London: Jessica Kingsley Publishers.

Graves, D. (2009) *Talking with Bereaved People*. London: Jessica Kingsley Publishers.

Hardy, T. (1994) *The Collected Poems of Thomas Hardy*. Ware: Wordsworth Editions.

Hardy, T. (2003 [1886]) *The Mayor of Casterbridge*. London: The Collectors Library, CRW Publishing.

Hedges, D. (2005) *Poetry, Therapy and Emotional Life*. Oxford: Radcliffe Publishing.

Hemingway, E. (2008) In R. Ferleischer and L. Smith (eds). *Not Quite What I Was Planning*. New York: Harper Collins.

Hilsdon, J. (2004) In G. Bolton, S. Howlett, C. Lago and J.K. Wright (eds). *Writing Cures: An Introductory Handbook of Writing in Counselling and Psychology*. Hove: Routledge.

Holub, M. (2002) 'The Door,' translated by I. Milner. In N. Astley (ed.) *Staying Alive*. Tarset, Northumberland: Bloodaxe Books.

Hughes, T. (1998) *Birthday Letters*. London: Faber and Faber.

Kübler-Ross, E. (2009 [1970]) *On Death and Dying*. Abingdon: Routledge.

Lawrence, D.H. (2002) *Piano*. Ware: Wordsworth Editions.

Lawrence, D.H. In E. Longley (ed.) (2010) *The Bloodaxe Book of 20th Century Poetry*. Tarset, Northumberland: Bloodaxe Books.

Lee, L. (2002 [1959]) *Cider with Rosie*. London: Penguin Books.

Lee, L. (1971) *As I Walked Out One Midsummer Morning*. London: Penguin Books.

McElhone, N. (2010) *After You*. London: Viking.

McGuinness, B. and Finucane, N. (2011) 'Evaluating and Creative Arts Bereavement Support Intervention; Innovation and Rigour.' *Bereavement Care 30*, 1, 37–42.

Mackay Brown, G. (2002) *Letters from Hamnavoe*. London: Steve Savage Publishers.

Mori, J. (2011) 'Poets and Blacksmiths.' *Interactions 18*, 5.

Moss, J. (2010) 'Sunflowers on the Road to NASA.' *Bereavement Care 29*, 2, 24.

Moss, J. (2012) In R. Neimeyer R. (ed.) *Techniques of Grief Therapy*. Abingdon: Routledge.

Neimeyer, R.A. (ed.) (2007, 5th edition) *Meaning Reconstruction and the Experience of Loss*. Washington, DC: The American Psychological Association.

Neimeyer, R.A., van Dyke, J.G. and Pennebaker, J.W. (2008) 'Narrative Medicine: Writing Through Bereavement.' In H. Chochinov and W. Breitbart (eds) *Handbook of Psychiatry in Palliative Medicine*. New York: Oxford University Press.

Parkes, C.M. (1987) *Bereavement – Studies of Grief in Adult Life*. Harmondsworth, Middlesex: Pelican Books.

Paterson, D. (ed.) (1999) *101 Sonnets*. London: Faber and Faber.

Pennebaker, J.W. (1990) *Opening Up – The Healing Power of Expressing Emotions*. London: Guilford Press.

Pennebaker, J.W. (2004) *Writing to Heal – A Guided Journal for Recovering from Trauma and Emotional Upheaval*. Oakland: New Harbinger Publications.

Pugh, S. (2002) 'What if this Road.' In N. Astley (ed.) *Being Alive*. Tarset, Northumberland: Bloodaxe Books.

Reeves, N. (2001) *A Path Through Loss*. Kelowna, Canada: Northstone Publishing.

Reid, C. (2009) *A Scattering.* Oxford: Arete Books.

Robinson, Edward A. 'The House on the Hill.' In S. Donaldson *A Poet's Life* (2007 [1894]) Chichester, West Sussex: Columbia University Press.

Rogers, C. (1967) *Client Centred Therapy.* London: Constable and Robinson.

Rosen, D. and Weishaus, J. (2004) *The Healing Spirit of Haiku.* Berkeley, CA: North Atlantic Books.

Sansom, P. (2007) *Writing Poems.* Tarset, Northumberland: Bloodaxe Books.

Schweitzer, P. (ed.) (2004) *Mapping Memories – Reminiscence with Ethnic Minority Elders.* London: Age Exchange.

Seatter, R. (2006) *On the Beach with Chet Baker.* Bridgend: Seren Books.

Shakespeare, W. (1951) Macbeth. In K. Muir (ed.) *The Arden Shakespeare.* London: Methuen.

Shuttle, P. (2006) *Redgrove's Wife.* Tarset, Northumberland: Bloodaxe Books.

Slater, N. (2007) *Eating for England.* London: Harper Collins Publishers.

Stroebe, M. and Schut, H. (1999) 'Dual Process of Grief.' *Death Studies 23*, 3.

Thompson, K. (2004) In G. Bolton, S. Howlett, C. Lago and J.K. Wright (eds) *Writing Cures: An Introductory Handbook of Writing in Counselling and Psychology.* Hove: Routledge.

Thompson, K. (2011) *Therapeutic Journal Writing.* London: Jessica Kingsley Publishers.

Thomas, D. (1955) *Quite Early One Morning.* London: J.M. Dent and Sons.

Thomas, D. In E. Longley (ed.) (2010) *The Bloodaxe Book of 20th Century Poetry.* Tarset, Northumberland: Bloodaxe Books.

Tonkin, L. (1996) 'Growing Around Grief – Another Way of Looking at Grief and Recovery.' *Bereavement Care 15*, 1, 10.

Walter, T. (1996) 'A New Model of Grief.' *Mortality 1*, 1, 7–25.

Walter, T. (forthcoming 2012) 'How People Who are Dying or Mourning Use the Arts.' In *Music and Arts in Action.* www.musicandartsinaction.net, accessed 16 April 2012.

Wiseman, E. (2010) 'Up Front: Eva Wiseman. How a Virtual Life Becomes a Virtual Death Thanks to Facebook's Memorialisation Process.' *The Observer.*

Worden J.W. (2004) *Grief Counselling and Grief Therapy.* Hove, East Sussex: Brunner-Routledge.

Wright, K. (2009) *The Magic Box – Poems for Children.* London: Macmillan Children's Books.

Woods, P. (1998) *Diary of a Grief.* York: Sessions of York.

Woodthorpe, K. (2011) 'Using Bereavement Theory to Understand Memorialising Behaviour.' *Bereavement Care 30*, 2, 29–32.

# Further Reading

---

The sources of inspiration are many and various. In this section I have drawn together some of the resources I find useful. It is a list that is constantly growing; I am sure you will add your own.

The books suggested here include anthologies and collections to draw upon when planning writing exercises; poems as starting points and sources from fiction and memoire that can provide stimulus. Some are published works by writers and others who have chosen to tell stories of bereavement (their own and others'). Not everyone wishes to read about others' loss, but some find comfort in comparing their own experiences.

I tend to steer clear of poetry and anthologies that are overtly about loss and sorrow (e.g. the kind sometimes consulted when seeking readings for the funeral service), but if people are drawn to these I would not discourage their use. The people you work with will suggest their own. Personally, I find more inspiration in writing that can be diversely interpreted. The list below is far from comprehensive but suggests some titles to start with.

## Bereavement, self-development and self-care

Bolton, G. (2011) *Write Yourself.* London: Jessica Kingsley Publishers.

Bolton, G., Field, V. and Thompson, K. (eds) (2011) *Writing Routes.* London: Jessica Kingsley Publishers.

De Salvo, L. (2000) *Writing as a Way of Healing.* Boston, USA: Beacon Press.

Gershie, A. (1991) *Storymaking in Bereavement.* London: Jessica Kingsley Publishers.

Hunt, C. and Sampson, F. (eds) (2005) *The Self on the Page.* London: Jessica Kingsley Publishers.

Killick, J. and Schneider, M. (2010) *Writing Yourself.* London: Continuum.

Lepore, S. and Smyth, J. (eds) (2009) *The Writing Cure.* Washington, DC: American Psychological Association.

Lewis, C.S. (1966) *A Grief Observed*. London: Faber and Faber.

Martin, T. and Doka, K. (2000) *Men Don't Cry...Women Do*. Abingdon: Routledge.

Parkes, C.M. (1987) *Bereavement – Studies of Grief in Adult Life*. Harmondsworth, Middlesex: Pelican Books.

Parkes, C.M. (2006) *Love and Loss, The Roots of Grief and its Complications*. Hove: Routledge.

Gibson, F. (2011) *Reminiscence and Life Story Work*. London: Jessica Kingsley Publishers.

Philips, Linington and Penman (1999). *Writing Well*. London: Jessica Kingsley Publishers.

Ramsay, G.G. and Sweet, H.B. (2009) *A Creative Guide to Exploring Your Life*. London: Jessica Kingsley Publishers.

Sampson, F. (ed.) (2004) *Creative Writing in Health and Social Care*. London: Jessica Kingsley Publishers.

# Creative writing

Feaver, V. In Anderson, L. (ed.) (2006) *Creative Writing; A Workbook with Readings*. Abingdon, Oxon: Routledge.

Earnshaw, S. (ed.) (2007) *The Handbook of Creative Writing*. Edinburgh: Edinburgh University Press.

Grenville, K. (2011) *The Writing Book*. London: Allen and Unwin.

# Memoire and life writing

Barratt, N. (2008) *Who Do You Think You Are?* London: Harper Collins.

Cline, S. and Angier, C. (eds) (2010) *The Arvon Book of Life Writing*. London: Methuen Drama.

Harvey Wood, H. and Byatt, A. (2009) *Memory, An Anthology*. London: Vintage Books.

Jansson, T. (2003) *The Summer Book*. London: Sort of Books.

Jansson, T. (2006) *The Winter Book*. London: Sort of Books.

Mackay Brown, G. (2002) *Letters from Hamnavoe*. London: Steve Savage Publishers.

Mackay Brown, G. (1992) *Rockpools and Daffodils*. Edinburgh: Gordon Wright Publishing.

Picardie, J. (2006) *My Mother's Wedding Dress, The Life and Afterlife of Clothes*. London: Bloomsbury, 2006.

Sayer, C. (2009) *Fiesta, Days of the Dead and Other Mexican Festivals*. London: British Museum Books.

Taylor, I. and Taylor, A. (eds) (2003) *The Assassin's Cloak*. Edinburgh: Canongate Books.

# Poetry

Astley, N. (ed.) (2004) *Being Alive; The Sequel to Staying Alive*. Tarset, Northumberland: Bloodaxe Books.

Astley, N. (ed.) (2011) *Being Human; More Real Poems for Unreal Times*. Tarset, Northumberland: Bloodaxe Books.

Cobb, C. (ed.) (2002) *The British Museum Haiku*. London: British Museum Press.

Darling, J. and Fuller C. (eds) (2005) *The Poetry Cure*. Tarset, Northumberland: Bloodaxe Books.

Emerson, S. (ed.) (2004) *In Loving Memory*. Tarset, Northumberland: Bloodaxe Books.

Gallagher, T. (2007) *Dear Ghosts*. Tarset, Northumberland: Bloodaxe Books.

Gillilan, P. (1986) *That Winter*. Tarset, Northumberland: Bloodaxe Books.

Longley, E. (ed.) (2000) *Bloodaxe Book of 20th Century Poetry*. Tarset, Northumberland: Bloodaxe Books.

Mabey, J. (2004) *Words to Comfort, Words to Heal*. Oxford: Oneworld Publications.

Washington, P. (ed.) (2003) *Haiku*. London: Everyman.

# *About the Author*

Jane Moss worked in the theatre and the Civil Service before moving into a career in writing and bereavement support. She is a visiting lecturer in creative writing at the University of Hertfordshire and runs writing workshops and courses in west London and Surrey. She has co-facilitated writing groups with the bereavement counselling team at Princess Alice Hospice in Esher, Surrey, and the Macmillan Bereavement Service at Meadow House Hospice in Ealing, west London. She is a volunteer for Cruse Bereavement Care. Jane is a board member of Lapidus, the UK organisation for writing and reading for health and well-being. She has been reading and writing for as long as she can remember and has MAs in Drama and Creative Writing in the Community. Brought up in Cornwall, with a Welsh heart and an English accent, Jane now lives in west London.

# Index

11414081R00143

Printed in Great Britain
by Amazon